Video and Filmmaking as Psychotherapy

While film and video have long been used within psychological practice, researchers and practitioners have only just begun to explore the benefits of film and video production as therapy. This volume describes a burgeoning area of psychotherapy that employs the art of filmmaking and digital storytelling as a means of healing victims of trauma and abuse. It explores the ethical considerations behind this process, as well as its cultural and developmental implications within clinical psychology. Grounded in clinical theory and methodology, this multidisciplinary volume draws on perspectives from anthropology, psychiatry, psychology, and art therapy, which support the use and integration of film/video-based therapy in practice.

Joshua L. Cohen has worked in film/video production for over 30 years, received a PhD in clinical psychology from Pacifica Graduate Institute, a master's in general psychology from Walden University, and a bachelor's degree in film and anthropology from Colorado College. He lives and works in Southern California, USA.

J. Lauren Johnson is a licensed psychologist and a filmmaker. She is also the founder of the Therapeutic Filmmaking Institute in Alberta, CA.

Penelope P. Orr is a board certified, registered art therapist in Edinboro, PA, USA. She is currently the director of the Edinboro University Masters in Art Therapy/Counseling Program.

Advances in Mental Health Research series

Books in this series:

The Clinical Effectiveness of Neurolinguistic Programming
A Critical Appraisal
Edited by Lisa Wake, Richard M. Gray and Frank S. Bourke

Group Therapy for Adults with Severe Mental Illness
Adapting the Tavistock Method
Diana Semmelhack, Larry Ende and Clive Hazell

Narratives of Art Practice and Mental Wellbeing
Reparation and connection
Olivia Sagan

Video and Filmmaking as Psychotherapy
Research and Practice
Edited by Joshua L. Cohen and J. Lauren Johnson with Penelope P. Orr

Video and Filmmaking as Psychotherapy

Research and Practice

Edited by Joshua L. Cohen and J. Lauren Johnson with Penelope P. Orr

Routledge
Taylor & Francis Group
NEW YORK AND LONDON

First published 2015
by Routledge
711 Third Avenue, New York, NY 10017, USA

and by Routledge
2 Park Square, Milton Park, Abingdon, Oxfordshire OX14 4RN

First issued in paperback 2016

Routledge is an imprint of the Taylor & Francis Group, an informa business

Library of Congress Cataloging-in-Publication Data

Video and filmmaking as psychotherapy : research and practice /
edited by Joshua L. Cohen and J. Lauren Johnson.
p. ; cm. — (Advances in mental health research series)
Includes bibliographical references and index.
I. Cohen, Joshua L., editor. II. Johnson, J. Lauren, editor.
III. Series: Advances in mental health research series.
[DNLM: 1. Psychotherapy—methods. 2. Sensory Art Therapies.
3. Motion Pictures as Topic. 4. Video Recording. WM 450.5.V5]
RC489.P56
616.89'165—dc23
2014036172

Typeset in Sabon
by Apex CoVantage, LLC

ISBN 13: 978-1-138-28696-2 (pbk)
ISBN 13: 978-1-138-78142-9 (hbk)

Contents

PART III
Research and Validity

PART IV
Tools for Practice Through Didactic Instruction

Figures

Tables

Foreword

In work with clients of all ages, I have witnessed a tremendous growth in the use of films and filmmaking as a form of reparation and recovery from emotional challenges and psychological distress. While reading *Video and Filmmaking as Psychotherapy: Research and Practice*, I was reminded of the growing demand for relevant and creative forms of therapy with military personnel who are often challenged by multiple deployments, the impact of active combat, and readjustment to life state-side. One way soldiers are taking charge of their psychological distress is through filmmaking as a means of telling their stories and confronting experiences that often include post-traumatic reactions, loss, depression, and traumatic brain injury. As one soldier told me, "You can put your story into a film, everything that you went through in combat and in a way that goes beyond words. It's your story. It's a way for me to tell my story without having to talk about it over and over. If people watch it, they can learn what happened to me. If other soldiers watch it, they will see that they are not alone and that we all have had the same experiences. Making my film helped me to move on from what happened. It has just made life a lot easier."

My core value as an expressive arts therapist and psychotherapist is the use of sensory-based approaches in work with individuals of all ages to make meaning of life's experiences; provide emotional relief; enhance resilience, self-efficacy, and self-regulation; and make desired behavioral changes. I have always found that engaging the senses in psychotherapy goes beyond what typical verbal transactions can stimulate; in other words, by appealing to clients' visual, auditory, and other senses, therapists can provide their clients with opportunities for self-discovery that are not found through words alone. As an expressive arts therapist I regularly use art-based approaches as key interventions with clients of all ages. In brief, individuals are encouraged to engage or experience some form of visual media as self-expression; traditionally, this involves constructing, arranging, mixing, molding, drawing, and painting (Malchiodi, 2012). Now, with the rapid increase in digital technology, like many other expressive arts therapists, I now have integrated newer forms of visual expression that depend on keyboards or a mouse, desktop computers, tablets, smartphones, and numerous "apps" [applications] that can be used as ways to draw, paint, and even sculpt in virtual space, as well as to make films and animations (Malchiodi & Johnson, 2013).

Why is the use of film and video particularly relevant to psychotherapy in general? In brief, they are forms of communication familiar to most individuals and are ubiquitous in contemporary culture. For example, as of this writing, more than a billion users visit the video-sharing platform known as YouTube each month and hundreds of hours of video are uploaded every minute. Almost everyone who owns a cell or smartphone now has the ability to create films at any time and edit and share them via social media within minutes. For the average person, smartphones have replaced traditional cameras because of their ease of use and high-quality lenses and image resolution. Webcams, camcorders, and other portable film cameras have also generated possibilities unimaginable only a decade earlier. Online apps make it easy for those with little to no filmmaking experience to integrate photo-images, sound, music, and text into professional footage through user-friendly commands and directions. Finally, almost everyone is influenced by and/or involved on a daily basis with digital media, including films, via social networking. In brief, digital technology is not only omnipresent and easy to use, clients generally already know how to access and use it.

In contrast, while film and video are ubiquitous forms of self-expression, relatively little has been written about the application of this type of media in psychotherapy, despite more than four decades of use. Historically, the term *videotherapy* has been used to describe the use of film in art therapy and psychotherapy and is sometimes used interchangeably with the term *cinematherapy*. Cinematherapy is generally defined as an intervention used by a variety of helping professionals that directs clients to watch specific movies for psychotherapeutic reasons and/or to report their impressions to their therapist for further discussion. It is similar to bibliotherapy (the use of books and stories to enhance understanding of emotional challenges and psychological difficulties) in that films can be used in similar and possibly even more potent, far-reaching ways. For example, when compared to books, movies not only contain the universal storylines found in books, they also are multisensorial. Along with their common themes, the sensory nature of movies can help clients achieve insights if the movies are strategically selected for relevance to the client's interests and needs in treatment. Films also evoke powerful projections—in other words, mental and sensory associations to one's life that may trigger a recall of emotion, memories, and experiences.

Film and video as forms of therapy also encompass the actual experience of client-created movies as part of treatment. Because of the accessibility of digital filmmaking, therapists can now capitalize on the idea that clients can become their own directors of films that express their life stories. For example, it is now possible for clients to film or record digital narratives, more commonly known as *digital storytelling*. These short, first-person autobiographical films are created by combining recorded voice, and still and video footage along with music and other sounds. With the involvement of a therapist, this type of film is essentially a contemporary interpretation of narrative therapy. Digital storytelling allows clients to communicate, create, and respond to personal stories through digital technology platforms as simple as webcams, smartphones, or tablets with video capabilities. As demonstrated throughout this book, clients can also engage in other types of filmmaking, including animation and "green screen" techniques. These experiences can be reparative within the context of psychotherapy because they constitute active, meaningful, and dynamic interventions involving self-discovery, self-awareness, and self-expression.

As Cohen and Johnson state in their introduction, "While there are different opinions on what film/video-based therapy is or even what to call it, this book is an attempt to build toward a consensus on both a theory and practice for developing this intervention. This book is not an endorsement of a single theory but rather a challenge to readers to think critically about a subject and the complexities of how this new intervention might be executed if it were peer reviewed" (p. 7). The consensus that the editors cite can be generalized into two possibilities for therapists who want to apply the power of film to their work with clients. First, the evocative nature of film has the potential to stimulate dialogue between client and helping professional as well as numerous applications for psycho-education, behavioral change, and personal insight. Second, there are multiple possibilities for actual filmmaking as a catalyst not only for clients to gain insight, but also for them to engage in a self-empowering, creative process for meaning-making and personal narrative.

Finally, films and videos, whether viewed, discussed, or created, capture the truth of many experiences and the day-to-day aspects of the human condition. They also touch on a wide range of sensory experiences through dialogue, lighting, special effects, cinematography, and music. Films reflect not only life's joyful, celebratory, or momentous events, they also mirror the array of experiences that bring clients to treatment—drug addiction and alcoholism, trauma and posttraumatic stress, grief and loss, violence, natural and man-made disaster, divorce and infidelity, phobias, and depression, among others. Ultimately, our clients may find it easier to address their own challenges if we give them the opportunity to literally see how others handle (or mishandle) similar situations via film. Or, like the soldier's experience with filmmaking that opened this foreword, clients can show us their experiences in a way that words alone cannot convey. These aspects compel all helping professionals to incorporate the insights and expertise of these authors' contributions into treatment and to appreciate the valuable role that film and video can have in a successful psychotherapeutic relationship between client and therapist.

Cathy A. Malchiodi, PhD, LPCC, LPAT, ATR-BC, REAT

REFERENCES

Malchiodi, C. A. (2012). Art therapy materials, media and methods. In C. A. Malchiodi (Ed.), *Handbook of Art Therapy* (pp. 27–41). New York: Guilford Publications.

Malchiodi, C. A., & Johnson, E. R. (2013). Digital art therapy with hospitalized children. In C. A. Malchiodi (Ed.), *Art Therapy and Health Care* (pp. 106–122). New York: Guilford Publications.

Acknowledgments

I want to thank my wife for her emotional and financial support. Without her, this book may not have been possible. Although Lauren Johnson and I are credited as the main editors of this collection, we also received a great deal of help in this task from Penny Orr, who spent many hours poring over our manuscript through several stages of revision and whose expertise and advice were so deeply appreciated throughout the entire editing process.

This book was a collaborative process from the beginning. In 1997, when I raised the money and flew Dr. Gary Solomon out to Colorado College in Colorado Springs to put on one of his seminars about the growing field of Cinematherapy, I introduced a panel of film theorists and filmmakers as well as an art therapist and discussed the idea of using films as a part of therapy.

In my master's and doctoral studies, I continued to pursue this goal of integrating films and healing, but in order for me to pursue this idea, I needed to continue to reach out to others for help. Many authors and practitioners who had been practicing in this field, somewhat independently, agreed to be interviewed for my dissertation. Brandon Brawner, who had been doing this work for several years before I started, gave me much needed advice and guidance and participated in the research in my dissertation, as did Amanda Alders/Pike, J. Lauren Johnson, Basia Mosinski, Jon Ehinger, and Brian Austin.

In addition to our recent work, Lauren and I both wish to thank the countless contributors over the past century and pay tribute to the pioneers in film and psychology who have tried to integrate psychology and film. This book is a collective vision stemming from the American spirit of the need to pioneer and has expanded to the rest of the world. Lauren and I both believe that this book is about asking questions and not answering them.

This book is intended to initiate the building of a community to support the growth of the theory and practice of film- and video-based therapies. The authors who contributed chapters to this book are the most visible part of this community, and as editors we cannot thank them enough for their ongoing efforts to support this growth. Without my dissertation chair, Michael Sipiora, and his continued support on writing my chapter, I may never have thought of the research design and the specific ways of collaborating and reaching out to others as he suggested.

In addition to the contributors whose names grace the pages of this book, we must acknowledge the great efforts and countless hours given to this project by the less visible members of our community. This book would not have gotten off the ground without the support of those who voluntarily took time out of their busy and professional schedules to review our proposals and their feedback and advice on how to improve this book in its earliest stages. We extend our thanks to Dr. Matthew Bennett from Pacifica Graduate Institute, Dr. Lynda Ross from Athabasca University, and Dr. Oksana Yakushko from Pacifica Graduate Institute for their generosity in helping us with our proposal.

We would also like to thank Stacy Noto and Lauren Verity from Routledge for their countless hours of assistance and answering questions. We would like to thank Ruth Cardinal de Ubiera for giving Lauren excellent advice and contributing to her work.

Additional credit goes to Catherine Highland Moon for allowing the inclusion of two chapters from her book, *Media and Materials in Art Therapy*, in this book and for her advice and guidance. Thanks also to Andrea Polard for her advice on positive psychology and happiness, Richard Himmer for his advice on leadership, and to Justine Frankel for her support and guidance over the years. Thanks to Doug Pray and Joel Kurahawa for permission to use the excerpt of dialogue from the video of the Dalai Lama I edited for them in 2001. Finally, thanks to Linda Buzzell, who came up with the idea to publish an edited book, and to John Izod, who referred me to Routledge. I personally thank Lauren Johnson for agreeing to participate in my dissertation project as well as in the difficult and often frustrating process of collaboration. Lauren volunteered to help with the book after I finished my PhD and without her support, this book may not have been possible.

Our hope is that this text will serve to inform, inspire, and advance the field of film-and video-based therapy and the growing community of researchers and practitioners. We hope for ongoing collaboration between art therapists, psychologists, and professionals from other disciplines as we continue to pioneer this field collectively.

Finally, this couldn't have been done without the help of the editors who constantly tended to grammar, APA style, and statistics.

We are deeply grateful for the dedication of others in this project, and sincerely look forward to witnessing the inevitable growth of this field in the future.

Josh Cohen, PhD
Lauren Johnson, PhD

Part I

Introduction

1 Introduction

Film and Video as a Therapeutic Tool

Joshua L. Cohen and J. Lauren Johnson

INTRODUCTION

Academy Award–winning actor and comedian Robin Williams's untimely death in August 2014 shocked the world. It appears that being in popular and profitable films was not enough to save him from depression and bipolar disorder. Jamison (2014) asserted, "The suicide death of Robin Williams has generated interest in the relationship between creativity and depression. No one knows the nature of Mr. Williams's problems" (para. 1). Jamison also stated that "he was suffering with early stage Parkinson's disease, but the possibility of a link between 'madness' and creativity is ancient and persistent" (para. 1). Indeed, Williams was a storyteller and a filmmaker, both of which are ancient art forms of healing. Films can be healing, but film- and video-based therapy is about much more than storytelling. It involves an ethical responsibility to clients.

Film has been used since its genesis as a therapeutic tool, because creating and watching a film often can speak directly to the human soul. Although we have felt a connection that tells us that film is therapeutic, we are just beginning to understand and use film intentionally as a therapeutic tool. Making films has evolved over time into an accessible activity, so films can range from professional blockbusters to private amateur films that people make in their backyards. Film is now being used intentionally as a therapeutic tool by social workers, therapists, psychologists, artists, and directors. As a result, film has become a therapeutic tool created and used by people from different disciplines and backgrounds. This book is a compilation of the experiences of therapists who are using film intentionally in practice to better understand the benefits of using film as a therapeutic tool.

As you read through this book, we invite you to reflect upon the various ways that the chapters relate to and are different from each other. If you are a practitioner, how might your approach fit into the work that is represented in these chapters? If you are a theoretician, what perspective(s) most closely align with yours? How might you make sense of film and video as therapeutic tools? How would you make them your own?

WHAT MAKES FILM THERAPEUTIC?

Film is a mass medium that reaches global audiences. Films can be created by large film studio companies for the masses or for smaller audiences or even for personal use through handheld devices. A film that combines elements of photography, theatre, music, literature, and other disciplines into a unified whole can be considered an aspect of art therapy. What makes any artistic medium therapeutic is that it is undertaken with therapeutic intent within the safe environment of therapy with credentialed and trained therapists. However, this use of film as a therapeutic tool should not detract from its use as entertainment, which is one reason it occupies a special place in our personal, artistic, and cultural experiences. Each culture has its own view of what art can be used for and what constitutes entertainment. Perhaps future researchers will engage other perspectives from more global sources.

This book was developed to explore the connection between the medium of film and the human experience from the points of view of people using film in the therapeutic setting. We used our own backgrounds in psychology and film to frame the content of this book to provide insight into how film and psychology influence each other. We discovered that film actually has a long association with psychology. Though psychology's interest in art grew along with a coinciding fascination with Jungian and Freudian concepts of the unconscious at the beginning of the 20th century, it was not until the 1940s that art therapy proper was founded in the United States by Margaret Naumberg and Edith Kramer (J. A. Rubin, 1999). Art therapy has its roots in psychoanalysis and focuses on the transference between patients and therapists using the third hand of the process and product of art making (Hogan, 2001; Hull, 1998). Though both of the founders of art therapy approached their work from a psychoanalytic perspective, the two women placed different emphases on art and therapy.

Margaret Naumberg approached art therapy from a psychoanalytic perspective, interpreting the art product as a form of symbolic speech similar to dreams. She conceived of art as both a diagnostic tool and therapeutic intervention that involves artistic creation and discussion between clients and trained therapists, in which clients can offer their insights. On the other hand, Edith Kramer approached art therapy from more of an artistic perspective, viewing art as a process through which people integrate conflicting unconscious and conscious forces.

Although Naumberg's art therapy reflected her emphasis on fostering insight into the unconscious for therapeutic gain, Kramer viewed art making itself as the therapeutic process through which psychological benefits naturally emerged (as cited in J. A. Rubin, 1999). From these roots, art therapy has grown to encompass many other theoretical perspectives and a myriad of artistic media. Art therapy can be used with couples, families, groups, and individuals to facilitate the safe release of uncensored and unconscious material to accelerate the therapeutic process (Cohen, 2007).

According to Malchiodi (2014),

> Art has the potential to transform lives and often in profound ways; research is demonstrating that art improves not only our quality of life, but also is effective in reducing pain, fatigue and stress and increasing cognitive abilities and emotional well-being. (para. 1)

WHAT MAKES VIDEO THERAPEUTIC?

Despite the relative novelty of film and video as therapeutic tools, their use in a therapeutic context is not new. They have been used to provide client feedback through the recording of group sessions reviewed and discussed later in the context of subsequent group sessions (Furman, 1990; McNiff & Cook, 1975). Widely available commercial films have been used as a cinematic form of bibliotherapy. In this form, clients are asked to view therapeutically relevant films between sessions and later discuss them as therapeutic metaphors with their therapists (Christie & McGrath, 1987, 1989).

Watching films can be healing as well. Solomon (1995) utilized movies to help treat his patients. He trademarked the term *Cinematherapy*, although the term was used earlier by Linda Berg-Cross, Pamela Jennings, and Rhoda Baruch (1990), who described this process as a way of stimulating discussion. Watching movies can also have a "direct therapeutic effect" (Wedding & Niemiec, 2003, p. 208). The idea for Cinematherapy is related to bibliotherapy, which utilizes individuals' reactions to the contents of books and other written material and employs exercises to help deal with symptoms of loneliness, guilt, hopelessness, and other symptoms of depression (Gregory, Canning, & Lee, 2004, as cited in Cohen, 2013, p. 15).

As a healing tool, creative video production in therapy might be efficacious in the treatment of many disorders (Cohen, 2013). According to artist and art therapist Rachel O'Rourke (2001), using video in art therapy can help people to heal from trauma through the creative process of video creation and environmental stimuli to encourage creative expression. Furman (1990) suggested that video therapy helps adolescents achieve therapeutic goals by providing greater feedback clarity, enhancing nonverbal responses, allowing adolescents to replay past group interactions, and generally deintensifying transference. Video techniques also can offer adolescents a more active part in their treatment by providing them with access to playback units, control of camera operations, and control over scripts. As reported by Chin et al. (1980), a group of 17- to 19-year-old high school dropouts who participated in a combination of art therapy and video therapy experienced elevated levels of self-worth and self-esteem. This result was supported by the findings of a pilot study on the use of therapeutic filmmaking, wherein the mechanisms of change that led to the achievement of therapeutic goals included feelings of mastery and changed perspectives of self (Johnson & Alderson, 2008).

Other clinicians have used video as part of therapy. Brawner (1993) used drama therapy in his work at the California Institute of Integral Studies to treat adolescents; art therapist McNiff (as cited in McNiff & Cook, 1975) used the term *video art therapy* to describe his work; Austin (2009) used animation with adolescents to inspire them to develop job skills and set goals for the future; and Gardano (1994) wrote about her work on the use of creative video therapy with adolescent girls with adjustment problems. Though the number of clinicians practicing film and video as therapeutic tools has been relatively small, it is a community that is growing rapidly, and we believe that this book will serve as the foundation for an expanding and increasingly socially relevant approach to therapy and healing.

CULTURAL DIFFERENCES IN THE BOOK

Although video therapy is a new intervention in various parts of the world, more countries than are represented by the authors in this book showed an interest in film- and video-based therapy during the writing process. Authors from Spain (Nera, 2013) and Argentina (Farias, 2007) are but two examples. Each country and culture have their own interpretations of healing, and even within a specific culture, there can be disagreements about what constitutes therapeutic interventions. This book is an attempt to understand and offer opportunities for dialogue among practitioners who are interested in using film as a healing tool in the therapy setting.

Many cultural backgrounds and ages are represented in this book: Johnson focused on First Nations populations; Cohen focused on clients with trauma backgrounds; Tuval-Mashiach and Patton, similar to Anderson and Wallace, focused on combat veterans; Mosinski focused on victims of domestic violence from different cultural backgrounds; Ehinger and Kavitski both worked with populations with severe mental illness; McGurl et al. and Kerem worked with adolescents who were dealing with grief and loss; and Austin worked with at-risk youth from various cultural backgrounds.

OUR CHALLENGE TO READERS, FUTURE FILMMAKERS, AND THERAPISTS

Although some art therapists (e.g., Austin, Ehinger, Kavitski, Mosinski, and Orr) have focused on the media and materials of using film, others have taken film beyond the therapy setting (e.g., Johnson, Tuval-Mashiach and Patton, and Kerem). Research has also been developed by McGurl et al. (Chapter 7, this volume) to show statistical analysis that might help one to establish interest in future empirical and qualitative research (Johnson & Alderson,

2008). The theoretical underpinnings of all of the collected art therapies seem to have one common construct, namely, film language, which is further explained through the art and process of editing in Chapter 3 (this volume).

Although opinions vary regarding what film- and video-based therapy is or even what to call it, this book is an attempt to build a consensus in understanding theory and practice so that this intervention can be developed. This book is not an endorsement of any particular theory; instead, it is a challenge to readers to think critically about the subject and the complexities of how this new intervention might be executed if it were peer reviewed. We challenge readers to ask questions and interact with the book. A website with a blog will allow readers to witness the video work and dialogue with each other about the nature of the content on theory and practice. The link to the webpage is http://www.filmandvideobasedtherapy.com/ and can also be found throughout the book.

Many of the contributors to this book first came into contact with each other through the small but growing body of literature on film- and video-based therapies that various theorists and practitioners have published. Scattered across the globe and often working independently from other experts in the field, we have all been working quietly in this field for a number of years. Although we have made contributions to the literature on film- and video-based therapies, our publications often have been isolated and have been difficult to review as a body of knowledge. The significance of this book is that it represents a broad survey of authors working in disparate fields, disciplines, and geographical regions on the topic of film- and video-based therapies.

Still, little agreement exists as to what term ought to be used to describe film- and video-based therapies: video art therapy (Mosinski, 2010), therapeutic filmmaking (Johnson & Alderson, 2008), or even video therapy (Furman, 1990)? Even less research has been conducted to develop a theoretical model for this kind of therapy. Though the field of art therapy has recently adopted the use of film and video as art media options, the need for more research in this area remains, particularly given the amount of research available on other artistic disciplines in this field (i.e., the use of photography, writing, drawing, music, and drama in a therapeutic context). This book is an investigation into the use of film- and video-based therapies by practicing clinicians who are emerging as experts in this new therapeutic intervention.

In This Book

This book is organized into sections, each with chapters that reflect the overall theme of the section in which they reside.

Part I: Introduction

This section highlights the importance of the ethical issues addressed therein. We encourage readers to review this chapter first, and then read subsequent chapters with these considerations in mind. We challenge readers to think about the potential of this intervention and to discuss the possible dilemmas that may occur.

Chapter 1: Introduction, by Cohen and Johnson. This chapter, as you know because you are reading it, provides an overview of the book, discusses its significance, and introduces concepts to think about as you read the following sections.

Chapter 2: A Challenge to Readers: Ethical Considerations in Film- and Video-Based Therapies, by Johnson and Cohen. This chapter addresses the ethical considerations that might arise when using film and video as therapy, as well as the concepts of health and wellness. Film- and video-based therapies have existed in some form for decades, yet little has been written about the ethical challenges that arise with the therapeutic use of these technologies. In this chapter, we outline the main ethical considerations in working with film- and video-based therapies, and then we discuss specific dilemmas that might arise for practitioners. We challenge readers by presenting these dilemmas without providing ready answers on ways to face them; instead, we invite readers to reflect upon their own ethical practices, professional guidelines, and jurisdictional considerations to guide their perspectives on these issues.

Part II: A Human Approach to Technology

This book includes a focus on theory and argues for the value of film- and video-based therapy from various perspectives, including a phenomenological approach. In this section, the contributors present theory and argue for the integration of art, psychoanalysis, and depth psychology combined with technology in this therapeutic intervention.

Chapter 3: Film/Video-Based Therapy and Editing as Process From a Depth Psychological Perspective, by Cohen and Orr. In this chapter, film/video-based therapy is explored from the perspective of using extant expressive art therapies and through the lens of a film/video editor from a depth perspective.

Chapter 4: Filming the Fantasy: Green Screen Technology From Novelty to Psychotherapy, by Ehinger. In this chapter, the author explores the use of green screen technology with various clients. He merges a unique blend of technology and psychoanalytic thinking into his version of play and art in therapy.

Chapter 5: Vision, Story, Medicine: Therapeutic Filmmaking and First Nations Communities, by Johnson. In this chapter, Johnson highlights some of the barriers that prevent First Nations individuals from accessing counseling services, introduces readers to therapeutic filmmaking, and argues why this approach to counseling might help to bypass these barriers.

Part III: Research and Validity

This section presents evidence for the efficacy of film- and video-based therapy in various settings and with different populations. The theoretical orientations represented here include the natural and human sciences. In combining qualitative and quantitative studies such as these, we attempt to improve the validity of future research on film- and video-based therapy.

Chapter 6: Expansive Palettes: A Client Video Media Experience, by Carlton. This chapter explores the topic of digital media in art therapy and describes a case wherein stop animation was used as a clinical tool. Several inherent qualities of digital video are isolated and described, and these qualities are discussed in the context of previous research outcomes that support these observations. Digital media in art therapy is further explored from the perspectives of art therapy practitioners who used this approach; the findings from an original qualitative study are summarized. The chapter concludes with questions regarding where digital media might progress as vital art forms, relational tools, and therapeutic processes in therapy.

Chapter 7: The Benefits of a Grief and Loss Program With a Unique Technological Intervention, by McGurl, Seegobin, Hamilton, and McMinn. In this chapter, the authors present compelling evidence that there is a statistical possibility that a video confessional helped to build specific skills and coping mechanisms in a group experiencing grief and loss. The authors investigated levels of hope and resilience reported by youth using a technological intervention within a grief program. The authors also analyzed the usefulness of the technological intervention in light of Worden's (1996) four tasks of grieving.

Chapter 8: Digital Storytelling as a Trauma Narrative Intervention for Children Exposed to Domestic Violence, by Anderson and Wallace. This chapter presents the use of digital storytelling as a trauma narrative intervention in the context of trauma-focused cognitive behavioral therapy for children exposed to domestic violence who received mental health services at a rural domestic violence agency.

Chapter 9: Special Education Students and Documentary Production: A Case Study, by Orr. Orr explored digital video use with students with special needs in an educational environment. Orr also explored the beneficial aspects, drawbacks, and strengths of digital video production for students with emotional, behavioral, and learning disabilities.

Chapter 10: Digital Storytelling: Using Videos to Increase Social Wellness, by Otañez and Lakota. In this chapter, an anthropological approach is used to tell the story of one woman's struggle with a family member who was suffering from mental illness. This retelling of her version of his story provided a catharsis that allowed the client to begin a discussion that might not have taken place otherwise. Although not intended as therapy, it opens up the discussion regarding when to refer someone to therapy.

Part IV: Tools for Practice Through Didactic Instruction

In this section, the contributors describe ways that video has been used in practice to promote social change by raising awareness of mental health services and individual wellness. Using the tools presented here, filmmakers along with psychologists and art therapists can work together to allow space for healing to take place in the production and editing processes.

Chapter 11: Video Art and Activism: Applications in Art Therapy, by Mosinski. This chapter presents a person-centered art therapy approach for adults using video art for learning, image making, processing life experiences, self-discovery, and empowerment. A brief discussion of video art and activism is presented to provide a context for the use of video in art therapy.

Chapter 12: Digital Storytelling: Healing for the YouTube Generation of Veterans, by and Tuval-Mashiach and Patton. This chapter focuses on a model for the use of collaborative digital video production (i.e., filmmaking) as an early intervention in the treatment of veterans coping with the stress of military service.

Chapter 13: Felt Sensing Video Art Therapy, by Kerem. In this chapter, Kerem describes therapeutic work via the creation of video art that combines two methods—namely, listening to the felt sense through the approaches of focusing and somatic experiencing. She explains the concept of the felt sense and the main principles of each approach, together with the way in which they blend in video art therapy.

Chapter 14: Expanding the Scope of Traditional Art Therapy with Green Screen Technology, by Kavitski. In this chapter, green screen technology is again introduced from practical and depth approaches. Patients in a hospital setting demonstrated that video therapy might help populations that are severely mentally ill. This chapter demonstrates how the green screen process allows patients to explore conscious and unconscious psychological themes and exhibits how using digital technology in a therapeutic context can expand the traditional scope of creative arts therapy effectively.

Chapter 15: Technology, Art Therapy, and Psychodynamic Theory: Computer Animation With an Adolescent in Foster Care, by Austin. This chapter addresses the integration of digital technologies with art therapy and psychodynamic practice. This case study, which focused on an adolescent male in foster care, demonstrated how playing video games might be used to promote the developmental task of mastering emotions and how the electronic screen might function as a therapeutic mirror.

CONCLUSION

The few clinicians who are already working in this field have demonstrated that it is possible to combine the existing traditional arts of painting, drawing, photography, music, and drama into the collaborative art of filmmaking for therapeutic purposes. Despite the work of the aforementioned art therapists and others, video therapy is not yet in popular use; however, with the increased interest in and use of social media and technology in psychology, interest in this approach could grow exponentially in the coming years.

We hope that the publication of this book might serve as a foundation for further reading, research, and practice in this area.

In this book, we focus specifically on the intersection of film- and video-based therapy. Although this book addresses theory and practice, the chapters on theory are specific to the theory of film and video as therapeutic practice. Throughout this book, different authors have very different perspectives that range from feminist to narrative to depth psychological on how and why film and video can be used in a therapeutic context. The authors represent three countries spanning two continents, and they work in the disciplines of psychology, anthropology, and art therapy. Our intention in compiling and editing this book is to illustrate the work being done in the field of film and video as therapy in the early 21st century. Our hope is that this book will serve as a review of the work completed during this time and provide inspiration for work yet to be created.

REFERENCES

Austin, B. (2009). Renewing the debate: Digital technology in art therapy and the creative process. *Journal of the American Art Therapy Association, 26*(2), 83–85. doi:10.1080/07 421656.2009.10129745

Berg-Cross, L., Jennings, P., & Baruch, R. (1990). Cinematherapy: Theory and application. *Psychotherapy in Private Practice, 8*(1), 135–156. doi:10.1300/J294v 08n01_15

Brawner, B. (1993). *The therapeutic use of video in the treatment of adolescents* (Unpublished master's thesis). California Institute of Integral Studies, San Francisco, CA.

Chin, R.J., Chin, M.M., Palombo, P., Palombo, C., Bannasch, G., & Cross, P.M. (1980). Project Reachout: Building social skills through art and video. *Arts in Psychotherapy, 7*(4), 281–284. doi:10.1016/0197-4556(80)90007-6

Christie, M., & McGrath, M. (1987). Taking up the challenge: Film as a therapeutic metaphor and action ritual. *Australian and New Zealand Journal of Family Therapy, 8*(4), 193–199.

Christie, M., & McGrath, M. (1989). Man who catch fly with chopstick accomplish anything: Film in therapy: The sequel. *Australian and New Zealand Journal of Family Therapy, 10*(3), 145–150.

Cohen, J. (2007). *The use of video therapy to treat depression in adolescent males* (Unpublished master's thesis). Walden University, Minneapolis, MN.

Cohen, J. (2013). *Film and soul: A theoretical exploration of the use of video and other film-based therapy to help transform identity in therapeutic practice* (Doctoral dissertation). Available from ProQuest Dissertations and Theses database. (UMI No. 3551606)

Farias, A. (2007). Arte terapia: Campo de conocimiento, campo de acción. Retrieved from http://www.elpsitio.com.ar/

Furman, L. (1990). Video therapy: An alternative for the treatment of adolescents. *Arts in Psychotherapy, 17*(2), 165–169. doi:10.1016/0197-4556(90)90027-N

Gardano, A. (1994). Creative video therapy with early adolescent girls in short-term treatment. *Journal of Child and Adolescent Group Therapy, 4*(2), 99–116. doi:10.1007/BF02548483

Gregory, R.J., Canning, S., & Lee, T.W. (2004). Cognitive bibliotherapy for depression: A meta-analysis. *Professional Psychology: Research and Practice, 35*(3), 275–280. doi:10.1037/0735-7028.35.3.275

Hogan, S. (2001). *Healing arts: The history of art therapy*. London, UK: Kingsley.

Hull, A. (1998). Art and transference: A comparative study of psychoanalytic transference and art and documentation of the exhibition memory, mammary, mummery. *Dissertation Abstracts International, Section A: Humanities and Social Sciences, 59*(1-A), 0009.

Jamison, K.R. (2014, August 15). Bipolar disorder and the creative mind. Retrieved from http://www.cnn.com/2014/08/14/opinion/jamison-depression-creativity/

Johnson, L., & Alderson, K.G. (2008). Therapeutic filmmaking: An exploratory pilot study. *Arts in Psychotherapy, 35*(1), 11–19. doi:10.1016/j.aip.2007.08.004

Malchiodi, C. (2014). Art therapy & expressive art therapy in trauma-informed practice and integrative approaches to practice. Retrieved from http://www.cathymalchiodi.com/#sthash.JlHnSrYy.dpuf

McNiff, S., & Cook, C. (1975). Video art therapy. *Art Psychotherapy, 2*(1), 55–53. doi:10.1016/0 090-9092(75)90027-7

Mosinski, B. (2010). Video art and activism: Applications in art therapy. In C.H. Moon (Ed.), *Materials and media in art therapy* (pp. 257–269). New York, NY: Routledge.

Nera, R.P. (2013). Video arte terapiael acto de grabar. *Arte Terapia: Papeles de Arte Terapia y Educación Artística Para la Inclusión Social, 8*, 83–103. Retrieved from http://dialnet.unirioja.es/servlet/articulo?codigo=4742563

O'Rourke, R. (2001). Anya's movies. *Afterimage, 29*(3), 9.

Rubin, J.A. (1999). *Art therapy: An introduction*. Philadelphia, PA: Brunner/Mazel.

Solomon, G. (1995). *The motion picture prescription*. Santa Rosa, CA: Aslan.

Wedding, D., & Niemiec, R.M. (2003). The clinical use of films in psychotherapy [Special issue]. *Journal of Clinical Psychology, 59*(2), 207–215. doi:10.1002 / jclp.10142

Worden, J.W. (1996). *Children and grief: When a parent dies*. New York, NY: Guilford Press.

2 A Challenge to Readers

Ethical Considerations in Film- and Video-Based Therapies

J. Lauren Johnson and Joshua L. Cohen

INTRODUCTION

It should come as no surprise to therapists practicing in this era of ubiquitous social media and Internet access that digital technologies have changed our profession. We are now able to advertise our businesses online; provide services remotely through e-mail, web chat, and video conferencing; and help our clients to cope with the overwhelming and constant barrage of work and social stressors that are a consequence of relentless connectivity. The development of these new technologies has been accompanied by many challenges to therapists, and these challenges have become especially relevant to therapists who use film- and video-based technologies as therapeutic interventions.

Although film and video have been used in therapy for decades (Johnson & Alderson, 2008, Cohen, 2013), little has been written about the challenges that these media have introduced to ethical professional practice. In this chapter, we intend to bridge that gap by exploring the ethical considerations of using film and video as therapeutic interventions. It should be noted that we do not presume that the content of this chapter provides definitive ethical guidelines to conduct video therapy, nor do we present ourselves as legal or ethical experts in this field. Rather, we are writing as practitioners of this burgeoning field who have encountered our own ethical questions and challenges in our work, and we hope that our experiences and reflections might give insight to others who are working in or considering working in this field. As such, we hope to challenge readers to think critically about the possible dilemmas that might occur while creating films or videos as part of therapy rather than as art or entertainment, and we welcome further discussion and debate about these pertinent and important issues. For this reason, we welcome readers to participate in this discourse through our online community (http://www.filmandvideobasedtherapy.com/), where we can take advantage of the dynamic and interactive capabilities of digital technologies to continue this discussion.

Though much has been written about the ethics of art therapy and the myriad art forms that might be included under that broad category, the media of film and video are unique in their combination of elements associated with performance, narrative, photography, drama, digital media, and music. Film and video are typically considered mass media, meaning that they are intended for mass distribution and consumption. As such, they have become increasingly implicated in the positive and negative therapeutic possibilities of the new and largely uncharted world of social media. With the increased use of film and video in therapy, ethical considerations now require that therapists not only reflect on what it means from an ethical standpoint to have clients represent themselves visually and aurally in their work but also consider the possibility that clients can instantly upload therapeutic films to YouTube, Facebook, and other social media sites. Therapists continue to be concerned about issues of ownership and privacy, but they now also must concern themselves with issues of access to and control of shared digital video, among others.

Film- and video-based therapies provide unique ethical challenges for therapists to consider, but we argue in this chapter that these challenges are not insurmountable. Rather, we welcome the ethical questions, dilemmas, discussions, and discomfort that might come from this distinct approach to practice. We believe that engaging in this dialogue could serve to strengthen the practice of film- and video-based therapies by collectively considering the positive and negative aspects of these legal and ethical dilemmas.

The two sections of this chapter address the considerations that we have encountered and addressed in our work as well as the questions and dilemmas that we hypothesize might occur in our work and the work of others. In the first section, we discuss the ethical considerations that arise when applying ethical principles to film- and video-based therapies, particularly with regard to informed consent, confidentiality, privacy, and ownership. We then discuss possible dilemmas to incite debate among readers and other practitioners of this work. These dilemmas include the issue of social media, the implications of working with special populations, and the appropriateness of using film- and video-based therapies with clients in crisis. Our intention in structuring the chapter this way is to provide a foundational understanding of the ethical principles at play in this work and then challenge readers to apply their own professional ethics, local jurisprudence guidelines, and personal morals to the possible dilemmas that follow.

ETHICAL CONSIDERATIONS

Informed Consent

One of the most pressing issues in any form of therapy is informed consent, which is especially important when working in relatively new areas of practice such as film- or video-based therapies. Therapists must inform clients of the novel nature of this approach, even though it is related to such established therapeutic approaches as psychodrama and art therapy, whose possible risks and benefits are more recognized. Despite being reasonably sure that film- or video-based therapies are no more risky than other forms of visual therapy, therapists do not yet know the long-term outcomes of this approach, so they must exercise full disclosure about their practice and the possible risks and benefits associated with it as best they can (Canadian Psychological Association [CPA], 2001). This information should be conveyed verbally to establish and protect the relationships between therapists and clients as well as in written form to ensure that legal interests are maintained. Through this verbal and written process, therapists can ensure that clients understand that participation in this type of therapy at this stage of its development might involve informed choices more than informed consent.

Ensuring that clients can make informed choices requires that therapists review with them the potential benefits and risks of participation, with the understanding that all of the outcomes of the therapy are simply unknown at this stage and that some outcomes might lead to unanticipated effects. Some clients might need to be made acutely aware that they are not playing or performing, but are participating in creative videos that are, in fact, therapy (Alders, Beck, Allen, & Mosinski, 2011; Cohen, 2013). Knowing the potential risks involved, including the fact that some risks are even unknown at this point, allows clients to decide whether to participate or decline. Participation ought to be based upon information given under full disclosure, meaning that nothing known by the therapists about the therapeutic approach, be it positive or negative, is kept from the clients.

One concern about the practice of full disclosure relates to the prospect of therapists showing clients' films or videos to audiences outside of the therapy room, thus allowing clients to be seen and heard by a broad audience (Brawner, 1993; Brawner & Emunah, 1992; Cohen 2013). If therapists can find ways to fully inform clients about the potential risks of this activity, including cyberbullying, exposure, and embarrassment, clients become more able to understand the potential risks and benefits, practice self-determination in deciding whether to proceed, and allow themselves to feel more emotionally safe in the therapy setting.

Each new social media technology presents ethical challenges. Many editing programs, including Final Cut Pro X, which was used by many of the authors who contributed to this book, have automatic sharing features that immediately upload videos to popular social networks such as YouTube, Vimeo, and Facebook. The ease with which people can make very private videos public ought to be a real concern for therapists working with video as a component of therapy.

The issue ought to be addressed at the informed consent stage and again when beginning the editing process. In this ongoing process, therapists would not only obtain informed consent at the beginning of the therapeutic process but also ensure that their clients are informed of the risks and benefits throughout the duration of therapy and that they have the opportunity to continue to participate in or withdraw from therapy.

Confidentiality

With this approach to therapy, one major concern lies in determining what constitutes confidential information. Beyond the confidentiality considerations associated with all forms of therapy, film- or video-based therapies share with other visual forms of art therapy the difficulty of distinguishing what might be considered confidential aside from the verbal communication exchanged during the therapeutic process. According to the Canadian Art Therapy Association's (CATA, 2003) standards of practice, art therapists are required to consider any information exchanged during therapy through verbal and visual avenues as confidential. Extrapolated to film- and video-based therapies, any films, clips, drawings, scripts, scenarios, and proposals produced during or for the therapeutic process ought to be treated as confidential information and require special consideration (CATA, 2003; CPA, 2001; Hammond & Gantt, 1998). In our clinical experience, such material, including electronic data stored on computers and on videotapes, has been kept confidential through the use of password-protected computer filing procedures and locked storage cabinets.

Privacy

Privacy is what makes intimacy possible in therapy. Beyond the therapy setting, privacy is also implicated in the broader context of human dignity and rights. The issue of privacy is addressed in the first and most important ethical principle that guides the practice of psychology in Canada, and plays a significant role in American ethics as well (APA, 2010; CPA, 2001). If clients choose to share their work, they as well as their therapists need to understand the possible consequences (Alders et al., 2011).

However, if clients choose not to share their work, their right to privacy should be honored by their therapists. The right to privacy has been recognized as a basic human right by the United Nations (2014). Given this fact, therapists working with film and video as therapeutic strategies ought to be especially concerned about protecting their clients' privacy.

At the same time, this particular type of therapeutic work poses challenges to the provision of therapeutic privacy. For instance, clients might record their own images in their therapeutic videos; record their therapists' images; and include images, personal information, audio recordings, and other representations of themselves and others in their therapeutic videos. The mere existence of these recorded representations might already be problematic in terms of privacy, even when they are held strictly confidential within the confines of the therapy session. What happens, then, if clients want to share their videos with others?

According to the APA's (2010) code of ethics, therapists must take reasonable measures to protect the privacy of their clients and ensure that they obtain permission from clients for any audio and/or visual recordings made in therapy. Therapists ought to take steps in advance to protect their clients' private information in the event that computers, cameras, or other devices are lost, stolen, or damaged. In the context of particularly heated sessions, clients might become involved in emotional outbursts and destroy equipment that contains other clients' material and information. Encrypted backups of digital information might mitigate such situations. It also might be prudent to store the material in secure locations, such as therapists' offices, rather than have clients store their own confidential material by, for example, allowing them to take home video cameras with therapeutic video footage on them.

Once therapeutic videos have been completed, what is done with the recordings? For some clients and therapists, privately sharing therapeutic work with select individuals, perhaps through private e-mail communications or just between therapists and clients, might be one option. However, Internet security is never guaranteed, and even the most limited sharing of electronic information requires some practice guidelines. In the United States, the Art Therapy Credentials Board's (ATCB, 2011) Code of Professional Practice states that art therapists must "address issues related to the difficulty of maintaining the confidentiality of electronically transmitted communications, and the difficulty in removing any information or imagery that has been posted electronically if consent is later revoked" (p. 12).

If therapists or clients want to share therapeutic work more publicly, such as by posting therapeutic work online, privacy becomes especially difficult to maintain. The American Art Therapy Association's (AATA, 2011) practice guidelines suggest that in the case of video- or film-based therapies, clients' images should remain private for legal and ethical reasons. However, a dilemma arises when some clients feel the need to be seen and heard for the therapy to be effective (Brawner, 1993; Cohen, 2013); as such, it might be therapeutic for clients to share their private therapeutic work in public settings.

In contrast to the AATA's (2011) guidelines, the ATCB's (2011) code, which is enforceable, stated that

> [Art therapists] must ensure that appropriate steps are taken to protect client identity and disguise any part of the notes, art expression or audio or video recording that reveals client identity unless the client or guardian specifically designates in the signed consent that their identity may be revealed. (p. 9)

This statement suggested a more lenient perspective toward the public display of therapeutic videos. In addition to the issues of privacy and confidentiality, the prospect of publicly sharing therapeutic videos raises questions of ownership and control. For example, as therapists, do we have the right to restrict what clients can do with their own therapeutic artistic works? In cases such as these, therapists might be faced with the prospect of pitting their own legal protection against what might be best for the clients.

Legally, limitations exist about what can be posted online in regard to health information. For instance, Beck (2009) asserted that health practitioners such as therapists "cannot use any information that links an individual to their specific health information" (para. 4). If a person can be identified as a therapy client with a particular diagnosis based upon a video-based therapy session that is posted online, that person's right to health information privacy has been compromised. As Beck argued, if one posts

> a video or pictures of a person in a way that makes it clear that they are a part of, for example, an autism group or receiv[ing] psychotherapy from a practitioner who specializes in eating disorders, it allows others to put [two and two] together. (para. 4)

One response to this concern was addressed by the ATCB code of ethics (2011) which stated that art therapists must "inform clients of the benefits and limitations of using information technology applications in the therapeutic process" (p. 12). This might involve allowing the clients or participants to understand the limitations of the technology as well as taking into consideration that their separate backgrounds in technology might influence their cognitive, physical, and emotional limitations throughout their work. Therapists should be aware of these limitations in video- or film-based therapies because they could influence how they work with clients clinically and ethically (Alders et al., 2011) as part of the informed consent process.

The CATA (2003) took a similar stance on privacy: The standards of practice stated that art therapists must make "[e]very effort . . . to avoid undue invasion of the client's privacy" (p. 3). Meanwhile, the CPA's (2001) code of ethics for psychologists dedicated six ethical standards to the topic of privacy, noting that psychologists must "take care not to infringe . . . on the personally, developmentally, or culturally defined private space of individuals or groups, unless clear permission is given to do so" (p. 12). Private space was interpreted broadly in this case, referring not only to physical space but also to any representation (i.e., image or sound) or information that was considered within the realm of privacy.

Informed Choice for Clients and Therapists

Regarding informed consent and the maintenance of the privacy of clients' identities, it is important for artwork that could identify clients to be disguised, according to Section 4.5 of the AATA's (2011) ethical principles.

However, if a video is used in research, this principle might not apply (Rosenstein, 2002) because video sessions in therapy can be used in studies. Proper consent forms would need to be obtained in order for the video material to be included in future research. In addition, any institution doing the research needs to approve the research of human subjects through the institution's ethics review board (Alders et al., 2011).

One simple solution to potentially infringing upon clients' privacy is to avoid the use of representative audio and images in therapeutic videos that have the potential to identify clients. However, we believe that this approach is pedantic and robs clients of the potential for growth from exploring the self via video representations. We prefer to discuss the issue of privacy with clients during the film- and video-making process and find ways to proceed while safeguarding their privacy. For instance, it might be worthwhile to develop a release form with clients so that even if the boundaries of privacy are pushed during the creation of a therapeutic video, permission has been received to do so and, as such, would still comply with the CPA's (2001) privacy principles already mentioned.

In the process of maintaining clients' privacy, it might be necessary to address the irreversible nature of information once it is posted online. Clients who have a strong need to be seen and heard may not be aware of the potential harm of putting their work on the Internet. In regard to this topic, both the AATA (2011) and the ATCB (2011) have clearly advised art therapists to remind clients that maintaining confidentiality when using the Internet can be difficult, if not impossible, once information is posted. Clients also must be made aware that they can revoke their consent to have their work posted online at any time.

Ownership

According to visual researcher Prosser (2000), "The issue of ownership and control is central since disconcertingly, and unlike in word-orientated research, not only do participants have the opportunity to see themselves interacting with each other, but so too do others" (p. 129). This assertion is equally true when visual material is used in therapy. This concern about ownership and control relates to how the visual material is handled and, more importantly, who decides what happens with the information.

Hammond and Gantt (1998) stated that the nature of the art produced in art therapy is extremely personal and that beyond concerns about confidentiality, it must sometimes be considered private information that should not be filed or shared with anyone who could misinterpret the contents. When the content of films or anything else produced during the process of therapeutic filmmaking is deemed potentially harmful, such as libelous claims about others or the use of people's images without their consent, material not suitably related to the purposes of the therapy, and/or material open to misinterpretation by others, this content could be entitled to protection as private information (CPA, 2001; Hammond & Gantt, 1998). As such, clients must be informed of their responsibility to protect their own rights as well as the rights of individuals who might be mentioned or featured in their videos. This responsibility could involve the creation of release forms for collateral parties and release forms that must be signed by all custodial parents of children whose images might appear in therapeutic films.

However, going back to Prosser's (2000) concerns about ownership and control, decisions about what is considered private and confidential should not be made by clinicians alone. Any information that could pose a risk to the privacy and confidentiality of the people involved ought to be addressed through ongoing consultations with clients regarding any potential harm, noting that harm is possible now and in the future, for example, when a child who is featured in a therapeutic film grows up. Through these discussions, clinicians and clients might mutually decide whether to include or remove material in films and/or in their files, including to what extent such material should be included, and how best to carefully store or ethically destroy that information.

According to the standards of practice established by the CATA (2003),

> Art therapists shall advise clients at the commencement of treatment about ownership of the artwork within the treatment mandate. Art therapists shall approach the release and/or disposal of artwork as a treatment issue and shall decide upon its release and/or disposal in consultation with the client (or legal guardian). (p. 2)

The AATA's (2011) guidelines agreed with the CATA's standards on this issue. As such, it would appear that although the issue of art ownership generally rests with clients, therapists ought to discuss the ownership, possession, and destruction of art materials with clients so that they can reach mutually acceptable decisions on these questions when they arise. A general reading of the CATA standards of practice suggests that such consultations ought to be ongoing and dynamic throughout therapy.

POSSIBLE DILEMMAS

We addressed some of the common ethical themes that arise when working with film and/or video as therapeutic tools in earlier sections. In this section, we move away from a discussion of the guidelines and standards and begin to consider the hypothetical concerns, possibilities, and questions that might arise as we continue our work in this field. As practitioners in a relatively new field, we have been asked many times to defend what we do and why we do it, and to consider how we know that what we do is ethical. We have been challenged to consider when it would be inappropriate to use this approach and to address whether aspects of this work might be discriminatory (i.e., against people with disabilities who might not be able to use filmmaking equipment directly). For instance, "TAP [The Animation Project] uses the theory of Kramer's third hand, an art therapy modality that is used when disabled clients are unable to do the artwork for themselves and need the therapist to do the work for them" (Austin, as cited in Cohen, 2013, p. 80). Given these experiences, we would like to pose some of these practical ethical questions to readers. We do not purport to have all of the answers to these questions, but we pose them because they are important to consider as we continue to expound on the legitimacy and acceptance of film and video as therapeutic tools. We welcome further discussion and debate about these issues in future publications and other modes of communication.

What Makes a Film Therapeutic?

Although we fully believe in the power of film and video to heal, it is possible for people who are filmmakers or artists who are not licensed or accredited as therapists to do harm by claiming to be doing therapeutic work with their films. To reduce this potential for harm, we must differentiate between films intended for health reasons and those meant to provide entertainment. For example, films intended for entertainment are typically intended to move an audience to feel something and to be a good return on an investment; therapeutic films are intended to be a form of personal exploration and expression, and are primarily made for the filmmakers alone.

Filmmakers who are not therapists have a very different ethical commitment than licensed professionals to society at large and to the people whom they claim to be helping. Filmmakers are not bound by the same ethical oversight that we are, making them more free to participate in potentially harmful practices, such as the exploitation of documentary participants. As therapists and psychologists, we have an ethical duty to work for the good of society as a whole, as well as our clients specifically, and to conduct ourselves professionally in our work.

We have a duty to protect our professions and practices from association with those who might do harm, intentionally or unintentionally, and to distinguish between filmmakers and therapists. For these reasons, practitioners of therapeutic filmmaking need to further discuss what makes therapeutic films different from documentaries or fictional films that are intended as art or entertainment, and to ensure that both the public and our own professions understand this difference.

Film- and Video-Based Therapies and Crisis Situations

If clients are actively suicidal or homicidal and are deemed at high risk to act upon their ideations, would video therapy be the best intervention for them? We have reflected on this question quite often in our practices.

This question is particularly challenging for therapists who are dealing with new clients. If clients have been seeing their therapists for years, the answer to this question will depend on the experience of the therapists and their familiarity with video therapy as an intervention. For instance, experienced therapists who have strong relationships with clients might be able to direct the clients' harmful ideations towards nonviolent expression through the video production process, possibly leading to insight, catharsis, and a reduction of risk. However, given the level of risk in situations like these, a film- or video-based approach might not be recommended. Instead, therapists might need to abandon creative methods temporarily and use directive approaches involving the development of safety plans, referrals to emergency services, and preparation for the possible need to break confidentiality.

Questions Regarding Posttraumatic Stress Disorder

Video-based therapies have been used in the treatment of posttraumatic stress disorder (PTSD), as detailed in this book in the chapters written by Tuval-Mashiach and Patton (Chapter 12) and Mosinski (Chapter 11). Some therapists working with this treatment issue have determined that guiding clients in telling their trauma narratives through video is helpful in their recovery from trauma. In addition, it is possible for therapists to use the production and editing processes as a form of exposure or flooding that might help clients to process their traumatic experiences. Indeed, the multistage process of making videos could be a progressive exposure technique in which clients are first asked to imagine and discuss their traumatic events, represent them visually, and then represent them using audio and visual techniques so that the traumatic experiences become more realistic and more challenging with each progression.

However, what might happen if clients are traumatized or memories are triggered by the images that they have produced? In this case, does the ethical issue become one of therapist competence and whether therapists have the training and experience to engage in certain therapeutic techniques such as exposure? Even if therapists have the training necessary to engage in exposure techniques, would psychologists specializing in behavioral or cognitive behavioral techniques be better trained to deal with potential crisis situations using more direct methods? These questions remain at the forefront of our consideration as we continue exploring this fascinating and potentially powerful area of practice.

Questions Regarding Working With Incarcerated Populations

Film- and video-based therapies have been used with incarcerated clients. For example, in an interview regarding the use of film and video in therapy, drama therapist Brawner (1993) discussed the ways in which correctional institutions can be safe environments for video therapy (Cohen, 2013).

However, Brawner suggested that therapists engaging in this work with incarcerated individuals should not refer to it as therapy, given that the stigma of being in therapy might prohibit clients' full participation and subsequently reduce the effectiveness of video therapy. This assertion brought about some pointed ethical questions for us: When faced with such a debilitating level of stigma, how can therapists ethically engage in video therapy? How can clients provide informed consent without agreeing that they are participating in therapy? How might one maintain the appeal of the project for clients who are resistant to participating in therapy without misleading them about what it is? Though these are questions that we have not addressed directly in our own work, we challenge readers to consider how the issues of stigma, consent, and confidentiality might intersect in the context of working with incarcerated individuals.

Questions Regarding Working With At-Risk Youth

In Chapter 15, Austin demonstrates through a case example how film- and video-based therapies might work with at-risk youth. However, the members of this population provide an ethical challenge for therapists using film- and video-based methods because if clients are under the age of 18 years, they typically require the consent of a parent or a guardian to participate in therapy. Gaining this consent is sometimes difficult, particularly if the parent or guardian is part of the reason that the youth is considered at risk.

Working with these clients presents unique challenges related to consent and privacy because of their age and vulnerability, but these challenges can be overcome. Austin explains in his chapter that through the use of film- and video-based therapies, the at-risk youth with whom he worked were able to transition into jobs and inhibit impulsive decision making. Nevertheless, many questions arose as we began to consider the prospect of working with members of this population, but rather than begin to answer them ourselves, we challenge readers to consider how they might answer them based upon their own professional standards and practices: How should therapists deal with accusations of abuse that might be recorded or dramatized in a video? What might the legal implications of accusations such as these be for the accusers, the accused, and witnesses to the accusations (i.e., therapists, the video's audience, etc.)? How can informed consent be obtained? Should informed assent to participate be obtained from the youth? If this therapy is conducted in a group setting, what considerations around confidentiality, privacy, and physical and emotional safety might arise?

Questions Regarding Working With the Issue of Domestic Violence

In this book, Mosinski (Chapter 11) explores the issue of using a video-based intervention with clients who are victims of domestic abuse, demonstrating that this intervention can be effective. Film- and video-based therapies can be used in a number of ways to help victims and perpetrators of domestic abuse. For instance, producing creative videos about their experiences might give clients important insights, improve communication skills, promote the development of empathy, and provide other possible benefits. However, producing videos focusing on domestic abuse could lead to various ethical dilemmas: What might happen if victims' videos were viewed by the perpetrators, who then objected to their portrayal? What might the legal and ethical implications be if accusations of abuse were disseminated through the public release of therapeutic videos? What steps should therapists take to ensure that their clients remain safe throughout the therapeutic process?

Questions Regarding the Use of Film- and Video-Based Therapies With Clients Who Are Severely Mentally Ill

Though some of the earliest therapeutic use of film took place in the psychiatric ward of a hospital in Switzerland (Muller & Bader, 1972), little has been written about using film- and video-based therapies with individuals who are severely mentally ill. Though documentation has been scarce, it does not mean that this approach to therapy cannot or should not be used with members of this population. For example, in Chapter 3 Cohen describes a client suffering from bipolar disorder who uses video editing to focus her manic energy. In Chapter 14, Kavitski describes a client diagnosed with bipolar disorder who was able to reflect on his videotaped behavior and gain important insights into his manic state. However, important ethical questions arise in engaging in film- and video-based therapies with clients who have certain diagnoses, such as those involving psychosis. For instance, might creative endeavors encourage the propagation of clients' delusions and fantasies, particularly when using technologies such as green screen, or could they provide safe ways of regulating the autonomic nervous system, as described by Levine (1997)?

In addition, how might issues of safety and reality testing be addressed? How might psychiatrists, physicians, nurses, and other members of multidisciplinary health care teams respond to and work with this approach to therapy? Responses might involve a combination of stabilizing clients by using medication first and then requiring that they participate in talk therapy before being approved to join a video therapy group. Although film- and video-based therapies might not be universally appropriate for all people suffering from severe mental illnesses, the chapters in this book provide hope that this approach can be appropriate and effective in working with these populations.

CONCLUSION

When faced with pioneering a new approach to therapy using technology, it is important to look back at what existed previously. Therapies using the expressive arts have helped to establish ethical standards and address ethical questions about the use of technology in therapy. Technology is becoming a more relevant and pervasive component of therapy, and with expansion of the Affordable Care Act in the United States and the use of electronic health records, along with other Internet-based and portable technologies such as Skype and iPads in therapy, we therapists must address the larger issue of how technology is changing the profession and how we ought to approach this change ethically.

We pose this question to readers: How should we approach the technical, legal, and ethical challenges related to film- and video-based therapies? We encourage readers to think of possible challenges as well as reasons to support this therapeutic intervention. We invite readers to explore the rest of the book with the curiosity of children but the critical analysis of thinkers, philosophers, scientists, and anthropologists by reading each chapter carefully and with equal consideration to find ways to make their own film- or video-based practice meaningful, ethical, and safe.

REFERENCES

Alders, A., Beck, L., Allen, P.B., & Mosinski, B.B. (2011). Technology in art therapy: Ethical challenges. *Art Therapy: Journal of the American Art Therapy Association, 28*(4), 165–170. doi:org/10.1080/07421656.2011.622683

American Art Therapy Association. (2011). *Ethical principles for art therapists.* Retrieved from http://www.americanarttherapyassociation.org/upload/ethical principles.pdf

American Psychological Association. (2010). Ethical principles of psychologists and code of conduct. Retrieved from http://www.apa.org/

Art Therapy Credentials Board. (2011). Code of professional practice. Retrieved from http://www.atcb.org/

Beck, L. (2009, September 20). *Ethics and the Internet* [Blog post]. Retrieved from http://www.lizbeck.net/

Brawner, B. (1993). *The therapeutic use of video in the treatment of adolescents* (Unpublished master's thesis). California Institute of Integral Studies, San Francisco.

Brawner, B., & Emunah, R. (1992). *Caring for the inner one: Self expression and self acceptance in drama therapy* [Video recording]. San Francisco: California Institute for Integral Studies.

Canadian Art Therapy Association. (2003). *Standards of practice.* Toronto, ON: Author.

Canadian Psychological Association. (2001). *Companion manual to the Canadian code of ethics for psychologists* (3rd ed.). Ottawa, ON: Author.

Cohen, J. (2013). *Film and soul: A theoretical exploration of the use of video and other film-based therapy to help transform identity in therapeutic practice* (Doctoral dissertation). Available from ProQuest Dissertations and Theses database. (UMI No. 3551606)

Hammond, L.C., & Gantt, L. (1998). Using art in counselling: Ethical considerations. *Journal of Counseling & Development, 76*, 271–276.

Johnson, J.L., & Alderson, K.G. (2008). Therapeutic filmmaking: An exploratory pilot study. *Arts in Psychotherapy, 35*(1), 11–19.

Levine, A. P. (1997). *Waking the tiger: Healing trauma*. Berkeley, CA: North Atlantic Books.
Muller, C., & Bader, A. (1972). Therapeutic art programs around the world IX: Filmmaking in a Swiss psychiatric hospital. *American Journal of Art Therapy, 11*(4), 185–189.
Prosser, J. (2000). The moral maze of image ethics. In H. Simons & R. Usher (Eds.), *Situated ethics in educational research* (pp. 116–132). London, UK: Routledge.
Rosenstein, B. (2002). Video use in social science research and program evaluation. *International Journal of Qualitative Methods, 1*(3). Article 2. Retrieved November 10, 2009 from http://www.ualberta.ca/~ijqm
United Nations. (2014). The Universal Declaration of Human Rights. Retrieved from http://www.un.org/en/documents/udhr/

Part II

A Human Approach to Technology

3 Film/Video-Based Therapy and Editing as Process From a Depth Psychological Perspective

Joshua L. Cohen and Penelope P. Orr

> The movies are far more efficient than the theatre; they are less restricted, they are able to produce amazing symbols to show the collective unconscious, since their methods of presentation are so unlimited.
>
> —C. G. Jung, 1984, p. 12

> As far as I'm concerned, editing is where the filmmaking process hits the road.
>
> —George Lucas, as cited in Clarkson, Daniels, & Shuper, 2004

INTRODUCTION

Like therapy, editing is a process. This chapter is a metaphoric and literal way of showing how filmmaking can be a process that is different from other art forms but one that also can include all of them. Film has traditionally been a method of expression on a scale meant to reach mass audiences. It also has been used to explore the innermost dimensions of the psyche in order to inspire and nurture the soul of the filmmaker (Brawner, 1993; Johnson & Alderson, 2008; Tosone, Gelman, & McVeigh, 2005). Film/video-based therapy (FVBT) fascinates therapists and clients because it is a modality for capturing and visually representing personal dreams and myths that reflect the collective unconscious. Although film is a contemporary art form, it encompasses storytelling, one of the oldest arts known. Storytelling is an ancient art form that is used in the writing and editing process in filmmaking (Murch, 2001). Because editing can be considered an extension of the writing process, the language of filmmaking should be studied in order to understand how it can be used therapeutically.

To explore the complex and often irrational aspects of the inner world of the unconscious, a language was needed to express and communicate the nature of the journey and what one discovers. Depth psychology provides such a language. Traditionally, depth psychology approaches to therapy have used writing, imagery, discussion, and amplification as the media for this exploration. Film production, particularly the editing process, might be well suited to expressing the personal and collective unconscious. Editing is a major component of the language of film that communicates in a way not found in traditional depth psychology approaches to therapy.

Film production, however, has many qualities in common with traditional expressive media that have been used in therapy for their healing potential. Editing in film is a process that creates and alters time, motion, and mood (Clarkson et al., 2004). Depth psychology focuses on what matters to people in life, but it also can be applied to what matters for people in the art-making process. Although my (Cohen) interviews with therapists using FVBT revealed many perspectives on how and why to use film and video within therapy, all of the therapists agreed that the language of film matters to people and that it can help in the healing process by conveying clients' stories (Cohen, 2013). Through a review of the literature and case studies from private practice, this chapter is an attempt to refine, criticize, and improve upon a theory of FVBT in which the medium and art of editing film can transform a message from an abstract unconscious form into a communicative storytelling event.

PART 1: THEORY

Researcher's Perspective

My name is Josh Cohen, and as a doctoral-degree-prepared researcher, my focus for the past 17 years has been to develop a theory on the use of filmmaking in therapy. I draw from my liberal arts and natural sciences background to structure counseling in a way that facilitates my clients' telling of their personal stories, a process that is vital to healing. In my work with clients, I use a variety of theoretical approaches (e.g., psychodynamic psychology, positive psychology, cognitive behavioral psychology, and depth psychology) to give my clients' inner feelings a voice, thus facilitating symptom relief and a way to thrive in their daily lives. Depth psychology is the approach that I most often use with clients when we work with film because it goes beyond symptom relief and works toward integration and wholeness.

Film is a distinctive medium in that it can express archetypal and sensual forms of nature that although not "healthy" in the sense of Western medicine, can provide a sense of health. Film engages people in a seductive dance with the dramatic so that a catharsis or purification, in the Greek sense, can be reached Cohen, (1998, 2000). In essence, the goal is to find a balance among desire, pleasure, discipline, and focus in a receptacle that can hold such passion. Film is a natural receptacle for this process. I have found this to be true in my own participation in the production of videos.

In 2001, documentary film director Doug Pray directed a film on the Dalai Lama and asked me to edit it. In the video (found on www.

filmandvideobasedtherapy.com), the Dalai Lama explains how monks at the Namgyal monastery helped to restore fungus-infested VHS tapes to a digital format in order to preserve his teachings. The monastery upgraded to a high-tech solution out of necessity. It was strange to watch the monks in their robes editing audio and video and burning DVDs; however, the Dalai Lama is known for claiming that science does not conflict with Buddhism. In the video, he stated:

> Wherever technology goes, if all human values are disregarded then, of course, there is a danger. If we human beings become slaves of the technology, of course this is wrong. Human value always remains above. Then, under that, to use technology in a maximum way to help achieve these goals is very good.
>
> (as cited in Kuwahara & Pray, 2001)

In an interview appearing in *The Huffington Post*, the Buddhist teacher, who has 8.5 million followers on Twitter, further discussed the use of technology, noting, "I think technology really increased human ability, but technology cannot produce compassion. We are the controller of the technology. If we become a slave of technology, then [that's] not good" (as cited in Alamendrala, 2014, para. 3).

The Dalai Lama's comments on technology referred not only to technology in general but also to the ways in which making movies can be helpful to humanity if one has human purposes in mind, such as the preservation of wisdom, as in the case of the digital restoration of his recorded teachings. Later in the interview, he stated that technology cannot produce compassion. In my published research on the use of filmmaking in therapy, I theorized that although one cannot create empathy, one can create the space for empathy within a safe therapeutic space that allows transformation to take place (Cohen, 2007b, 2013).

The entire film production process allows clients to tell their stories by facilitating the development of a language that merges conscious logic with unconscious aspects of the psyche. Editing film is a process similar to what clients might go through when putting together the pieces of their life stories.

Editing as Language

Editing film involves a language that has its own grammar (Bowen, 2013). The scenes of a film are usually shot out of order, so it becomes the editor's job to put the pieces together, just as it is the job of therapists to help clients to put together the pieces of their lives and psychic material that emerges in the course of therapy.

In feature films, the grammar of editing, direction, and writing can allow one to see the unconscious through the filmmakers. The director and screenwriter of *A Beautiful Mind* "interpreted Nobel Laureate John Nash's subjective view of his schizophrenic hallucinations and delusions through acting, digital effects, writing, and directing, a process that allowed the viewer to empathize with Nash during the experience" (Cohen, 2007a, p. 3). In addition, Howard and Grazer (2001) used editing and special effects to bring the viewers into the mind of John Nash. Using this unique technique of editing and direction and writing, one could empathize with the perspective of the protagonist. "The filmmakers used techniques of audio editing to allow viewers to experience Nash's hallucinations as he mostly likely did. For a schizophrenic, appearances are preceded by audio hallucinations, according to Howard" (Cohen, 2007a, p. 3).

It also seemed natural to use audio editing because the hallucinations were auditory and visual, meaning that they could be represented in both media. Editing is somewhat unique as an art form in that it can combine audio and visual elements, whereas other arts are limited.

"Through the editing process, Howard made sure that throughout the film, whenever the hallucinated figure of Charles appeared, viewers would hear him before seeing him, thus indicating that Nash's audio hallucinations may have preceded the visual hallucinations" (Cohen, 2007a, p. 3).

From a depth point of view, image plays an important role. In psychoanalytic theory, a form of depth psychology, "the ego involves a perception of the external world, self-awareness, problem solving, control of motor functions, adaptation to reality, memory and reconciliation of conflicting impulses and ideas" (APA, 2007, p. 317). The filmmakers used image and audio to bring about an internal perception of the external world. Specifically, they used "computer graphics to visualize John's thought process, thereby giving the viewer an opportunity to empathize with his perspective and recognize the prodromal symptoms of the illness. The filmmakers used light flashes to indicate his insights" (Cohen, 2007a, p. 3). This example of filmmaking illustrates how the editing process, with its manipulation of sound, light, effects, and pacing, is critical in conveying unconscious elements of the human story.

Many believe that storytelling in film is accomplished only in the writing and directing phases; however, the editing process is equally, if not more, essential for creating the overall tone and pace of a film. Composing a language using images and sounds together requires many elements that make the film editing process unique. The emotional language of editing employs many different levels of arts and technology combined to bring one coherent story to life. Walter Murch (2001), editor of *Apocalypse Now, The English Patient*, and many other films, stated that he cuts on emotion when he integrates the arts into a narrative that flows together.

Art Making as Therapy

The postproduction process in film usually includes any processes that occur after shooting the film or video. One such process is editing, which involves several stages of integration of different arts in a specific order. The editing process can bring emotional clarity, and the structural stages of the process can provide boundaries, direction, and a feeling of safety in the repetitive actions involved. When film editing is included in a therapeutic process, clients with a diagnosis of bipolar disorder, for instance, might find this structure useful in providing focus and direction. Each art form that is integrated in film through the editing process has been used within therapeutic specialties such as art therapy, music therapy, narrative therapy, dance therapy, and drama therapy.

What makes films different from other media employed in arts therapies and talk therapy is the combination of arts in the editing process. FVBT might integrate existing expressive art therapies that range from drama (Emunah, 1997) to painting (Plante, Cote, Saint-Jean, & Pilic, 1979); drawing (McNamee, 2004); journaling (Progoff, 1973a, 1973b); photography (Stewart, 1979); poetry (Gorelick, 2005); music therapy (Hillecke, Wormit, & Bardenheuer, 2004; (Kerem, Chapter 13, this volume); Lehtonen, 2002); and animation (Austin, 2010). The process of editing the various expressions of these activities into a film is still being explored for its therapeutic potential. Because "the audio and visual images allow clients to symbolize and organize inner chaos in some form" (Kerem, Chapter 13, this volume), FVBT is concerned with the inward journey into the unconscious through the language of depth psychology using film and editing as media to give it form.

> Editing requires that clients themselves choose what comes first, what comes second, and so on, until the end. Clients decide what will go beside what, what will be in front and what will be on the sides, and what will receive a great deal of screen time and what will receive less.
>
> (Kerem, Chapter 13, this volume)

My intent in writing this chapter is not to describe the process of editing or the use of filmic language, but to explain how the use of FVBT, along with depth psychology's perspective on the significance of imagery in myths and dreams, can be used with clients, with a particular emphasis on video editing. The value of video editing in therapy is that it "permits repeated approaches at various levels of processing that promote [the processes of] inner observation and internalization. It is a crystallizing experience" (Kerem, Chapter 13, this volume).

A JUNGIAN APPROACH TO FILM: MYTHOLOGY

> I think that the movie is the perfect medium for mythological messages. The medium is so plastic and pliable and magic things can happen. And then the combination . . . of fantastic landscape and possible modes of action and voyaging that we can hardly conceive of in good solid

> terms. . . . That's a mythological realm, and movies could handle this kind of thing.
>
> —Campbell, 1997

Because editing is part of the directing and writing process, it is important to understand how essential imagination, dreams, and myths are to Jungian or depth psychology. The Jungian approach toward film involves looking within, that is, to one's unconscious. This is done in therapy partly by examining clients' transference in sessions, keeping track of their dreams, or working with images made by the client. Symbols and metaphors are the basis of much of depth psychologist Jung's work in describing the unconscious, and mythology is central to that language.

To understand how depth psychology applies to editing, the role of mythology in depth psychology must be acknowledged. Mythologist Campbell (1988) used mythology and dreams to guide people toward their own adventures in life and thus help them to find their bliss. As therapists working with clients, we are always looking for ways to draw out and hear their stories. The editing process is a way of emphasizing and facilitating the expression of clients' stories, including any trauma that they might have endured. Depth psychology, like Campbell's approach to mythology, is more optimistic than traditional Freudian analysis in that it welcomes many possibilities of interpreting the unconscious. Video provides a way of literally and figuratively representing clients' stories in ways that allow clients and therapists to see the positive and negative aspects of trauma. The purpose of Campbell's mythological approach is not only to find happiness but also to acquire a serene sense of self that puts one in the moment, experiencing life as a heroic journey (as cited in Campbell, 1988).

The way film editing relates to the unconscious and myths also can be seen through the use of dream interpretation. Like Jung, Campbell (1988) believed that myths and dreams come from the same source, namely, humanity's collective unconscious. Depth-oriented psychotherapists are always alert for the expression of their clients' stories. Film and video provide a way of representing clients' stories literally and figuratively so that clients and therapists can see and hear them. Through the FVBT process, clients' personal myths are articulated, including the archetypes that dwell in the unconscious. When one tends to a dream, one is creatively interacting with images, much in the way that an editor would tend to a movie.

Emphasizing themes in the footage is an aspect of the film editing process. The hero's journey is a common theme in many narratives and stories in popular and independent films. Jung (1952/1983) stated, "The hero symbolizes a man's unconscious self, and this manifests itself empirically as the sum total of all archetypes and therefore includes the archetype of the father and of the wise old man" (p. 333). In Campbell's (1949) book, *The Hero With a Thousand Faces*, he outlined the path of the hero in the myths of many different cultures and pointed out the common themes of the hero's story. Campbell identified the hero myth as the *monomyth*.

Filmmaker George Lucas emphasized new forms of editing in the production of the *Star Wars* saga (1977–2005) as well as in his writing. Lucas stated, "When I sit down, I don't just cut a movie. I actually rewrite it and redirect it. As far as I'm concerned, editing is where the filmmaking process hits the road" (as cited in Clarkson et al., 2004). In his narrative, Lucas used Campbell's outline of the monomyth to help construct his epic film series. Lucas was followed by other filmmakers who saw the potential of this heroic structure in modern film; however, the hero myth goes far beyond the more contemporary heroes we might see in today's cinema to more subtle themes and other genres. By using a heroic journey for a structure, one can see a simple yet complicated pattern of departure, fulfillment, and return. In the final stages, the hero brings the boon to society, which is also the role of the editor and the therapist in taking the "undigested remnants" (Hillman, 1983, p. 28) of experience that dwell in the psyche and integrating them into some sort of meaning that makes it possible to deal with trauma.

In the book *The Writer's Journey: Mythic Structure for Writers*, film development executive Christopher Vogler (1998) explicated a way of interpreting Campbell's (1949) mythological motifs to help screenwriters, among other types of storytellers. Stuart Voytilla (1999), a writer, script consultant, and teacher of acting and screenwriting, believed that filmmaking and, therefore, writing and editing, plays a large role in the development of a modern mythology. Extending Vogler's ideas defining the stages of the hero quest, Voytilla discussed 11 genres of motion pictures: action adventure, western, horror, thriller, war, drama, romance, romantic comedy, comedy, science fiction, and fantasy. Voytilla noted that both Jung and Campbell recognized artists as powerful influences in preserving mythologies. Campbell (1988) said, "Myths are so intimately bound to culture, time, and place that unless the symbols, metaphors, are kept alive by constant recreation through the arts, the life just slips away from them" (p. 59). Voytilla claimed that film is one form of art that keeps myths alive because it is a public expression of a collective myth or dream.

FVBT perhaps fascinates therapists and clients because it is a modality for capturing and visually representing personal dreams and myths, which also reflect the collective unconscious. When clients edit their films, they might be able to slow down the process of thought physically and emotionally and take the opportunity to play with ideas usually found only in abstraction. Through the technology found in editing, they can tangibly deal with metaphors, symbols, and ideas from the personal and collective unconscious that words might not be able to access.

Myth Making From a Depth Perspective: Written Form

In my work with clients in the entertainment industry, I asked them to begin a written journal to express their ideas and explore their inner worlds. I saw this as a way of actively engaging the unconscious in order to help them return to a state of creativity that might improve their lives and creative potentials. It is my passion to help others to realize their potential in their own creative processes, so I consider journaling a concrete tool to help to focus the narrative of the internal process toward personal growth. Psychotherapist Ira Progoff (1973a, 1973b) used journaling with his patients as a way to explore his theories related to depth psychology and transpersonal psychology (Gestwicki, 2001). He worked with Jung from 1963 to 1965 and developed a specific journaling method that he used not only for increasing self-awareness but also for exploring unconscious behaviors, including dreaming.

Progoff's goal was to introduce individuals to a process that allowed them to achieve transcendence and change through exploration (as cited in Epple, 2003). His work with Jung and the theories of depth psychology, as well as transpersonal psychology, influenced his concepts of journal writing (as cited in Gestwicki, 2001; Progoff, 1973a, 1973b). Progoff's method, along with other methods of art therapy, can be combined to form a depth approach toward filmmaking. In the process of FVBT, clients might be able to examine their own behaviors and develop self-empathy. Film can be used as a journaling tool because it is a means of telling a story.

When working with filmmakers in this deeply personal way, one can explore waking dreams and thoughts, and the technical aspects of the craft of editing can provide ways of expressing these through the language of film. Editing thus becomes a gateway to open up the language of the unconscious mind through dreams, fantasies, and the imagination, and allows patients to develop self-empathy (Cohen, 2007b).

Editing: Tending to the Image and the Unconscious

Because films are like a collective dream, it is appropriate to take a depth psychological approach toward tending to a dream using mythological motifs when applied to FVBT. Editing in film mirrors the depth psychological process in the therapy room because its recognition and use of metaphor and symbols create a narrative whereby the unconscious is portrayed consciously. Symbolic thought is important to editing because the unconscious mind does not always process ideas from a rational perspective.

James Hillman (2010), an associate of Campbell and Lucas, was a renegade Jungian analyst and a student of Jung who taught extensively in many American universities. He developed archetypal psychology and also saw the value of editing in therapy as well as in the arts. Hillman wrote that editing (i.e., psychotherapy notes) and archetypal psychology share a similar process of tending to the soul. He felt that the image is the language of the psyche and the soul.

The editing process is complex and involves putting together as well as taking out. In the film industry, professionals in postproduction understand that editing is actually part of the writing process, not just "where you take out the bad bits" (Murch, 2001, p. 10). Walter Murch, a film editor, director, and writer, described the editing process as similar to the creative writing process in the revising stages but also different because it often involves collaboration with others, which helps to develop interpersonal skills. Murch commented that "there are frequent times when two or more editors are working simultaneously, sometimes with equal authority" (Murch, 2001, p. 29). Editing film involves learning to play and work with image, sound, and meaning. Archetypal psychology lends itself to interpreting works of art, another component of editing.

PART 2: PRACTICE

Using the process of editing in therapy can help clients to bring certain concepts together and integrate the expressive art therapies. The following case studies from my practice (Cohen) and association with filmmakers are examples of how editing and working with images from a depth psychological perspective can be used to heal.

Case Study: The Stigma of Mental Illness

Another example of how editing mirrors the process of integration of the unconscious in therapy was found in my treatment of a documentary filmmaker who was suffering from psychosis and depression. She gave me consent to discuss her case here, but the details of her identity are concealed to maintain her privacy.

This woman's grief was so severe when she approached me that she could barely concentrate and needed to be prescribed Lexipro. She was already taking antipsychotic medication, but after I consulted with the psychiatrist, we both determined that the main cause of her grief was the end of a recent romantic relationship. She is a successful filmmaker who was in the process of making a film on bringing awareness to the stigma of mental illness. In her profession, she usually works at editing film on a daily basis. Once she was able to shift her focus back to the filmmaking process and the positive relationships that would happen in her future, she spent less time worrying about the past. She still had to do the therapeutic work involved, including taking medications, attending support groups, and reaching out to other support in her life. She even did some art interventions with me, but in the end, her passion for documentary film allowed her to focus on finding meaning in the loss of one relationship and refocus on her calling or purpose. Her process in therapy, along with her editing work, allowed her to focus on moving forward as well as being more present in the moment and sublimating into art her frustration regarding the breakup that had triggered her depression.

Case Study: Grounded Through Editing

Another filmmaker, editor, and producer whom I saw as a client used journaling as a way of getting in touch with and managing her scattered thinking. This practice grounded her in a way that allowed her to control the symptoms of her bipolar disorder. Instead of labeling her grandiosity and ideational flights as a disorder, I retermed the disorder a *condition* rather than an *identity*. She then adopted journaling to help to focus her attention on the narrative of her work. She discussed editing techniques and her passion to edit in a more creative way. Editing and producing were important to her because they gave her a way to cope with the disorder. She was quite concrete in her thinking, in that she needed to see results in order to become excited about the possibilities in her work. She could make plans for large projects but was very careful about the details. Her interest in editing was profound, and she viewed it as another aspect of the creative writing process. This case demonstrated that individuals with manic energy can channel it and their attention into a focused activity like editing if they are compliant with medication and thus able to concentrate. Once she was focused on editing, she was able to concentrate with passion, and it brought hope for the future by giving her concrete goals as well as tools for being in the moment.

Case Study: Breathing

In a clinical case study supervised by James Hillman, I presented a client who was suffering from severe trauma and posttraumatic stress. He had been shot in the jaw and stomach, and he was dealing with physical and psychological pain. With Hillman supervising, we used a depth psychological approach to view the client's situation.

When asked how important therapy was to him, the client stated that therapy was like breathing, figuratively and literally. Having to go through surgery and physical pain caused him much suffering, but through therapy, he felt that this "breathing" opened up the space for him to feel safe and explore the root causes of his suffering. He said that the breathing allowed him to feel as if the room were larger.

Hillman (2010) responded to this statement by asking me the following:

> Is it possible that within the larger room, working at that within the fantasy of the larger room that the larger room could pull other kinds of people, forces, images, that some of which as you said could be negative? So as long as it is kept in the larger room and the sorts of forces that used to get him upset, could be allowed into the larger room. So without changing doctrine in any way, within the realm of the imagination, those forces can come in and he doesn't have to disappear psychologically in order to . . . there is space for them, psychic space for

> them. To hang out. The fact that the psychic space has expanded, the question you raised could be held without him compromising his ideals, his religion, or anything. It's all done within the realm of the image. (audiorecording)

This process of integration of image and allowing space, or a stage upon which the images within can safely appear, is the same process that allows one to heal by using fiction, according to Hillman (1983), who once said, "The essence of theater is knowing it is theater, that one is playing, enacting, miming in a reality that is completely a fiction" (p. 39). Hillman considered art (and, by association, film) as a way of viewing things differently, and that when one views things differently, one can act differently (Cohen, 2013, p. 26).

How we see our clients, said Hillman (1983), is reflected in the words that we use in our psychotherapy notes. In his book *Healing Fiction*, Hillman expressed the opinion that we therapists should spend more time "re-writing and editing" (p. 28) our notes so that our clients do not become static entities, but remain full of character. He wrote about not losing sight of the humanity of our clients by characterizing them by diagnosis rather than by their full histories that capture the essence of the whole person.

During the supervision session, Hillman, who made comments and offered suggestions on how to tend to my client, compared the editing process when writing case notes to a fiction-writing process, which also could be applied to film editing. This also pertains to film and video editing because they both produce narratives about our clients that influence how we see them. By changing the narrative, such as in reframing the story in a session or in a movie, the depth approach, in the case of my traumatized client, softened the sensations of the trauma and allowed him to begin to confront it. The integration of the images of "the larger room" and "breathing" helped him to become brave enough to face his trauma. Even without a physical editing system, we were engaged in the process of integrating images and using depth psychology to help the client to approach a sense of wholeness again.

By using my knowledge of depth psychology and film editing in regard to images, I discovered that opening up one's space to "hang out" and allow a playful sense of safety and imagination to return to the therapy process can help to heal any condition, even trauma. The client needed to feel safe before he could be creative and openly explore ideas through images; the imagination process and the film editing process do not function without that opening-up process.

I returned to the client after the supervision session without a particular approach, but I focused on the images of the breath and the larger room. This approach gave the client a safe place to explore the trauma, and because I used a language with which he could identify, he became more capable of facing the trauma. Depth psychology's emphasis on the use of the imagination and playful approaches to image also is essential to the art of editing film.

CONCLUSION

The literature and case studies reviewed in this chapter support the notion of editing as an inherent quality that makes film unique among traditional arts used in therapy. A second inherent quality that film possesses is its integration of several different arts within the filmmaking and editing processes.

This chapter discussed FVBT using editing in conjunction with a depth psychological approach. Editing is basically a process that uses images; depth psychology also focuses on images in its use of imagination, dreams, and myths. In the process of editing, clients can talk about and project their fantasies in ways that allow them to make meaning of them, as well as to make up a new script for their lives through a more powerful way of relating to issues or topics that concern them. They are the writers and directors of their lives, and they have all of the arts at their fingertips, including acting, drawing, music, dance, writing, and FVBT, which facilitates combining various expressive art therapies into one therapy.

Many people have reported feeling empowered and connected to others through the collaborative art of filmmaking (O'Rourke, 2001). Because art therapy techniques that use writing, painting, poetry, photography, drawing, music, and drama can serve as tools for the filmmaker, video maker, or client in therapy, it is reasonable to conclude that a collaborative approach toward this type of therapy is essential. Editing is a shared process that combines the previously existing art forms into a new language that can be used therapeutically. One way that language can be explored is through a depth psychological process, which helps to create meaning for filmmakers, film editors, and therapeutic clients alike.

REFERENCES

Alamendrala, A. (2014, February 26). Dalai Lama on Hollywood: It's bad for my eyes and a waste of time. *The Huffington Post*. Retrieved from http://www.huffingtonpost.com/

American Psychiatric Association. (2007). *APA dictionary of psychology*. Washington, DC: Author.

Austin, B. (2010). Technology, art therapy, and psychodynamic theory: Computer animation with an adolescent in foster care. In C.H. Moon (Ed.), *Materials and media in art therapy* (pp. 199–213). New York, NY: Routledge.

Bowen, C.J.G. (2013). *Grammar of the edit* (3rd ed.). New York, NY: Focal Press.

Brawner, B. (1993). *The therapeutic use of video in the treatment of adolescents* (Unpublished master's thesis). California Institute of Integral Studies, San Francisco, CA.

Campbell, J. (1949). *The hero with a thousand faces*. New York, NY: Bollingen.

Campbell, J. (with Moyers, B.). (1988). *The power of myth*. New York, NY: Doubleday.

Campbell, J. (with Toms, M.). (1997). *The wisdom of Joseph Campbell* [4-CD set]. Santa Rosa, CA: New Dimensions.

Clarkson, W., & Daniels, P. (Producers), & Shuper, A. (Director). (2004). *Edge codes* [Motion picture]. USA: Travesty. Available at https://vimeo.com/15059269

Cohen, J. (1998). Catharsis: A video seminar [Video]. Retrieved from http://tiger.colorado college.edu/

Cohen, J. (2000). Catharsis: Film-healing: Collaborative art-therapy. Retrieved October 20, 2006, from http://www.copyright.gov/records/cohm.html

Cohen, J. (2007a). A beautiful mind*: A case analysis* (Unpublished paper). Argosy University, Orange, CA.

Cohen, J. (2007b). *The use of video therapy to treat depression in adolescent males* (Unpublished master's thesis). Walden University, Minneapolis, MN.

Cohen, J. (2013). *Film and soul: A theoretical exploration of the use of video and other film-based therapy to help transform identity in therapeutic practice* (Doctoral dissertation). Available from ProQuest Dissertations and Theses database. (UMI No. 3551606)

Emunah, R. (1997). Drama therapy and psychodrama: An integrated model. *International Journal of Action Methods: Psychodrama, Skill Training, and Role Playing, 50*(3), 108–134.

Epple, D.M. (2003). *The creative inner voice: A study of the Intensive Journal (TM) process* (Doctoral dissertation). Available from ProQuest Dissertations and Theses database. (UMI No. 305444269)

Gestwicki, R. (2001). Ira Progoff (1921–1998): The creator of the intensive journal method and a new profession [Obituary]. *Journal of Humanistic Psychology, 41*(3), 53–74. http://dx.doi.org/10.1177/0022167801413005

Gorelick, K. (2005). Poetry therapy. In C.A. Malchiodi (Ed.), *Expressive therapies: A framework for using art in therapy* (pp. 117–140). New York, NY: Routledge.

Grazer, B. (Producer), & Howard, R. (Director). (2001). *A beautiful mind* [Motion picture]. USA: Imagine/Dreamworks/Universal.

Hillecke, T.K., Wormit, A.F., & Bardenheuer, H.J. (2004). Schmerz = pain. *Musik-, Tanz-und Kunsttherapie, 15*(2), 92–94. http://dx.doi.org/10.1026/0933-6885.15.2.92

Hillman, J. (1983). *Healing fiction*. Woodstock, CT: Spring.

Hillman, J. (2010, April 16). Supervision session [Audiorecording]. Pacifica Graduate Institute, Carpinteria, CA.

Johnson, J.L., & Alderson, K.G. (2008). Therapeutic filmmaking: An exploratory pilot study. *Arts in Psychotherapy, 35*(1), 11–19. http://dx.doi.org/10.1016/j.aip.2007.08.004

Jung, C.G. (1983). *Symbols of transformation*. In H. Read, M. Fordham, G. Adler, & W. McGuire (Eds.), *The collected works of C.G. Jung* (R.F.C. Hull, Trans.; 2nd ed., Vol. 5, pp. 299–337). Princeton, NJ: Princeton University Press. (Original work published 1952)

Jung, C.G. (1984). *Dream analysis I: Notes of the seminar given in 1928–1930* (W. McGuire, Ed.). Princeton, NJ: Princeton University Press.

Kuwahara, J. (Producer), & Pray, D. (Director). (2001). Dharamsala [Unreleased video]. Film clip.

Lehtonen, K. (2002). An interview with Kimmo Lehtonen (Interview by M.F. Shaughnessy). *Music Therapy With Adolescents, 4*(1), 13–20.

Lucas, G. (Producer, Director) (1977–2005). *Star wars* [Motion picture series]. USA: Lucasfilm.

McNamee, C.M. (2004). Using both sides of the brain: Experiences that integrate art and talk therapy through scribble drawings. *Art Therapy, 21*(3), 136–142. http://dx.doi.org/10.1080/07421656.2004.10129495

Murch, W. (2001). *In the blink of an eye* (2nd ed.). New York, NY: Viking.

O'Rourke, R. (2001). Anya's movies. *Afterimage, 29*(3), 9.

Plante, G., Cote, H., Saint-Jean, M., & Pilic, I. (1979). Free painting as therapy for children from a disadvantaged urban area. *Canadian Psychiatric Association Journal, 23*(8), 567–571.

Progoff, I. (1973a). *At a journal workshop: The basic text and guide for using the intensive journal*. Oxford, UK: Dialogue House Library.

Progoff, I. (1973b). *Jung's psychology and its social meaning*. Oxford, UK: Anchor.

Stewart, D. (1979). Phototherapy: Theory and practice. *Art Psychotherapy, 6*(1), 41–46. http://dx.doi.org/10.1016/0090-9092(79)90019-X

Tosone, C., Gelman, C.R., & McVeigh, L. (2005). Through their own eyes: A media-based group approach to adolescent trauma. *International Journal of Group Psychotherapy, 55*(3), 415–432. http://dx.doi.org/10.1521/ijgp.2005.55.3.415

Vogler, C. (1998). *The writer's journey: Mythic structure for writers* (2nd ed.). Studio City, CA: Wiese.

Voytilla, S. (1999). *Myth and the movies: Discovering the mythic structure of 50 unforgettable films*. Studio City, CA: Wiese.

4 Filming the Fantasy

Green Screen Technology From Novelty to Psychotherapy

Jon Ehinger

INTRODUCTION

When my family came to visit New York to celebrate my completion of a master's degree in art therapy, we visited Madame Tussaud's Wax Museum. Near the end of the tour was an interactive green screen exhibit that simulated museum visitors flying over New York like Superman. Madame Tussaud's exhibit encapsulated what I spent all year attempting to explain through my thesis research, entitled, *Exploring Dreamspace Through Video Art With At-Risk Youth*. The foundation of the work was that through the use of video technology and computer effects, green screen technology digitally transports clients and offers them different ways of experiencing themselves kinesthetically and perceptually. Once filtered through live video depictions, clients featured on the green screen can embody their art as interactive moving images: Their art becomes objects through which they can express unique emotions, reenact histories and experiences, and create fantasy narratives. Even with my then-limited therapy experience, I intuitively knew that the green screen could normalize intense fantasies, feelings, and fears, thus allowing the healing process to begin. Clients can use the green screen in the therapeutic setting as a stage for their life stories to be unveiled, recreated, or rewritten (see Figure 4.1, also at www.filmandvideobasedtherapy.com).

STORYBOARDING

To avoid the green screen's novelty (i.e., new technology is exciting for clients, but its newness can be a therapeutic distraction, and clients' initial eagerness can become a form of therapeutic resistance), I work with clients to create their storyboards first, allowing them to fully imagine their movies in a series of sequential squares. Each storyboard square represents a different scene of the actual green screen stage. Creating a storyboard is how ideas are sketched and rapport is established with clients before we even step into the green screen studio, where their ideas to come to life (see

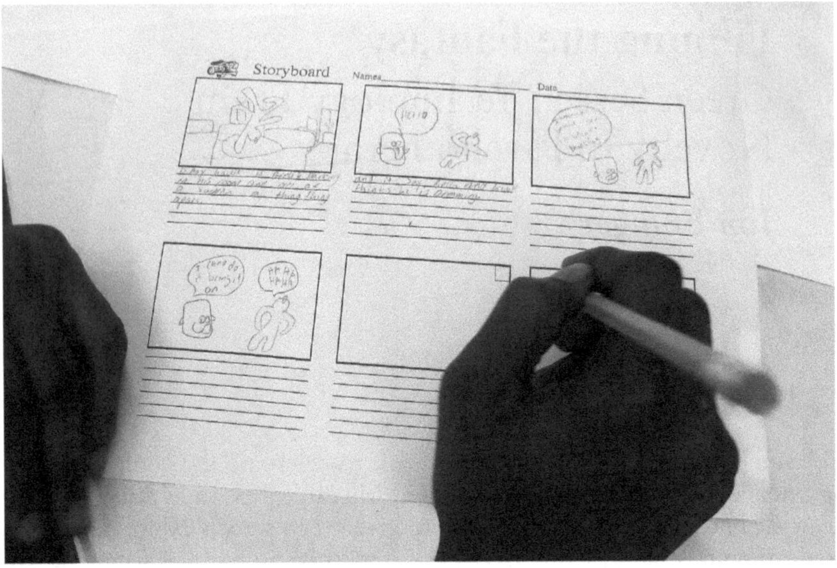

Figure 4.1 Storyboard created during green screen thesis research, 2009

Figure 4.2, also at www.filmandvideobasedtherapy.com). This process of sketching clients' ideas with paper and pencil is reminiscent of traditional creative arts therapy modalities and harnesses clients' ideas into more manageable parts of their stories. It also provides a clear sense of containment for clients, allowing their emotions, fantasies, and traumas to exist within the squares of the storyboard narrative.

By creating images inside storyboard squares and adding related text or dialogue, clients can develop their ideas and consider their fantasies. The creation of storyboards is its own unique therapeutic process, where many of the "whys" are explored. For example, walking on water or flying in the air is a fantastical ability that frequently emerges during these early storyboard sessions. By breaking down these ideas into smaller parts, therapists can explore why they are important to clients and what exactly these parts of the stories mean, inviting processing about fantasy, wish fulfillment, and unconscious dream life made conscious.

Speaking in practicalities, storyboarding also is capable of teaching clients valuable and transferable life skills. Creating stories or narratives in a step-by-step sequential process teaches organization and orienting, meaning that clients must plan before they act. In addition, clients learn about what it means to collaborate, and while the clients are in the creative director's chair, their therapists are responsible for searching for the items or images required to fulfill the clients' creative visions. Compromises must sometimes be made, possible technological limitations might need to be negotiated, and clients have to learn to manage feelings of disappointment.

Figure 4.2 Green screen therapy studio

TECHNOLOGY

The use of technology in psychotherapy is a relatively new adventure. The detached and emotionless experience that computers can offer seems at odds with the emotionally rich human response that therapists are trained to provide. By using green screen technology in therapy sessions, therapists and clients use the computer not as an objective object, but an integral tool. The computer, the green screen, the camera, and the software all become the art materials that express the inner workings of clients' psyches.

Simply put, the setup operates as follows: A camera films a client in front of the green screen. This camera is connected to a computer that holds the images that the client would like to enter. This composite image of the client in his or her virtual environment is then displayed on a TV screen (or monitor or projection) so that the client can then see it and interact with it (see Figure 4.3, also at www.filmandvideobasedtherapy.com).

Technically speaking, the computer senses the unique color green of the screen while the camera simultaneously replaces this green color with any images of the therapists' or clients' choosing. These new scenes then have the potential to transcend everyday life with their special effects and

Figure 4.3 Client witnessing the effects of a green shirt sensed by green screen computer software

movie-made environments. This is especially apparent when bringing the outside world into an in-patient setting, as discussed later in this chapter.

In an effort to remain authentic to the issues at hand, during sessions that involve creating therapeutic videos together, the clients make the creative decisions, and the therapists operate the software. The subject matter is at the clients' discretion, and they decide what fantasies (conscious or unconscious) they need to express, what wishes they need to fulfill, or what they want to physically experience differently. This approach promotes authenticity and meaningful journeys, and avoids the Hollywood sensationalism of feature films.

THEORETICAL FRAMEWORK

The green screen process is, in a sense, a new world of perceptual potential. It provides clients with distancing while they simultaneously experience the immediate connectivity that comes with composite video projections in their likenesses. Sessions that allow clients to view themselves as newly imagined video images are rich with therapeutic potential and the possibility of intervention. The green screen process invites explorations of ideas of the self and Other, considering the camera/therapist and background landscapes that occupy the space as "Other." These explorations help clients to come to terms with the Other, a process Jung (1970) called worthwhile because "in this way we get to know aspects of our nature which we would not allow anybody else to show us and which we ourselves would never have admitted" (para. 706).

The real benefit to therapists who use digital media in their practices is that they can witness clients' authentic reactions to a myriad of emotions. Depending on clients' affective states during such sessions, therapists can easily join clients in their fantasies or passively engage them, as in traditional psychoanalysis. In talk therapy, emotions are discussed, and in art therapy, they are drawn, but in film, they are lived. By entering the green screen space, clients can enact their fantasies and truly inhabit them, thus gaining more in-depth understanding of their urges, ideas, daydreams, and desires. How clients handle their bodies in physical space communicates their experiences of self and other boundaries, intrapsychic space, and interpersonal space (Wrye, 1993).

Using green screens in therapy is based upon the belief that everything that clients say or do is meaningful and expresses something within their unconscious minds or emotional landscapes. The green screen process is an active and interactive art medium that heightens awareness of all five senses, thus altering clients' states of mind (Emunah 1983). The role of therapists is to help clients to understand what is available to them from the inside out. Therapists help their clients to understand why they chose a particular subject matter for their videos, process the choices that they are making, and acquire the technical expertise to make their fantasies come to life.

Green screen therapy can be viewed as a modern application of active imagination, a process that facilitates the use of imagination and creativity to better understand the unconscious mind. According to Jung's (1961) theory, active imagination is a creative bridge between the unconscious and the conscious mind: Engaging in fantasy allows clients to bring their unconscious thoughts, feelings, and wishes forward into consciousness. What might have initially felt like a stream of consciousness or free association to them when they were storyboarding was actually full of unconscious meaning. When clients enter the green screen space, their unconscious choices, urges, and impulses become more clear and meaningful to clients and therapists.

Although the traditional use of active imagination relies heavily on clients' observation of egos, Jung (1961) also required clients to enter their experiences and respond to any changes in their fantasies or scenes authentically. The green screen takes Jung's active imagination process out of the mind and allows clients to actually live it for a few moments. This process becomes a way to build ego strength, create a greater sense of mastery, and spawn deeper personal exploration.

For Jung (1969), the green screen can be adapted into a mandala (see Figure 4.4, also at www.filmandvideobasedtherapy.com) to activate the imagination using this technology. Jung's (1933) study of individuation

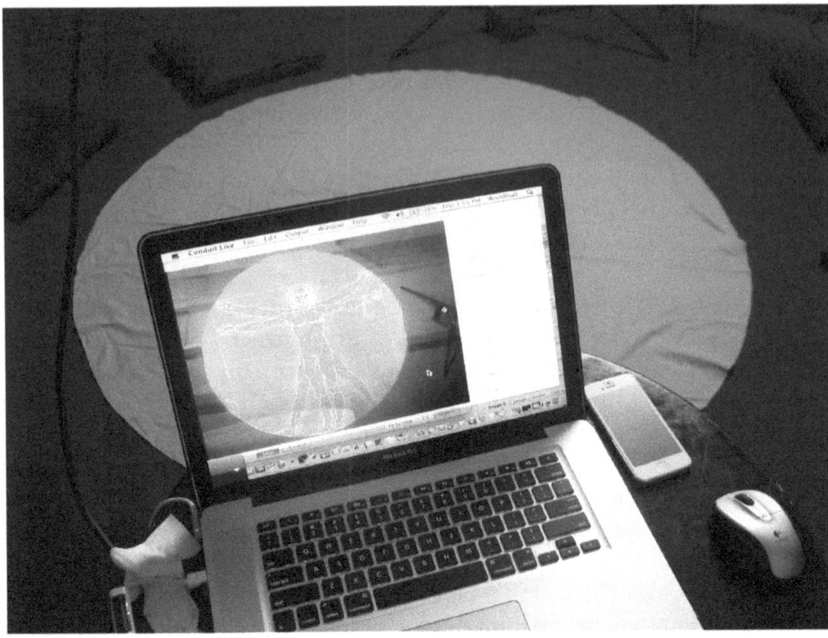

Figure 4.4 Green screen mandala presented at 2012 Expressive Therapies Summit

recognized the circle as a mandala, the psychological expression of the totality of the self on a journey toward wholeness. The potential of working with the green screen fashioned in a mandala shape holds vast possibilities for individual and group work. With the camera mounted above the mandala green screen and facing downward, clients can sit, lie, or stand within its bounds. Taking the mandala green screen from the floor back to its upright wall position creates a circular portal for clients' use. Following Jung's idea of mandalas, this application of the green screen gives clients the opportunity to experience a sense of wholeness.

From a Freudian or Winnicottian object relations standpoint, most theorists describe unconscious fantasies about internal objects that often are violent or sexual in nature. These are what Klein (1975) termed phantasies because they are completely unconscious. These phantasies act as a defense against more intense feelings of rage and sexuality, providing a possible cathartic release. Defense mechanisms are not inherently bad: They provide safety and emotional protection, especially in the clinical setting (or the green screen environment). The changes and healing come from how the defense phantasies are processed and understood consciously by clients.

Winnicott's (1971) psychoanalytic theory made an important impact on the creative arts play-world that transcends time as transitional space in which inner and external realities contribute to intermediate states of being. As the spaces and scenes change with clients' own imaginations, facilitated by the green screen effect, the feelings that arise are processed, and the creative choices made by clients during filming are discussed. Making videos has the potential to facilitate enormous change in clients, particularly in the areas of fantasy, wish fulfillment, and play, because the green screen acts as a transitional object.

According to Winnicott (1971),

> The essential feature of my communication is this, that playing is an experience, always a creative experience, and it is an experience in the space-time continuum, a basic form of living. The precariousness of play belongs to the fact that it is always on the theoretical line between the subjective and that which is objectively perceived. (p. 50)

In 1967 Winnicott (Rudnytsk 1993) wrote about the importance of play within the therapeutic relationship, which he later termed *prelogical*, a fusion of subject and object that underlies all interpersonal relationships. In this way, therapeutic use of the green screen works directly with the prelogical; that is, in combination with the use of active imagination, the green screen explores ways of relating to the world not given to logical formation.

Use of the green screen in therapy is comparable to Winnicott's postulation of the potential space between infants and their mothers (Rudnytsk 1993). Winnicott contended that the potential space contrasts with the inner world and actual external reality. This is the play space. A similar triangulation is used in green screen therapy: Clients' inner worlds are projected out, highlighting their prelogical relationships with their therapists. Unconscious fantasies, relationships with therapists, and the medium of the green screen combine to allow therapy to happen. Winnicott stated, "Psychotherapy takes place in the overlap of two areas of playing, that of the patient and that of the therapist. Psychotherapy has to do with two people playing together" (p. 38).

GREEN SCREEN MECHANICS AND CASE VIGNETTES

Green screen background images encapsulate all that the clients' images are, and they fill the space around human beings as the ever-changing Other in this work. People's immediate environments can directly affect their moods; this idea also holds true in the green screen environment. Because of this fact, the discussion now turns to the creation or selection process of green screen backgrounds in three ways: (a) the use of handcrafted backgrounds through fine art means (e.g., client-created artwork or photographs); (b) the use of found imagery that includes magazine collages as well as video clips via Internet sources; and (c) the use of either a simple solid color generated by the computer or no background at all represented as black (this works especially well for group therapy).

Most importantly, backgrounds need to have structure that can support the clients' visions (likely already considered and discussed in their storyboards). Just as in traditional art therapy images, the green screen images often need a ground line that can give clients a strong and stable foundation from which to work. Otherwise, clients risk being seen in their artwork as floating; oftentimes, the clients are left feeling unstable and unsafe emotionally, unless, of course, the desired effect is outer space or some other gravity-defying exploration. Once a featured client steps inside and decides to be seen as a figure supported by an object (e.g., a doorway, a path, etc.), the therapist might then intervene with suggestions to assist in the client's overall concept to facilitate the idea to ensure the desired effect. However, sometimes, ground lines are not needed when clients wish to be featured in extreme close-up or medium shots (i.e., from the waist up).

Let us begin by entering the green screen space with images handcrafted by clients. In my early years of piloting green screen work with clients, the Internet was not always available, so we had to create our own backgrounds in which to be featured. This process is enormously powerful for clients and is a source of rich information. Not only does the artwork have inherent meaning but also the ways in which clients interact with and physically respond to the work provide additional experiences to unpack therapeutically. As clients interact with their own paintings, drawings, and clay works, it is important that their therapists understand the potential for heightened emotional experiences and modulate the therapy accordingly.

An example that comes to mind is a 56-year-old female with dementia who drew a colorful botanical garden during an art therapy group session in an in-patient psychiatric unit. In the middle of her picture, she drew a slide. In discussing her image, she disclosed that as a child, she loved slides. I draped a chair with the green screen fabric and instructed her to sit in the chair. Her image was projected onto a TV monitor, and as I moved the camera, the resulting effect simulated her sliding down the slide that she had created. She was joyful and experienced her creative self without needing the symbolic overlays that she might not have been capable of accessing; the feeling of happiness and her creative involvement were enough to be healing, a reflected integration of wholeness described by Jung (1933) and Winnicott (1971). Her experience was perceptual and affective, in accordance with the reverse developmental process of Alzheimer's disease, and she engaged in kinesthetic and sensory activities without the fragmentation of images (Hinz, 2009). This experience would not have been possible without the use of the green screen.

Continuing with this idea of entering the green screen with a client-created rendered image, the experience of another client comes to mind. Police brought a 17-year-old male with conduct disorder issues into the psychiatric emergency room in handcuffs. The client had several outstanding warrants for his arrest and was very limited cognitively. With some individual assistance, he was able to grasp the concept of the green screen in his therapy sessions. His storyboards depicted his recent arrest, a violent event that included hiding in the bushes for hours, being pursued on foot by police, and possessing a gun. In his ending scene, he drew a court with a jury and created a place for himself on the witness stand. In his video, he told his side of the story, in which he admitted that a series of destructive decisions led to his arrest. The jury that he had created found him guilty, and the judge sentenced him to prison. In this case, the client enacted his greatest anxiety, namely, that he would be sent to prison. Taking the stand and then sentencing himself to the inevitable outcome provided him with some relief from his anxiety, but it also was important for him cognitively. The video helped him to understand his actions and his situation from the perspectives of the judge, the jury, and the police officers.

Clients also can use Internet images to create their backgrounds. These images are instant, high quality, and close to their ideas. One advantage of using a basic web search for images is that it significantly expedites the filming process because clients can create videos from idea inception to edited completion within one session. It is a technique that I have used frequently on in-patient psychiatric units. With the average length of stay of patients on these units being 10 days, time is not a luxury that we always have. Plus, I have no assurance that I will see a client more than once. However, the instantaneousness of this method also is its largest drawback in that it can feed the culture of instant gratification and "quick fix therapy" rather than promote deeper, insight-oriented work necessary to get to the root of the problem. In the most psychologically defended clients, Internet-based images offer them a safe way to begin the therapeutic process.

Group work in green screening is different from other types of group work because green screen groups often are more about client placement and feelings of belonging within the artistic process. It follows the same line as verbal group therapy: Where do I fit in this group? What is my role here? and What can this group do for me? Personal space becomes important, as does paying close attention to the scale of background images so that they do not over- or under-whelm the group.

In my experience of green screening with groups, I have found that the green screen process results in heightened roles within the group: The state of interdependence that influences group members' behaviors and attitudes is more intense not only because of the close physical proximity of the group members but also because the video process allows them to behave in ways that they might not ordinarily manifest because it is "for the camera" or they're "playing a part." However, when verbally processing the green screen experience with the group, it can become clear that "playing a part" actually involved enacting an unconscious urge, usually rooted in the id.

The following example is a more in-depth case study of a 12-year-old boy diagnosed with hyperactivity attention deficit disorder (ADHD) who came to my private practice explicitly for green screen therapy. His parents stated to me that he had been "slipping lately," that is, throwing uncharacteristic

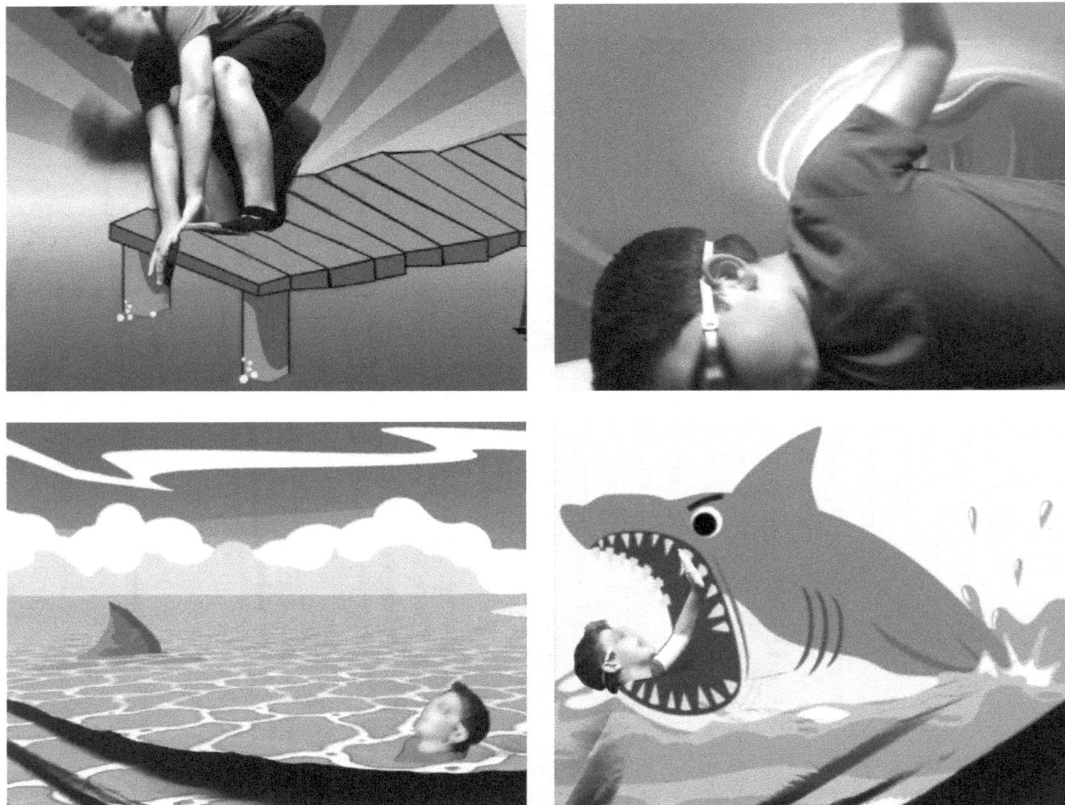

Figure 4.5 Selected screen shots from client green screen video narrative

tantrums that included ripping off his shirt in public and throwing furniture from windows. For the purposes of protecting his anonymity, I will call this client Jose. Like many ADHD symptomatic children with whom I work, Jose resisted the early storyboard planning. After my repeated insistence that he create a storyboard in order "to help me understand your ideas better," he reluctantly did.

Jose decided to create the character Miguel Phelps, a champion swimmer modeled after Olympic swimming champion Michael Phelps. Jose was to play Miguel on screen.

The video would depict an important swimming meet between Miguel and a cartoon shark. Jose's storyboard was hurriedly and loosely sketched, with Miguel being a stick figure bobbing in the water and the shark being an enormous figure with angry eyebrows and pointy teeth. The plot of the video was simple: In an epic swim meet, Miguel Phelps would race a shark. In an unexpected twist, Miguel would lose the meet and would ultimately be eaten alive by the shark (see Figure 4.5, also at www.filmandvideobasedtherapy.com).

Jose insisted that his backgrounds be cartoons taken from the Internet. When I asked him about this, Jose's only response was that "it would be cool." This statement served as our therapeutic in: Jose was communicating that he had hope for the therapy to be successful. He was not concerned with the images looking realistic; in fact, he pointedly stated that he liked how the shark did not look realistic. In addition, he wrinkled the green screen, creating huge black swipes across the bottom of the composite image. Again, this was how Jose wanted the image to look: He wanted the black to break up the water and thus lose the seamless effect.

I understood these imperfections to be rich with meaning. Jose flailed and struggled to swim in the rough waters in his video, desperate to keep his head above water and stay one stroke ahead of the shark. This metaphor was clear: Jose knew that he was struggling in his life, desperately trying to stay above the fray of the intensity of his own emotions. In his video, Jose was quite literally consumed by his shark, just as he was frequently consumed by the intensity of his own feelings. The creative choice to make the shark a cartoon provided him with an element of safe distance to his projection (i.e., a cartoon shark could not actually eat him), and the messiness of the green screen served as a metaphor for the imperfections in his home life and a visual reminder that this was a simulation. In this way, Jose was able to enact his fears and communicate his feelings effectively while simultaneously regulating the experience to one that he found tolerable.

CONCLUSION

Green screen technology in art therapy is useful in allowing clients to explore and understand fantasies as well as enter into them, that is, dynamically participate in their own creative and unconscious processes. The combination of Jung's (1933) theories of individuation and the self's search for wholeness with his (1961) ideas of active imagination and mandala making (1968) together with Winnicott's (1967, 1971) idea of a play space and the importance of play in the therapeutic relationship make green screen therapy a potentially effective intervention for clients from different populations. Through use of the green screen, clients' intense fears and feelings can be normalized, and new ways of understanding the self can be unveiled as histories are rewritten or relived.

REFERENCES

Emunah, R. (1983). Drama therapy with adult psychiatric patients. *Arts in Psychotherapy, 10*(2), 77–84. http://dx.doi.org/10.1016/0197-4556(83)90033-3

Hinz, L.D. (2009). *Expressive therapies continuum: A framework for using art in therapy*. New York, NY: Taylor.

Jung, C.G. (1933). *Modern man in search of a soul* (C.F. Baynes, Trans.). New York, NY: Harvest Books.

Jung, C.G. (1961). Freud and Jung: Contrasts. In H. Read, M. Fordham, G. Adler, & W. McGuire (Eds.), *The collected works of C.G. Jung* (R.F.C. Hull, Trans.) (Vol. 4, pp. 333–342). Princeton, NJ: Princeton University Press. (Original work published 1931)

Jung, C.G. (1969). Concerning mandala symbolism. In H. Read, M. Fordham, G. Adler, & W. McGuire (Eds.), *The collected works of C.G. Jung* (R.F.C. Hull, Trans.) (2nd ed., Vol. 9i, pp. 355–384). Princeton, NJ: Princeton University Press. (Original work published 1950)

Jung, C.G. (1970). Mysterium coniunctionis: An inquiry into the separation and synthesis of psychic opposites in alchemy. In H. Read, M. Fordham, G. Adler, & W. McGuire (Eds.), *The collected works of C. G. Jung* (R.F.C. Hull, Trans.) (2nd ed., Vol. 14). Princeton, NJ: Princeton University Press. (Original work published 1955–1956)

Klein, M. (1975). *Love, guilt and reparation and other works 1921–1945*. London, UK: Karnac Books.

Rudnytsk, P. L. (1993). *Transitional objects and potential spaces: Literary uses of D.W. Winnicott*. New York, Chichester: Columbia University Press. (Original work published 1967)

Winnicott, D.W. (1971). *Playing and reality*. New York, NY: Basic Books.

Wrye, H. (1993). Hello, the hollow deadspace or playspace? *Psychoanalytic Review, 80*(1), 101–122.

5 Vision, Story, Medicine

Therapeutic Filmmaking and First Nations Communities

J. Lauren Johnson

WORKING WITH ABORIGINAL CLIENTS

Tansi. Please allow me to introduce myself, as many of the people I work with appreciate knowing who I am and where I come from. My name is Lauren Johnson. Though I currently live in Edmonton, Alberta (Canada), I have lived in several other cities throughout Canada and am originally from Toronto, Ontario. I am a mother and a psychologist.

For the past three years, I have developed a specialization in working with First Nations clients, working largely in Cree communities in Northern Alberta and as the clinical director at a treatment center for Aboriginal girls in Central Alberta. I felt called to this work as a feminist practitioner sensitive to issues of injustice and inequality, as a survivor of childhood trauma, and as a member of a minority Jewish population that has experienced its own historical oppressions. As a teenager, I was at one point the only Jewish person in my school of 1,600 students, and felt deeply saddened when another singular minority whom I had met, an Aboriginal girl who shared my fondness for horses, left our school after less than a year because of racial bullying. This experience taught me that although I could easily pass with my blue eyes and Anglican last name as a member of the majority in a culture that privileged European-descended, middle-class, Canadian-born people, many others could not. I hoped that I might use my privileges of race, class, and education to work with those whose voices still too often are oppressed and ignored.

In my years of working with members of First Nations, I have learned that particular challenges exist in these communities that I had not encountered in the largely Caucasian, middle-class, urban communities in which I was trained to work. First Nations people in Canada are over-represented in virtually all risk groups associated with social and economic problems, including "homelessness, poverty, addictions, violence, chronic illness[,] and diseases that include tuberculosis, HIV/AIDS[,] and diabetes" (Chansonneuve, 2005, p. 5). According to the 2006 Census (Gionet, 2009), First Nations people make up 2.2% of the Canadian population. Compared to non–First Nations people, First Nations people are typically young (median age is 25 compared to the non–First Nations median age of 40), less educated, more frequently unemployed, and tend to earn substantially less money (Gionet, 2009). Nearly one-third of Canadian Aboriginal people, including First Nations, Inuit, and Métis, have a disability, and their rate of diabetes is among the highest in the world (Chansonneuve, 2005). As one Statistics Canada author put it: "[T]he best-off First Nations communities compare only with the worst-off areas of non-Aboriginal Canada" (Armstrong, 1999, p. 17). Aboriginal people's health and economic problems, then, are associated with some of the lowest standards of living in the country.

Professionals working with Aboriginal people need to be cognizant of the long-term effects of historical trauma, systemic shame, and ethnocide, and how these have affected indigenous people. Many Aboriginal people have been directly and indirectly affected by historical trauma, which may be understood as the collective emotional and psychological injury, experienced over a life span and across generations, resulting from a cataclysmic event in history (Aboriginal Healing Foundation [AHF], 2001). As Gone stated: "In addition to violence, widespread loss of indigenous language, culture, and ceremony has combined with multigenerational disruptions in parenting practices to yield a harrowing legacy of distress and disability for contemporary Native peoples" (2009, p. 752). For Canadian Aboriginal people, the cataclysmic historical event that continues to cause historical trauma is the ongoing legacy of colonization, which includes the multi-generational effects of residential schools. In these schools, Aboriginal children were taken from their families, where they were raised in often-abusive, church-run, government-sanctioned schools; assimilated into Western, Christian traditions; and taught to reject the culture and language of their families. These residential schools existed for over 120 years in Canada, with the last closing in 1996.

According to the Indian Residential Schools (IRS) Data Project (Indian and Northern Affairs Canada [INAC], 2004), approximately 106,000 residential school survivors were still alive in 1991. Gone (2009) described the effect of colonization and residential schooling as the "collective, cumulative, and intergenerational transmission of risk for adverse mental health outcomes that stem from the historical unresolved grief or 'soul wound' inflicted by experiences of colonization" (p. 752). Given the historical period over which these schools operated and the number of Aboriginal people who were affected in that time, it is understandable that intergenerational historical trauma has resulted from these systemic abuses.

Despite a need in many Aboriginal communities for mental health services to help people heal from these historical traumas, a number of barriers to effective mental health services exist (McCabe, 2007). These barriers include cultural disconnection, limited access to services, underutilization of services that are available, and a lack of culturally relevant interventions (Gone, 2009; McCabe, 2007). A significant barrier is that typical methods of counseling and therapy represent a Eurocentric worldview, and Aboriginal clients' refusal to accept this worldview may be punished through the assignment of labels, such as unnecessary diagnoses or being dismissed as "resistant" to therapy. Todd and Wade (1994) described this process as "psycholonization," in which colonial professional discourses "produced the [Aboriginal person] as a deficient and therefore exploitable subject; a subject to be contained, civilized[,] and assimilated into normative (i.e., European) modes of conduct" (p. 37). It is imperative for professionals working with First Nations clients to be cognizant of this perspective and to work actively against these colonialist practices by, for instance, adopting an *indigenist* perspective, which "acknowledges the colonized or fourth world position of [Aboriginal people]," a perspective that is empowering and that acknowledges their sovereignty (Walters & Simoni, 2002, p. 520).

In my experience, I have learned that there exists a great need to develop a personal relationship with the people and communities with whom I intend to work. This relationship may push the boundaries of what staunch critics of dual relationships may consider ethical practice; however, without such a relationship, a therapist runs the risk of being seen by wary community members as a threatening representative of a non-Aboriginal, colonial profession. An elder who agreed to review this chapter for me noted that many professionals, including "social workers, police, health professionals, etc., have a long history of many negative outcomes as a result of their interactions with Aboriginal people [that is] largely because of the clash of two worldviews" (Personal Communication, July 2, 2014). This, in turn, may lead to the substantial under-use of available services by Aboriginal people.

How, then, might a therapist work with Aboriginal clients in a culturally relevant way, and how might he or she do this while developing a working relationship with clients that is not reminiscent of colonial practices? In this chapter, I argue that therapeutic filmmaking may represent a productive modality for working with Aboriginal clients, given the nature of film as a storytelling medium and its capacity to contribute to spiritual experiences for the filmmaker and members of the audience. In what follows, I first introduce therapeutic filmmaking as an approach before beginning my argument.

INTRODUCTION TO THERAPEUTIC FILMMAKING

Before describing the ways in which I believe therapeutic filmmaking represents a culturally relevant, non-colonial therapeutic modality for working with Aboriginal clients, it may first be helpful to describe what it is. Therapeutic filmmaking is an arts-based therapeutic approach that combines talk therapy techniques with the client's creative first-person, or *autodocumentary*, filmmaking. This is an approach that I developed as a film student, when I took the opportunity to reflect upon my intensely private and personal experience of childhood trauma in the context of an externalizing, creative, visual story told in a supportive environment. In doing this, I found that the process of filmmaking allowed me to make sense of an event that I had experienced without words and that I felt too deeply in my body for it even to register in my mind. This process gave voice to a part of me that had been unable to speak. The burden I had lived with for many years suddenly was outside of me, disclosed to and shared with others, understood, and accepted. Through this journey, I celebrated my strengths of courage, forgiveness, and resilience; stood in awe before the strength of countless other survivors of trauma; and came to believe in the power of film as an artistic, therapeutic, communicative medium.

Therapeutic filmmaking is related to other creative arts therapies. For example, early film therapy pioneer Stewart (1979) contended that photo therapy shares many commonalities with film- and video-making and suggested that the theory and practice of photo therapy can easily be applied to the use of film and video in therapy. Although therapeutic filmmaking shares with other creative arts therapies the ability to foster expression, disclosure, insight, self-awareness, and self-efficacy, it also differs in important ways. One of the most important differences between therapeutic filmmaking and other forms of expressive arts therapies is the former's nearly exclusive focus on process rather than outcome of the creative endeavor. Filmmaking is essentially a five-stage process:

1. Development (i.e., developing and writing the story that the filmmaker wants to tell);
2. Pre-Production (i.e., preparing to shoot the story; this stage involves storyboarding, creating shot lists, etc.);
3. Production (i.e., the process of filming);
4. Post-Production (i.e., picture and sound editing, adding digital effects, etc.); and,
5. Exhibition/Distribution (i.e., making copies of the finished film and exhibiting and/or distributing it to others).

I contend that the entire five-stage process of filmmaking is an excellent context in which the therapeutic process may unfold. It is through the writing, re-writing, visual exploration, visual and aural storytelling, and continual processing and analysis of the film that therapeutic goals are met. As such, the *product*—the finished film—represents an important keepsake and a helpful record of the therapeutic process, but it is not necessarily used as the subject of further analysis. However, it may be helpful to return to a therapeutic film at a later time to reflect upon any changes that have occurred within the client after the completion of the project.

Another significant difference between therapeutic filmmaking and other expressive arts is film's unique combination of the dimension of time with tangible, stage-specific documentation, and storytelling. Creating a photograph or drawing a picture requires a certain creative process and may take some time to perform. However, the product itself does not take place through time—it is unmoving, static, and disconnected from the passage of time. Meanwhile, psychodrama, dance, and music occur over the span of time—a gesture, a musical note, a bodily motion occurs at one distinct moment of time, followed by another with a separate and distinct position on the time continuum. These art forms are time-dependent, and without resorting to the use of digital or analog recording, they disappear as the forward momentum of time pushes them into the past. Film and video have the paradoxical distinction of being timeless, like sculpture, drawing, and photography—capable of repeated viewings in various contexts and multiple points in time—and time-based, such that the film itself plays out over a span of time. This unique combination positions filmmaking as multiply therapeutic—it has the benefits of the timeless arts (i.e., the documentation of a singular moment in time for reflection and analysis at a distinctly separate moment in time, such as in editing or in viewing), in addition to those of the time-based arts (i.e., fluidity of expression, the depiction of change over time, the ability to tell a story). In this way, I argue that filmmaking has the potential to be especially therapeutic.

Lastly, because of its paradoxically timeless yet time-based nature, film shares some common elements with the widely used and popular form of therapy known as narrative therapy (Epson & White, 1992). As mentioned previously, filmmaking is a medium through which stories are told. Storytelling is at the core of narrative therapy, though typically it has been relegated to written and oral, rather than visual, media. With the introduction of therapeutic filmmaking, a powerful connection can take place between art therapy and narrative therapy—at the juncture of time, documentation, and story.

METHOD AND RESULTS OF PILOT STUDY

Under the supervision of Dr. Kevin Alderson, I conducted a qualitative pilot study on therapeutic filmmaking for my master's thesis (Johnson, 2007), later published as an article (Johnson & Alderson, 2008). This phenomenological study was conducted at a post-secondary counseling center with three participants. The chosen methodology "emerged out of a growing discontent with a philosophy of science based exclusively on studies of material things, a science that failed to take into account the experiencing person and the connections between human consciousness and the objects that exist in the material world" (Moustakas, 1994, p. 43). Through rigorous methods of data collection and analysis, phenomenologists aim to "return to experience," privileging subjectivity rather than focusing on objective material observations, in order to provide a "reflective structural analysis that portrays the essences of the experience" under study (Moustakas, 1994, p. 13).

In this study, I focused on the phenomenon of therapeutic filmmaking in order to understand clients' essential experience of this therapeutic modality. As such, three participants seeking counseling at a post-secondary counseling center consented to participate in this pilot study by first undergoing a period of therapeutic filmmaking in lieu of more traditional talk therapies, then participating in recorded and transcribed interviews on their experiences of that therapy. Based on these in-depth interviews with participants, I analyzed 80 distinct comments and organized them into 11 themes, representing two broad categories. The first category, *Mechanisms of Change*, encompassed themes that expressed the participants' subjective experience of undergoing therapeutic transformation through the use of therapeutic filmmaking. This category included the following themes:

- *Positive Experiences:* This theme encompassed participants' global observations about their experience with therapeutic filmmaking, what worked about therapeutic filmmaking, and their overall positive experiences with this modality.
- *Feelings of Mastery:* Participants' perception was that this form of therapy helped them gain a sense of accomplishment and mastery of a new skill through the task of learning how to make films.
- *Observations on Perception:* This theme encompassed comments that addressed participants' observations about the shift in perception afforded through the addition of an objective camera's lens to their own subjective perspective. They described this as a valuable shift in perspective that shed new light on themselves and their situations, and encouraged them to develop a new perspective on both.
- *Changed Perspective of Self:* Viewing themselves and their situations from different perspectives, as noted above, allowed participants to learn about themselves in meaningful ways and embark on therapeutic change.
- *Changed Perspective on Interactions:* Participants described experiencing a shift in perspective that shed new light on their interactions with others. With the video camera as feedback, participants were able to gain a different perspective on how they saw and were seen by others in their lives.
- *Humor as Healing:* By representing themselves and their situations in a more humorous light than they initially experienced them, participants were able to externalize and find the lighter side of otherwise traumatic situations, thereby decreasing the impact of the trauma.

The second category, *Experience of Therapy*, encompassed themes that addressed the content of the films and what was discussed in session with the participants' counselors, as well as the participants' subjective experiences of how the filmmaking and talk therapy sessions affected each other. The themes in this category included the following:

- *The Personal as the Subject in Filmmaking:* Participants noted that what was filmed often became fodder for therapeutic exploration with their counselors because of the personal nature of the content.
- *Film as a Focusing Agent:* Participants noted that making films about themselves impacted their ability to focus on particular aspects of their lives during the course of therapy. For example, some used an idea or theme that arose during the filmmaking process as a spring-board from which to jump into deeper discussion and processing with their counselors.
- *Film as a Catalyst for Discussion:* Participants described the film as a form of expression from which therapeutic conversation freely flowed, wherein they used their film to bring up difficult issues with their therapists.
- *Comparison to Other Experiences of Therapy:* Participants noted differences between therapeutic filmmaking and other forms of therapy they had experienced, describing it as "fun," "non-directive," and "active" compared to other therapies.
- *Suggestions for Improvement:* Participants made recommendations primarily related to issues of resources (i.e., time allotted with cameras, wanting to participate for a longer period, etc.). Participants appeared to enjoy their therapeutic experience and wanted to remain engaged in the process for a longer period.

Given the results of the pilot study, I observed that there are a number of ways that therapeutic filmmaking may be an appropriate therapeutic modality for working with Aboriginal clients. Indeed, I argue that, with its focus on a side-by-side rather than a face-to-face relationship between therapist and client, the focus on storytelling, the client-directed approach to the creative process, the inclusion of audio-visual representations that may aid communication where language barriers exist, and the inclusion of explorations and representations of self, culture, and historical context in the project, therapeutic filmmaking is an excellent modality for working with Aboriginal clients. In the following pages, I describe other ways that therapeutic filmmaking may represent an anti-oppressive, culturally relevant approach to working with Aboriginal people. First, I describe the connection with storytelling. Second, I argue that the act of filmmaking may be experienced as a spiritual practice.

THE MEDICINE REEL: FILM AS STORYTELLING

Early in my work with therapeutic filmmaking, I theorized that one strength of film and video is the capacity to use these media for storytelling. I saw a distinct kinship between therapeutic filmmaking and narrative therapy, an approach to therapy pioneered by Epson and White (1992). In narrative therapy, clients are encouraged to tell and re-tell their stories, to externalize their internal struggles through the use of story, and to understand their experiences through the conventions of story. Because narrative therapy engages the client's perspective and worldview, it tends not to impose a "fixed, generalized view of what is right or wrong or introduce or impose a culturally constructed view of the world" (Stock, Mares, & Robinson, 2012, p. 158). As such, it may be a preferred method for therapists working from cross-cultural, anti-oppressive, feminist, and other post-modern counseling perspectives.

In therapeutic filmmaking, clients are encouraged to develop films about their own personal experiences; to work with these narratives through the externalizing processes of writing, filming, and editing; and to analyze these narratives from the perspective of a filmmaker rather than of the person living the experience. As such, one may easily see the similarities between these two approaches. I would like to note here that in therapeutic filmmaking, clients do not necessarily have to make narrative films, which may distinguish therapeutic filmmaking from other film/video-based therapy approaches discussed in this book that are more closely aligned with narrative structure, such as digital storytelling. Indeed, just as Kerem describes in her chapter on video art therapy (see Chapter 13, this volume), I believe there is much insight and healing that can be gained through the creation of experimental and other forms of non-narrative films. However, in my experience, clients tend to prefer making narrative films, and the capacity for storytelling with the media of film and video may be part of the appeal of this approach for many clients. I argue here that this also makes this therapeutic approach particularly fitting for use with Aboriginal clients.

Aboriginal people have a long history of storytelling and oral traditions. "Indigenous people are embedded in traditions of storytelling, both in everyday social life and in the upbringing and education of their children" (Stock et al., 2012, pg. 158). Thus, the art of storytelling serves an important cultural purpose for Aboriginal people. It is through storytelling that they share their histories, beliefs, and cultural traditions with each other and between generations. By using storytelling with Aboriginal clients in therapy, holistic understandings of emotional reactions, physical symptoms, spiritual experiences, and family and community expectations can be achieved (Agius & Hamer, 2003).

Inviting Aboriginal clients to engage in film- or video-based storytelling as part of their therapy may represent a modern interpretation of traditional methods of communication and healing. Additionally, the audio-visual aspects of film and video may provide opportunities for Aboriginal clients to bring together elements of traditional storytelling, including the use of voice, artifacts, and traditional arts, in a way that honors these important cultural elements. Further, the valued intergenerational transmission of the art of traditional oral storytelling may be aided with the introduction of technology-based methods, allowing elders to work together with technology-savvy youth to continue these important traditions. Given that the Aboriginal population in Canada is distinctly young, the use of video technology to bridge gaps between youth and elders, as well as between traditional and modern life, may represent a fitting and powerful tool in the post-colonial reclamation of Aboriginal culture.

FILM AS SPIRITUAL EXPERIENCE

In addition to being a storytelling medium that fits well with Aboriginal storytelling traditions, therapeutic filmmaking may also be seen as a spiritually relevant therapeutic approach for working with indigenous populations. Hill (1992) described cinema as mythic, using the term "cinemyth" (p. 3) to describe how films convey important information about morality and belief systems, among other things, from filmmaker to audience. He described the audience's collective participation in film as a form of spiritual devotion, and described the movie theatre as a "tribal dream house" (p. 4) similar to the sweat lodge of traditional cultures: "The dark cave of the cinema is reminiscent of a ceremonial sweat lodge . . . [i]t is the communal meeting place where tribal strangers of like mind meet to explore the inner reaches of the soul" (p. 20). Though I take issue with Hill's use of the term "primitives" to describe early peoples because of the pejorative use of that word in relation to Aboriginal people, I do appreciate his perspective on the cultural and even spiritual role that the mass media of film and video can play in a culture. If one agrees with Hill that film and video play a mythic role in a culture and that the movie theatre (and, I would argue, the darkened editing room as well) may be seen as a spiritual space similar to the sweat lodge, one can make the argument that one's participation in film/video as either creator or viewer may represent a spiritual experience. This, in turn, leads to a consideration of the power of spirituality in Aboriginal healing traditions.

The sweat lodge is considered by many Aboriginal people to be the central healing experience, providing health remedy and maintenance through the cleansing and purification of mind, body, and spirit (Ryback & Decker-Fitts, 2009). Through the process of inhaling medicinal steam vapors in the darkened, dome-shaped, womb-like enclosure of the lodge, this ceremony "is used for purification by embracing the natural powers of the Universal Circle, giving thanks and requesting blessings for others and oneself" (Portman & Garrett, 2006, p. 463). Additionally, some see this particular ritual as a rebirth of sorts, being a ceremony that "honours the process of transformation and healing, and is central to the modern-day practice of Native traditionalism across nations" (Portman & Garrett, 2006, p. 463). This ceremony provides an opportunity for participants to commune with their ancestors, other spirits, and the Creator in an atmosphere that is somewhat other-worldly, with its darkness and humidity and heat, functioning as a conduit between the natural and the spirit worlds.

In both the sweat lodge and the darkened realms of film creation and consumption, participants are invited to experience new and sometimes unreal events and to make sense of these beyond the literal, beyond the common, within the liminal space between reality and belief. The creation of a film within the dark room or the editing room provides the filmmaker an opportunity to commune with his or her inner life in a similar way that the sweat lodge participant is invited to commune with his or her spiritual life—outside the realm of lived experience, in the world of meaning and symbol. Thus, the process of making a therapeutic film or video with the guidance of a therapist (rather than a traditional healer, as would be the case in a ceremony) may be experienced as a spiritual event. In this way, the act of therapeutic filmmaking may be well suited both culturally and spiritually as a therapeutic approach for working with Aboriginal clients.

When I requested that a respected elder review this chapter for me, she noted that the comparison above may be "stretching it" (Personal Communication, July 2, 2014). However, she acknowledged that although she has a great deal of experience with sweats, she has never experienced the process of personal filmmaking. She invited me to converse further about this with her and another person who is well versed in both sweat lodge ceremonies and personal filmmaking. At the time of this writing, I am preparing for this meeting by collecting offerings and gifts.

CONCLUSION

In this chapter, I have noted that working as a therapist with Aboriginal clients can involve specific barriers. This is particularly the case for therapists working from a Eurocentric treatment perspective, who may inadvertently further colonialist practices against this client population through the implementation of culturally irrelevant and insensitive therapeutic practices. I have argued here that therapeutic filmmaking represents an approach to working with Aboriginal clients that may fit in close alignment with Aboriginal cultural and healing practices, and as such may be a useful practice approach for therapists working with Aboriginal people. As I continue my work on First Nations reserves, and particularly as I continue directing the work of my colleagues who aim to help Aboriginal teens at a residential treatment center, I will continue to implement this approach and assess its ongoing fitness for use with this population. I hope, as more clients reclaim their voices, languages, and cultural practices, that their words, stories, and films will stand as a lasting representation of the change of which they—and this medium—are capable.

REFERENCES

Aboriginal Healing Foundation (AHF) (2001). Aboriginal Healing Foundation program handbook (3rd ed.). Ottawa, ON: Aboriginal Healing Foundation.

Agius, T., & Hamer, J. (2003). Thoughts on narrative therapy contribute to Indigenous mental health. *PPEI Magazine, 18*(2), 8–9.

Armstrong, R. (1999). Mapping the conditions of First Nations communities. *Canadian Social Trends*. Statistics Canada. Retrieved Monday, January 27, 2014 from http://publications.gc.ca/site/archivee-archived.html?url=http://publications.gc.ca/Collection-R/Statcan/11-008-XIE/0039911-008-XIE.pdf

Chansonneuve, D. (2005). *Reclaiming connections: Understanding residential school trauma among aboriginal people*. Ottawa, ON: Aboriginal Healing Foundation.

Epson, D., & White, M. (1992). *Experience, contradiction, narrative and imagination: Selected papers of David Epson & Michael White 1989–1991*. South Australia: Dulwich Centre Publications.

Gionet, L. (2009). *First Nations people: Selected findings of the 2006 Census*. Statistics Canada: Canadian Social Trends. Retrieved Monday, January 27, 2014 from http://www5.statcan.gc.ca/bsolc/olc-cel/olc-cel?catno=11-008-X20090011 0864&lang=eng

Gone, J.P. (2009). A community-based treatment for Native American historical trauma: Prospects for evidence-based practice. *Journal of Consulting and Clinical Psychology, 77*(4), 751–762.

Hill, G. (1992). *Illuminating shadows: The mythic power of film*. Boston, MA: Shambhala Publications, Inc.

Indian and Northern Affairs Canada (INAC) (2004). *Report of the Royal Commission on Aboriginal Peoples, Vol. 1: Looking forward looking back, part one—The relationship in historical perspective*. Chapter 5—Stage two: Contact and co-operation. Retrieved Monday, January 27, 2014 from http:///www.ainci nac.gc.ca/ch/rcap/sg/sg11_e.html

Johnson, J.L. (2007). Therapeutic filmmaking: An exploratory pilot study (Unpublished master's thesis). University of Calgary, Calgary, AB.

Johnson, J.L., & Alderson, K.G. (2008). Therapeutic filmmaking: An exploratory pilot study. *Arts in Psychotherapy, 35*(1), 11–19.

McCabe, G.H. (2007). The healing path: A cultural and community derived indigenous therapy model. *Psychotherapy: Theory, Research, Practice, Training, 44*(2), 148–160. doi:10.1037/0033-3204.44.2.148

Moustakas, C. (1994). *Phenomenological research methods*. Thousand Oaks, CA: Sage.

Portman, T.A.A., & Garrett, M.T. (2006). Native American healing traditions. *International Journal of Disability, Development and Education, 53*(4), 453–469.

Ryback, C., & Decker-Fitts, A. (2009). Theory and practices, understanding Native American healing practices. *Counselling Psychology Quarterly, 22*(3), 333–342.

Stewart, D. (1979). Photo therapy: Theory & practice. *Art Psychotherapy, 6*(1), 41–46.

Stock, C., Mares, S., & Robinson, G. (2012). Telling and re-telling stories: The use of narrative and drawing in a group intervention with parents and children in a remote Aboriginal community. *The Australian and New Zealand Journal of Family Therapy, 33*(2), 157–170.

Todd, N., & Wade, A. (1994). Domination, deficiency, and psychotherapy. *The Calgary Participator, Fall*, 37–46.

Walters, K.L., & Simoni, J.M. (2002). Reconceptualizing Native women's health: An "Indigenist" stress-coping model. *American Journal of Public Health, 92*(4), 520–524.

Part III

Research and Validity

6 Expansive Palettes

A Client Video Media Experience

Natalie R. Carlton

EXPANSIVE PALETTES

Through experimentation as well as trial and error, I have developed reflective practices with diverse media that support clients' goals and creative drives. I briefly describe a direct example of using digital media in therapy from my own reflective practices before I present the findings from my phenomenological study. At the time of this clinical example of digital video use, I was a private practice therapist applying for future doctoral study. One reason that I wanted to pursue a doctoral degree was to learn about and apply research to questions that I had as a practitioner experimenting with digital media in art therapy. This chapter details how a particular application of digital video media facilitated the progress of therapy and how this case example connected to later research that qualified some of what I perceived in the therapeutic engagement and outcomes.

A CLIENT-THERAPIST VIDEO MEDIA EXPERIENCE

I worked as an outpatient, private practice art therapist with an 8-year-old boy who was seeing me for issues related to behaviors of aggression at home and school. One year into our therapeutic work, he chose digital video as a process and creative material because of his interest in computers and curiosity about my studio photography equipment. I chose this medium because of perceived therapeutic benefits such as opportunities for structure, collaborative interactivity, and self-observation inherent in the tools and process.

My young client and I began to use digital video as an interactive tool to record and play back a story of superhero sand play characters throughout a series of art therapy sessions for 3 months. After sequential sessions of photographing characters and placing raw footage into a digital editing computer program, the client requested to play back either portions or the entire video on the computer and viewed unedited footage in the camera repeatedly. These repetitive viewings became a ritualized part of ongoing sessions, allowing him to look and listen, objectify, or "observe self at a distance with projections of self displayed through the character play" (McNiff & Cook, 1975, p. 56). In sessions, we explored technological tools and techniques through collaborative and autonomous efforts that developed his ability to manipulate the technology, story, environment, and therapeutic relationship (Ehinger, 2009; O'Rourke, 2001). The technology's gear and structure, such as how to set up and work the camera or methods of editing in a software program, not only challenged him but also provided him with problem-solving situations to gain a "sense of control and ego mastery" (Tosone, Gelman, & McVeigh, 2005, p. 426). He learned media literacy experientially through self-directed and collaborative camera operation, video editing activities, and soundtrack creation (Ehinger, 2009; Mosinski, 2010). Moreover, the client dually controlled the video as observer and creative processor through directing and editing (Ehinger, 2009; Mosinski, 2010; Tosone et al., 2005) to create a dynamic story of superhero powers, conflict and battle, teamwork, and death to rebirth.

We found video to be a powerful art medium for capturing self-narrative imagery because it gave my client choices about what he wanted to photograph. The tools of video processing also were a dynamic in directing how we chose to edit and sequence his imagery and sound recordings to build the story into a time line. Moreover, the making and editing of the imagery and self-generated soundtrack were multilayered processes that formed his creative visions and were "driven" (Austin, 2010; Edmunds, 2012; Ehinger, 2009) by me only when technical needs arose. My client showed many instances of self-direction by setting up the equipment and reviewing his video numerous times. He activated collaboration by asking me to participate, record, and witness his actions and character play unfolding in the sand play. The creation of the stop-animation video project seemed to grant him, along with his aggressive and sometimes destructive play, a newfound sense of order, safety and containment, and a distancing from chaotic internal and external forces.

The medium of video structured our relational interactions and inspired creativity and learning for both of us. After this project, I had many reflective questions as to how the qualities of the material advanced the therapeutic goals. The following discussion is of the doctoral study that I completed to reflect on the queries that this and other experiences with video had raised. The findings are summarized and placed alongside other research findings to illustrate how various digital media might be applied intentionally in therapy sessions.

DIGITAL MEDIA USE IN ART THERAPY INTERVIEWS

For Stage 1 of my doctoral research, I studied four art therapists who were using digital photography, video, and animation in their clinical and educational settings. The phenomenological interviews were conducted, respectively, at the participants' studio apartments, an art therapy site, and a public venue after a workshop session on digital video green screening methods (full transcripts of the interviews can be found at www.filmandvideobasedtherapy.com). Interviewees described the positive and negative qualities inherent in the digital media that they used: digital video, photography, and animation.

The need to balance the liabilities and limitations of technology with the strengths and integration of clinical, creative, and technological abilities was one overall conclusion of my research. For example, the interviewees noted how the technological quality of immediacy could be beneficial to clients through the creation and immediate observation of seriated photographs or videos in their therapeutic sessions. In contrast, the same media quality that supports instant gratification through a multitude of self-directed imagery choices could be perceived as a drawback when working with clients who might need therapeutic distancing elements or containment in the selected media.

Clients of diverse ages and circumstances might become overwhelmed by having too many choices or by recording their likenesses and hearing their own voices recorded. Clients and therapists might choose video media to tell stories because of their interest, skills, or accessibility to equipment, but care must be taken to safeguard against and think through any adverse effects that particular media can bring to therapy or the therapeutic relationship (Alders, Beck, Allen, & Mosinski, 2011). The interviewees characterized digital media as contemporary tools and applications that are relevant for therapists to learn. They also described how their learning with digital media evolved and how they became more cognizant of and skilled in how to drive and amplify creative tools, therapeutic opportunities, and inherent qualities.

"Digital Media Use in Art Therapy Interviews" (Carlton, 2013), (available at https://vimeo.com/89563621 and www.filmandvideobasedtherapy.com), as a research video product, allows viewers to "see and hear" the interviewees and engage the video art form as a way of exploring and knowing (S. A. McNiff, personal communication, May 9, 2014). It also integrates themes and ideas related to how computer arts media are being applied for therapy. The following themes and subthemes emerged from the synthesis of the interview data:

1. Omnipresence of technology with a subtheme of digital divides in art therapy.
2. Photography and video as an access to memory with a subtheme of storytelling.
3. Inherent qualities of technology, including immediacy and playback, emotional distancing and pause elements, movability, mobility, and re-presentation.
4. Hybrid nature of digital art therapists.

5. Fluid parameters in digital media, along with a subtheme of fluid boundaries in the ethical use of digital media.

Following is a discussion of each theme that emerged from the study.

Omnipresence of Technology

All of the interviewees described the ubiquitous nature of technology as an undeniable presence in their evolving creativity, professional tasks, and work, as well as in the parallel lives of their clients. All of the interviewees characterized digital media as an additional tool that can be used to modernize art therapy palettes and expertise. Necessary technology assimilation, adaptation, and learning were emphasized, as was reflection on what various individuals and communities are experiencing in regard to technological innovations and their broad presence.

The case was made repeatedly that clients outside of therapy are already using video media contained within smartphones and readily available computer software and that these personal devices and technological practices can be used in ways that bridge therapy and real life. All of the interviewees noted the many ways in which clients and art therapists are using technology to aid communication, access information, and form new digitalized visual and auditory languages and culture. In addition, all the interviewees spoke to the ways in which diverse populations of people are evolving with technology and why this is a valuable topic for them to explore and understand as artists and therapists.

Digital divides. Art therapists might choose to engage with the social networks, musical preferences, and other audiovisual representations of self brought by clients to therapeutic sessions through cell phones, laptop computers, iPods, and iPads, or, they might ask clients to leave these devices outside of the sessions (Klorer, 2009; Potash, 2009). The subcategory of digital divides emerged from the interviewees' descriptions of how accepting and knowledgeable therapists are about technology as an art form and the interests of their clients. The interviewees saw therapists as either open to actively learning about digital media or not interested in exploring, owning, or using technology with clients because of such divisive and complex issues as affordability and accessibility; generational experience; educational exposure; professional identity; and negative perceptions of, or experiences with, the media.

Previous research has shown that although increasing numbers of art therapists own and use technology for professional practice reasons, smaller numbers are using these same tools with clients as dynamic art forms or to achieve clinical goals (Orr, 2006b, 2012; Peterson, 2010). All four interviewees reported that responses to digital media and informed knowledge of digital media among therapy professionals seem to run along wide continuums. They also described some of their professional experiences teaching digital media workshops and colleagues' responses to their writing on the subject. The following themes emerged: resistance and interest; growing research and training needs contrasted, with some lack of both; growing digital culture participation for younger clients and art therapy students; and ongoing dialogue needed to address the benefits and costs of a technological world that is expanding outside of therapy. The interviewees invited curious individuals to reserve judgment about the use of digital media through informed experiences gained from self-experimentation and ongoing community dialogue.

Photography and Video as Access to Memory

All of the interviewees spoke about the power of still and moving imagery to access memory through clients' affective and visceral experiences of recording, watching, and listening. Media manipulation of images and sounds within video processes might employ the following choices or others not listed: layering, reviewing, amplifying, or fading, and transparencies, deletions, and juxtaposing and cutting up elements. Autonomy and mastery are inherent in the basic manipulations of video editing because clients are in control of their video time line material. They can readily enact power through the digital tools that they decide to use and how they sequence their memories in representational or direct ways through the media. One interviewee spoke about observing video editing to mimic memory processes and, importantly, granting control to the client through the tools of manipulation used to form the final product. Another interviewee discussed how potently photographic imagery can access memory because visual language is the first language in human development.

Storytelling. In the development of an individual or a group narrative over time and through multiple art therapy sessions, clients' photography and video work also were characterized in the subtheme of storytelling, where video content was not directly associated with reviewing personal memories. One interviewee described the ways in which the youth participants in therapeutic animation groups often used many aspects of the media for their collective storytelling. He also related how their narratives evolved and changed through the process of engaging with the media and each other over several weeks of structured sessions. Another interviewee similarly described how his green screening video work with youth and adults formed complex storytelling through the collaborative application of digital recording equipment and editing software, theatrical staging, lighting, stock to self-made virtual backdrops, and recorded visual movement and sound.

Inherent Qualities of Digital Media

Inherent qualities of digital media identified in this study were immediacy and playback; emotional distancing and elements of pause; movability; mobility;

and re-presentation. Media qualities existed on a continuum according to their valuation under certain conditions and devaluation in other situations to match the needs and circumstances of clients, including their stage of development. For example, the media benefit or deficit changed in relation to the ages, skills, experiences, concerns, and abilities of the clients.

Immediacy and playback. The interviewees reported photo and video work as having positive immediacy effects because digital formats facilitated instantaneous imagery, that is, no time lapse between taking and seeing the imagery. In contrast, analogue film media can result in lagging interest from clients because of the more protracted process of waiting for imagery to be developed or processed. As mentioned previously, inherent qualities often have a continuum of perceived positive and negative impacts. One interviewee mentioned that art therapists should be cautious and discerning in their use of technology because of possible media overexposure that clients and students might be experiencing. On the other hand, showing interest and openness toward media that clients are excited about using and engaging with can be seen as a digital culture consideration (Carlton, 2014; Orr, 2010).

The interviewees also described playback as a therapeutic tool in which client-driven actions initiate the process of viewing and reworking the video content numerous times to generate evaluation and editing within digital media art forms. Reviewing and changing parts to make a more cohesive whole is exactly how painters rework images. The interviewees in this study, similar to previous researchers, perceived the benefits of the playback process, including self-observation (McNiff, 1981; McNiff & Cook, 1975); client desensitization around certain images (Mosinski, 2010); and the ability of clients to form and build their own stories to achieve the goals of empowerment and trauma resolution (Cohen, 2013; Ehinger, 2009; O'Rourke, 2001).

Emotional distancing and elements of pause. The subthemes of emotional distancing and elements of pause were related to the ways in which digital media might heighten and support the containment of affect and impulse control for clients. One interviewee discussed his work with youth and explained that they have to engage in a long-term process to learn and experiment with the digital animation tools and media to create their finished products at the end of several weeks. These slow processes and complex media learning, creativity, and practiced application can support positive developmental skills and tasks such as frustration tolerance and delayed gratification. Two interviewees viewed digital media as offering a structure and "a screen to hide behind," because not all clients benefit from accessing or displaying affect in therapy.

Movability. The subtheme of movability came from the interviewees' descriptions of visceral and movement sensations, the integration of traditional and digital media, and the various image and sound possibilities of creative works. For example, watching themselves on recorded videos allows clients to assess their own ability to move and to experience sensations by watching their own movements, sound, and interactions. Likewise, static images drawn on paper can be photographed and brought into a video time line as a backdrop to moving elements, or they can be made to appear fluid and/or transparent with visual effects, image filters, and accompanying sound.

Mobility. Mobility in the digital medium of video might refer to clients' ability to take recorded segment examples and combine them with other video segments to make DVDs to be taken home or transferred to personal computers. The interviewees considered mobility a tool of technology that is literally transportable from place to place. Mobility also refers to the ways in which creative digital products can be uploaded, shared, printed, or placed with other materials through manipulative digital file format choices.

Re-presentation. In its simplest form, one interviewee noted that artists use digital media to re-present and archive artwork to show to others later. Digital media also lend themselves to multiple product choices of dissemination and formats in the multiple possibilities of reappropriation. Re-presentation using digital media could involve the process of clients digitally photographing original paintings, sculptures, or drawings; making them digital files; and then recreating or transforming them into multiple possible formats, such as posters, t-shirts, or comic book pages. One interviewee explained how the photo manipulation directives gave students a way to alter their feelings and thoughts by re-presenting and manipulating old images.

Hybrid Nature of Digital Art Therapists

All of the interviewees in this study described the need for mixed skill sets in their backgrounds and ongoing learning to stay current about technology. Three interviewees remarked that they had obtained degrees in and/or had pursued careers in technology before they became art therapists. It might be that hybrid interests and backgrounds created a strong mix of technological, clinical, and artistic skills that these art therapists could not use in isolation. The hybrid skills and interests of the interviewees was an emergent theme that needs further investigation because understanding how therapists come to use technology and digital media also can be critical in explaining how sophisticated use of the media can be nurtured and expanded.

Fluid Parameters in Digital Media

How digital media and artwork can change formats, unlike traditional media, was a concern expressed by some interviewees. This theme often becomes a challenge for art therapists in learning digital tools and software and then applying them according to professional ethical codes. Staying current in digital media or any art media use requires openness to ongoing learning curves in self-study or with learning groups and colleagues. Digital media ethical considerations and best practices are being defined somewhat behind the exponential development of the use of these media in therapy. This lag in the development of ethical guidelines is creating challenges for practitioners using the media because they are sometimes defining boundaries, protocol, and ethical dilemmas while also developing their reflective practices alone or in informal work communities (L'Esperance, 2014).

Fluid boundaries in the ethical use of digital media. Ethical considerations regarding technology and social media have sometimes confounded art therapists' ability to use them. Many ethical concerns about digital art therapy processes and products have focused on protection and privacy concerns for clients because these fluid media test privacy boundaries in ways that traditional media do not. Additional considerations are related to safe storage and encryption, professional and personal identity fusions, and safe practices for Internet communication, to name but a few. This is an exciting and often daunting element of digital media because the products and systems of technology continue to emerge and evolve. Developing ethical codes of conduct to use such media can be difficult because even after guidelines are established, the products continue to change and precipitate new challenges.

CONCLUSION

From this study, as well as previous research, expert reflective practitioners have expounded on how the inherent qualities of video media can work well for diverse clients in varied settings, along with the specific creative qualities and relational impacts that traditional media can and cannot provide (Cohen, 2013; Edmunds, 2012; Ehinger, 2009; Mosinski, 2010; O'Rourke, 2001; Orr, 2005; Tosone et al., 2005). Moreover, the results of my study supported previous findings showing that video media can concretize client memories and personal to collective storytelling and why specific qualities of the media can promote certain goals and positive outcomes (Ehinger, 2009; Mosinski, 2010; O'Rourke, 2001; Orr, 2006a; Wolf, 2007).

In contrast, some previously surveyed art therapists have generalized that because digital photography, video, and animation media lack a critical art feel, their use has been deemed limited because of their intangible nature or lack of physicality in virtual spaces (Edmunds, 2012; Kuleba, 2008; Orr, 2006b, 2012; Peterson, 2010). The interviewees in my study countered these characterizations by naming specific sensory qualities of the media. They also spoke about broader queries regarding the relationships between technology and creativity as well as the certainty of human interactivity with and need for both of them.

The two sides of the dialogue seem not to understand each other's point of view because of contrastive self-experimentation levels and exposure to digital media. Previous research has concluded that technology requires assimilation and adaptation (McNiff, 1999; Orr, 2006b, 2012; Peterson, 2010; Wolf, 2007). The results of this study similarly highlighted how adaptation must be based upon informed experimentation and learning. I contextualized how knowledge and the skilled application of digital media were embodied by the participating art therapists, who mixed hybrid interests and professional experience with dual fine arts and technology drives and talents. The interviewees described how their life and work experiences had allowed them to integrate technological learning with other pursuits to form strong visions and expertise as art therapy clinicians and educators using digital media. Many questions raised by this research highlight the ways in which technology can affect therapists and clients diversely, and inspire lively dialogue about its relevance for use in contemporary therapy.

As therapists advance their use of digital media with clients, as well as for their own purposes, they must acknowledge that the social complexities relevant to such use of technology require awareness and active participation (Austin, 2010; Kapitan, 2009). Moreover, some art therapists have insisted that digital media are the future of creative materials in therapy because they are multileveled art forms that are sensory rich and relevant to increasing numbers of individuals, particularly young people (Austin, 2010; Ehinger, 2009). Like other possible media choices, digital materials are integrative to art therapy reflective practices that emphasize awareness of the impact of media properties and the skills necessary to facilitate sessions that include the media, clients, and related therapeutic goals (Austin, 2010; Choe, 2014; Edmunds, 2012; Ehinger, 2009; Moon, 2010; Orr, 2005, 2010, 2012; Wolf, 2007).

Expressive art therapist and educator Knill (2008) mused excitedly, "In the Internet, the whole globe is at hand and through a mouse without ever having to encounter a concrete object" (p. 41). The creation of digitalized media can similarly defy physical constraints through "intermodal editing and shaping" processes limited only by copyrights and the "polyaesthetic skills necessary to make the edits work" when "adding a soundtrack, a subtitled poem, doing color manipulations, theatrical effects, playing with movement and time and framing" (Knill, 2008, p. 41).

The ability to layer digital media such as audio, still and moving images, and graphics into a time line or an edited video is part of the polyaesthetic skills referred to by Knill (2008). Knill also discussed some common criticisms of digitalized imagery, where the imprinted or painted canvas, for example, becomes the pixilated or representational imagery of the same image on a computer screen. This difference in the materials and how art forms are created, stored, and disseminated is often judged as "virtual reality" (Knill, 2008, p. 39) and thought of as a degradation when compared to other media or fine art aesthetics. This author and others view digital media as distinct forms of expression and tools that reflect sensory-altering creativity and products. These media embody inherently different modes and means of crafting art forms and are further differentiated from earlier media by distinctive creative processes, products, and pathways of connection. "The transition from paintbrushes and cellos to digital tools alters our sense of what creativity is by changing our relationship with production and dissemination" (Blythe, Light, & O'Neill, 2007, p. 6).

Human beings make art and engage in creativity not simply through the media or because of the materials chosen. Multisourced storytelling and personal narratives can be conveyed through the use of digital video software programs that integrate still images, music, recorded sounds or voices, and moving imagery recorded by clients in or outside of therapy (Mosinski, 2010). In addition, Mosinski (2010) discussed the ways in which the physical product of the video concretized clients' internal worlds and explained that her (Mosinski's) role was to support this experience of self-discovery and efficacy.

Adjustments, deletions, and experimentations can occur, and multiple seriated versions of video, audio, text, and stills can be manipulated and placed on a cumulative media file time line (Ehinger, 2009). Videos can be saved, shared, and stored on external hard drives or portable flash drives. Completed and in-progress projects can be restarted or reviewed later as documentation of treatment or treatment closure, as well as for periodic client and therapist reviews (Alders et al., 2011). Digital files and completed artwork can be taken home immediately or upon project completion, as well as for therapy closure.

Expansive Palettes

The interviewees in this study articulated several inherent qualities of digital media. Particular focus was on qualities distinct from traditional arts media parameters and boundaries. Future researchers of digital media should consider giving careful consideration to whether and how clients perceive differences and distinct therapeutic qualities in computer-based art forms compared to traditional art forms. Another area of critical study could focus on tangible media effects from the increasing omnipresence of technological gear and devices, and communications, information, and commerce platforms and how these might have positive or negative impacts in therapy. Since the 1980s, technology has been shaping cultural norms in the physical world and in the ways that individuals think and interact. Technological devices can be turned off, but the power and influence that have resulted in major cultural shifts cannot be ignored. "Digital culture includes multiple sets of values and evolving worldviews, therefore art therapists must confront and define the differentiating and joining elements of media on many levels" (Carlton, 2014, p. 44).

It seems important not only to find and cultivate the benefits of technological creative art forms but also to be aware and informed of the adverse effects of technology. Digital media can bridge therapy and real life with vital creative materials and connectivity platforms that offer broader access and application than traditional fine art materials of paint or activities of drawing. The choices of art therapy material have remained individualized or appropriate to the settings, groups, treatment rooms, and studios in which therapists work, but are the specific needs and interests of clients also being considered? More than choosing media that therapists themselves consider valuable and therapeutic, art therapists have an important responsibility to work with clients, taking into account the media skills and preferences that they bring to therapy.

REFERENCES

Alders, A., Beck, L., Allen, P., & Mosinski, B. (2011). Technology in art therapy: Ethical challenges. *Art Therapy: Journal of the American Art Therapy Association, 28*(4), 165–170.

Austin, B. (2010). Technology, art therapy, and psychodynamic theory: Computer animation with an adolescent in foster care. In C.H. Moon (Ed.), Materials and media in art therapy (pp. 199–213). New York, NY: Routledge.

Blythe, M., Light, A., & O'Neill, S. (2007). Untitled: Emerging cultural form in the digital age. *Human Technology, 3*(1), 4–11.

Carlton, N.R. (Producer). (2013). Digital media use in art therapy interviews. Available from https://vimeo.com/89563621 and http://www.filmandvideobasedtherapy.com

Carlton, N.R. (2014). Digital culture and art therapy. Arts in Psychotherapy, 41(1), 41–45.

Choe, S. (2014). An exploration of the qualities and features of art apps for art therapy. Arts in Psychotherapy, 41(1), 145–154.

Cohen, J. (2013). Film and soul: A theoretical exploration of the use of video and other film-based therapy to help transform identity in therapeutic practice (Doctoral dissertation). Available from ProQuest Dissertations and Theses database. (UMI No. 3551606)

Edmunds, J.D. (2012). The applications and implications of digital media in art therapy: A survey study (Unpublished master's thesis). Drexel University, Philadelphia, PA.

Ehinger, J.F. (2009). *Exploring dreamspace through video art with at-risk youth* (Unpublished master's thesis). Pratt Institute, New York, NY.

Kapitan, L. (2009). Introduction to the special issue on art therapy's response to techno-digital culture. Art Therapy: Journal of the American Art Therapy Association, 26(2), 50–51.

Klorer, P. (2009). The effects of technological overload on children: An art therapist's perspective. Art Therapy: Journal of the American Art Therapy Association, 26(2), 80–82.

Knill, P.J. (2008). When pictures move, are we moved too? In E.G. Levine & P. Antze (Eds.), In praise of poiesis: The arts and human existence (pp. 32–46). Toronto, CA: EGS Press.

Kuleba, B.A. (2008). The integration of computerized art making as a medium in art therapy theory and practice. (Unpublished master's thesis). Drexel University, Philadelphia, PA.

L'Esperance, N. (2014). Current practices: A Delphi study concerned with current technology use in art therapy. Manuscript submitted for publication.

McNiff, S.A. (1981). Video enactment in the expressive therapies. In J.L. Fryrear & B. Fleshman (Eds.), Videotherapy in mental health (pp. 79–92). Springfield, IL: Charles C. Thomas.

McNiff, S.A. (1999). The virtual art therapy studio. *Art Therapy: Journal of the American Art Therapy Association, 16*(4), 197–200.

McNiff, S.A., & Cook, C. (1975). Video art therapy. Arts in Psychotherapy, 2(1), 55–63.

Moon, C. (2010). A history of materials and media in art therapy and theorizing materiality in art therapy. In C.H. Moon (Ed.), Materials & media in art therapy (pp. 3–88). New York, NY: Routledge.

Mosinski, B.B. (2010). Video art and activism: Applications in art therapy. In C.H. Moon (Ed.), Materials & media in art therapy (pp. 257–270). New York, NY: Routledge.

O'Rourke, R. (2001). Anya's movies. Afterimage, *29*(3), *3*, *9*.

Orr, P.P. (2005). Technology media: An exploration for inherent qualities. *Arts in Psychotherapy, 32*(1), 1–11. doi:10.1016/j.aip.2004.12.003

Orr, P.P. (2006a). A documentary film project with first-year art therapy students. *Arts in Psychotherapy, 33*(4), 261–287. doi:10.1016/j.aip.2006.03.002

Orr, P.P. (2006b). Technology training for art therapist: Is there a need? *Art Therapy: Journal of the American Art Therapy Association, 23*(4), 191–196.

Orr, P.P. (2010). Social remixing: Art therapy media in the digital age. In C.H. Moon (Ed.), Materials & media in art therapy (pp. 89–100). New York, NY: Routledge.

Orr, P.P. (2012). Technology use in art therapy practice: 2004 and 2011 comparison. Arts in Psychotherapy, 39(4), 234–238. doi:10.1016/j.aip.2012.03.010

Peterson, B. (2010). The media adoption stage model of technology for art therapy. *Art Therapy: Journal of the American Art Therapy Association, 27*(1), 26–31.

Potash, J.S. (2009). Fast food art, talk show therapy: The impact of mass media on adolescent art therapy. *Art Therapy: Journal of the American Art Therapy Association, 26*(2), 52–57.

Tosone, C., Gelman, C.R., & McVeigh, L. (2005). Through their own eyes: A media-based group approach to adolescent trauma. *International Journal of Group Psychotherapy, 55*(3), 415–432. doi:10.1521/ijgp.2005.55.3.415

Wolf, R. (2007). Advances in phototherapy training. *Arts in Psychotherapy, 34*(2), 124–133. doi:10.1016/j.aip.2006.11.004

7 The Benefits of a Grief and Loss Program With a Unique Technological Intervention

Carolyn McGurl, Winston Seegobin, Elizabeth Hamilton, and Mark McMinn

The grief process, difficult for anyone, is especially challenging for children and adolescents because they integrate loss differently from adults both in terms of cognition and emotion (Webb, 2011). Studies have found that bereaved children and adolescents are at high risk for depressive symptoms, anxiety, somatic complaints, and academic difficulties, compared with children and youth who are not grieving (Cohen & Mannarino, 2004; Dowdney, 2000). It is therefore important to provide effective intervention. While researchers have found age-appropriate and developmentally relevant strategies that help children and adolescents navigate the grief process (Rosner, Kruse, & Hagl, 2010; Sandler et al., 2010), additional data-based studies to explore optimal therapeutic services for these youth can provide new choices.

This chapter contains a review of existing developmentally based models used to conceptualize children's grief processes and a discussion of empirical studies concerning child and adolescent adaptation to loss, with a special focus on our recent study of a novel technological intervention. The chapter also includes a discussion of directions for future work.

CHILD AND ADOLESCENT GRIEF MODELS

Webb (2011) offered a developmental conceptualization based on Piagetian cognitive development stages. During the preoperational stage (ages 2–7), children are egocentric; they view death as temporary, and they engage in magical thinking. In the concrete operational stage (ages 7–11), children begin to understand the finality, irreversibility, and universality of death. In the formal operational stage (ages 9–12), more logical and abstract thinking emerges, leading to an increased understanding of the death process. In the adolescent years, children begin to form complex conceptual frameworks for coping with death.

Worden's Task Model

Data from the Harvard Child Bereavement study guided the development of a task model that includes flexibility for youth progressing at developmentally appropriate rates (Silverman & Worden, 1992, 1993). Their first task is to accept the reality of the loss, a task contingent in part upon the emergence of operational thinking around age 7 (Webb, 2011). The second task is to experience the pain of the loss; the third is adjusting to life without the loved one; and the fourth is to discover ways to memorialize dead loved ones, in a sense relocating them in their lives. Worden (1996) pointed out that each child resolves these tasks developmentally and that resolution occurs most effectively with the help of an adult who can regularly aid in the grief process.

EFFECTIVE INTERVENTIONS

Although therapeutic literature on intervention strategies for bereaved children and adolescents is available, empirically guided research is not so common (Currier, Neimeyer, & Berman, 2008). One exception is a meta-analysis conducted by Rosner, Kruse, and Hagl in 2010 to provide support for treatment models incorporating music therapy and brief school-based psychotherapy focused on grief.

Other researchers have identified several therapeutic interventions for facilitating children's and adolescents' grieving processes. Narrating personal stories and integrating feelings can lead to children understanding death (Cohen & Mannarino, 2004; Scaletti & Hocking, 2010). Art, bibliotherapy, play therapy, and multimedia are also beneficial therapeutic formats (Morgan & Roberts, 2010; Webb, 2011). Relevant support groups can be instrumental in helping grieving youth maintain a sense of connectedness and a positive outlook of the future (McNess, 2007). Cognitive-based interventions can help children who are dealing with more complicated grief adapt: Specifically, family-based programs have yielded positive results over time for parentally bereaved youth who had adopted maladaptive grief responses (Sandler et al., 2010).

The Role of Technology

The current societal trend of using the Internet to obtain information and support has led to research concerning the viability of technological interventions for dealing with grief. Researchers have begun to evaluate the ethical and appropriate use of technology in therapy, and to explore whether technological interventions can be helpful, while also maintaining professional standards of care (McMinn, Bearse, Heyne, Smithberger, & Erb, 2011; Van Allen & Roberts, 2011). Quality research is required to assess the potential benefits of the rapidly increasing number of technological interventions available (Jones, 2014).

Some researchers have suggested that children and adolescents often use the Internet when dealing with stress resulting from the death of a loved one (Leung, 2007). Children and adolescents increasingly use technology in ways that expose them to risk if they reveal personal information (Livingstone, 2008). The full implications of processing emotions in an online forum are unclear (Williams & Merton, 2009). Adolescents are not always aware of privacy settings—a lack of knowledge that can place them in vulnerable positions if they reveal personal information. Despite the potential dangers, however, the Internet may still be a positive tool for grieving individuals because of its instant availability, information, and support (Gilbert & Horsley, 2011).

Some researchers support the incorporation of multimedia components in interventions for bereaved youth. For example, a review of developmentally appropriate interventions for bereaved adolescents suggests that creative arts, including visual arts, drama, and music provide needed benefits (Johnson & Alderson, 2008; Slyter, 2012). In a recent exploratory pilot study, participants in therapeutic filmmaking activities adjunct to university counseling services reported positive benefits, including increased sense of mastery and changes in perspective (Johnson & Alderson, 2008). Cohen (2007, 2012) and Marsick (2010) suggest that video-based therapies, including Cinematherapy (Solomon, 2001) may yield therapeutic benefit for adolescents within the field of expressive art therapies. In another study, researchers identified the efficacy of mobile phone self-monitoring in decreasing depressive symptoms (Kauer et al., 2012). Ortiz, Cozza, Fullerton, and Ursano (2013) found positive support for the effects of *Talk Listen Connect*, a self-directed multimedia program for children who had lost a parent.

In many cases technological interventions, either incorporated into traditional psychotherapeutic formats (Anderson, Spence, Donovan, March, & Kennedy, 2012) or used as distinct approaches (Kauer et al., 2012), have led to demonstrated positive therapeutic effects. *The Confessional* videotape technique described below is another example of how technology can be used effectively to treat bereaved children and adolescents.

Hope and Resilience

Hope can be conceptualized in terms of *agency*, or motivation towards a goal, and *pathways*, finding ways to reach the goal (Snyder, 2000). Although Cutcliffe (2004) demonstrated that therapists' hope is vital for the reemergence of hope in bereaved adults, research concerning the role of hope in the grief process of children and adolescents has been scant.

Sapienza and Masten (2011) defined resilience in youth as "the capacity of a dynamic system to withstand or recover from significant challenges that threaten stability, viability, or development" (p. 268). Others have conceptualized resilience as a sense of mastery, a sense of relatedness, and moderated emotional reactivity. A sense of mastery includes optimism, self-efficacy, and adaptability. A sense of relatedness includes a sense of trust, perceived access to support, comfort with others, and tolerance of differences. Emotional reactivity includes sensitivity, recovery, and impairment (Prince-Embury, 2007).

THE CURRENT STUDY

Within this context, we investigated the use of a technological intervention, *The Confessional*, which allows young people to speak to a camera behind a two-way mirror. The Confessional is a creative bereavement intervention tool such as those reviewed by Slyter (2012). It has elements of Gestalt therapy (being rooted in a phenomenological construct, using an empty chair approach, and involving psychodrama) and allows individuals to respond freely to open-ended questions and prompts. We measured the effects of engagement in the Confessional by noting self-reported accomplishment of Worden's grieving tasks (Worden, 1996).

This unique intervention provided a safe, relevant medium for youth to process grief verbally. We examined hope and resilience before and after participants' time in the program, hypothesizing a significant increase in hope, sense of mastery, and sense of relatedness, along with a significant decrease in emotional reactivity. We also expected that the technological intervention would facilitate accomplishing the four grieving tasks (Worden, 1996).

METHODOLOGY

Participants

Participants entered the study through a grief support program facilitated by a grief and loss center for children and adolescents in Pennsylvania. They participated in the program for 8 weeks. Forty-nine children and youth in three separate programs (summer, winter, and spring) were recruited, including 16 boys and 33 girls ranging in age from 6 to 18 years. The majority of the young people in the program had lost their loved ones 3 to 6 months prior. Of the 49 participants, 33 had lost a parent, 4 had lost a grandparent, 5 had lost a sibling, 3 had lost a cousin, 2 had lost a great grandparent, 1 had lost an uncle, and 1 had lost a friend. Causes of death included illness (22), suicide (2), sudden death (12), homicide (8), and accidental death (4).

Instruments

The grief and loss program in this study facilitated children learning healthy ways to express their feelings about bereavement. Coping skills were taught and encouraged through engagement in program activities that included a visit to a funeral home that provided appropriate information. The program culminated with a review and a celebration of life ceremony that included a balloon release. During this time, children were empowered to be "wisdom givers" to others in their communities who were experiencing grief. These interventions are similar to those that were empirically supported in a bereavement camp where a balloon release, memorial service, and journaling were implemented (McClatchey & Wimmer, 2012).

Children's Hope Scale. The Children's Hope Scale contains six self-report items for children aged 7 to 16 years, resulting in an overall score, a score for pathways, and a score for agency (Snyder, 2000). Administration and scoring took approximately three minutes. Response options followed a Likert format and included the items none of the time, a little of the time, some of the time, a lot of the time, most of the time, and all of the time. The measure was filled out by the children alone or with the aid of readers available to help those without the requisite reading skills (Snyder et al., 1997). Our original study design included using the Adult Dispositional Hope Scale for participants over the age of 16 years and the Young Children's Hope Scale for children under the age of 7 years. However, analysis of data from these two age ranges was precluded by low numbers of participants (only four adolescents and one 6-year-old child).

Resiliency Scales for Children and Adolescents. The Resiliency Scales for Children and Adolescents contain three subscales (20 to 24 items each) that measure (a) sense of mastery, (b) sense of relatedness, and (c) emotional reactivity in youth aged 9 to 18 years (Prince-Embry, 2007). It took approximately fifteen minutes to complete. Respondents answered questions on a Likert scale containing the elements never (0), rarely (1), sometimes (2), often (3), and almost always (4).

Confessional Questionnaire. Study participants filled out five-item questionnaires developed specifically for this study following each use of the Confessional. Four questions related to Worden's (1996) four tasks of grieving and one related to their overall experience. Respondents answered these questions on a Likert scale between not helpful (1) and very helpful (5). See Table 7.3 for specific Confessional Questionnaire items.

Procedure

The 8-week support program in which the children and youth participated was facilitated by a grief and loss center for children and adolescents. Each week, the age groups (elementary: 6–11 years; middle: 12–14 years; and adolescent: 14–18 years) met for 1.5 hours. The participants in these groups were encouraged to cope with their grief by engaging in various activities that were designed to increase their coping skills, enable emotional expression, and encourage memory sharing. The program is not considered formalized therapy, but rather a multifaceted supportive program to help youth navigate grief.

Participants were invited to take part in this study to investigate the efficacy of video-based technology. Parents or caregivers as well as the children provided consent and assent, respectively. All participants responded to the Resiliency Scales for Children and Adolescents and we analyzed answers appropriately for each participant's age. Children aged 7 to 16 years responded to the Children's Hope Scale. We distributed all forms both pre- and post-participation.

The participants had the unique opportunity to confidentially use the Confessional, a room with brightly painted walls, a couch, a television monitor, and a one-way mirror with a camera. They could choose to use the Confessional alone, with a friend, with their entire age group, with their group facilitator, or with the program director. They were encouraged to speak freely, read something aloud, play an instrument, play with toys, or respond to questions on the television monitor. The program director regularly reviewed video footage to ensure the safety of all participants. No other individuals viewed the footage and it has been kept confidential. Each time the participants used the Confessional, they filled out the Confessional Questionnaire described above.

Statistical Analysis

The process described above resulted in the variables in Table 7.1. The first variable, time, was the grouping variable. The two hope measures—agency and pathways; the resiliency measures—sense of mastery, sense of relatedness, and emotional reactivity; and measures related to the Confessional Questionnaire provided the means for close statistical analysis of the program's efficacy.

We performed one-tailed paired *t* tests to measure changes in overall hope, agency, pathways, mastery, relatedness, and emotional reactivity. A one-tailed test was appropriate because we specifically hypothesized increases or decreases in the variables. Pairing was appropriate given that we had two readings (before and after) for each participant. For the Confessional Questionnaire, we examined the mean values for each of the five items on the survey to ascertain how the children responded to the intervention.

Results

Descriptive statistics. Table 7.2 contains the sample sizes (*N*), means (*M*), and standard deviations (*SD*) for each of the hope and resilience scales and Table 7.3 contains the means and standard deviations for each element of the Confessional Questionnaire.

Analysis. We performed one-tailed paired *t* tests to identify changes in the hope and resilience variables from the beginning to the end of the program. The Confessional Questionnaire provided descriptive information that showed to what extent participants who used the tool found it to be helpful.

Table 7.1 Variables used in this study

Variable		Variable Type	Group or Minimum	Group or Maximum	Instrument	Number of Readings
Hope	Overall Hope	Scalar	6	36	CHS*	2
	Agency	Scalar	3	18	CHS	2
	Pathways	Scalar	3	18	CHS	2
Resiliency	Sense of Mastery	Scalar	0	80	RSCA†	2
	Sense of Relatedness	Scalar	0	96	RSCA	2
	Emotional Reactivity	Scalar	0	80	RSCA	2
Confessional		Scalar	5	25	CQ‡	Dependent upon how many times participants used the Confessional

*Children's Hope Scale (CHS)
†Resiliency Scales for Children and Adolescents (RSCA)
‡Confessional Questionnaire (CQ)

Table 7.2 Means and standard deviations for pre- and post-measures

	Pre			Post		
Measures	N	M	SD	N	M	SD
Hope (Ages 7–16)	41	24.95	5.26	41	26.92	5.36
Agency	41	12.44	3.07	41	13.78	3.07
Pathways	41	12.51	2.78	41	13.14	2.96
Resilience (Ages 9–18)						
Sense of Mastery	36	49.25	9.04	36	52.39	10.62
Emotional Reactivity	35	53.43	9.56	35	51.60	11.54
Sense of Relatedness	36	50.06	8.44	36	50.64	7.94

Table 7.3 Means and standard deviations for questions on the Confessional Questionnaire

Question	M	SD
1. My time in the Confessional was helpful.	4.45	0.86
2. My time in the Confessional helped me accept the death of the person who died.	3.74	1.23
3. My time in the Confessional helped me to feel the hurt I have from losing the person who died.	3.63	1.38
4. My time in the Confessional helped me to get used to life without the person who died.	3.93	1.11
5. My time in the Confessional helped me to find ways to remember the person who died.	4.25	1.12

Hope. Using one-tailed paired *t* tests ($1 - \beta = .93$), we found that overall hope and agency increased during participation in the program with statistical significance, $t(40) = -2.454$, $p = .010$ and $t(40) = -2.820$, $p = .004$. Overall hope increased by 1.97 and agency by 1.34.

Resilience. Again using a one-tailed paired *t* test ($1 - \beta = .90$), we found that children's sense of mastery increased with participation in the program, $t(35) = -2.128$, $p = .020$. Mastery increased by 3.14.

The Confessional. As shown in Table 7.3 and in Figure 7.1, data indicated that the Confessional aided participants in accomplishing Worden's (1996) four tasks of grieving. Ten participants used the Confessional once, 14 used it twice, 7 used it three times, and 6 used it four times.

Discussion

In this study, we explored factors that could promote healing after the deaths of loved ones among children and adolescents participating in a bereavement program that made use of a unique technological intervention.

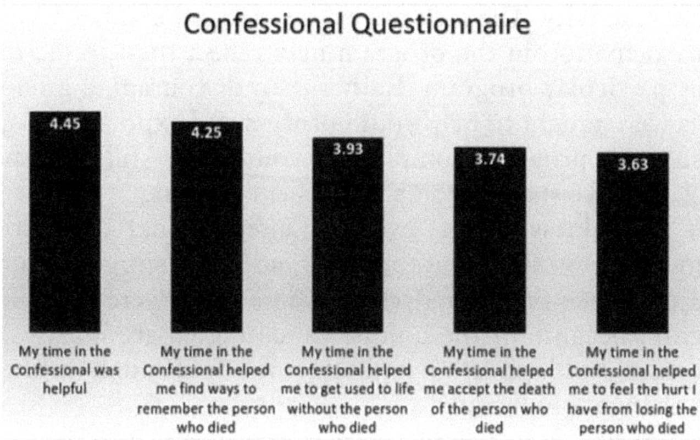

Figure 7.1 Average responses to questions on the Confessional Questionnaire

Overall, the data provided evidence of the clinical utility of the grief program as indexed by multiple therapeutic changes.

Researchers have used empirical studies to identify themes of healthy bereavement, including open communication, peer connection, and emotional catharsis (McClatchey & Wimmer, 2012). A child bereavement camp also has provided evidence that grief is a process that includes coping, empowerment, and hope (Swank, 2013). These themes were congruent with the significant factors that emerged in this study.

Hope

Significant changes were observed in overall hope and in agency for children aged 7 to 16 years. In addition, program alumni offered hope and validation to current participants, and at the close of the program, youth were encouraged to share with others the wisdom and skills that they had gained. It is reasonable to state that the need for hope drew families to the program in this study for various reasons congruent with Snyder's (2000) framework.

Resilience

Sense of mastery. Johnson and Alderson (2008) identified sense of mastery as one of the mechanisms of change that contributed to the positive therapeutic effects of using film as therapy for young adults. The use of the Confessional in this study leads to the new question of whether children might gain a greater sense of mastery when they are able to use tools such as the Confessional to create a narrative for themselves. The use of the Confessional in our program could explain why the children gained a greater sense of mastery than they did a sense of relatedness and why emotional reactivity did not change as much as sense of mastery did.

Emotional reactivity. The lack of change in emotional reactivity over the course of participation in the program may reflect the specific therapeutic goals of this particular program. Rather than discouraging grief reactions, coping skills were taught to help youth process and express their grief effectively. As such, at program completion, youth may still have been in an emotionally sensitive stage in the bereavement process.

Sense of relatedness. High levels of interpersonal connections were quickly formed within the program. Trust, access to support, comfort with others, and tolerance of differences are values that were established early in the program because of the unique validating environment. A sense of relatedness started at high levels and remained so throughout the program but did not change significantly.

Technology: The Confessional

Confessional Questionnaires completed by participants demonstrated that each item was rated with a mean greater than 3 ("above average") out of 5. The young people in this program said that using the Confessional especially helped them to accept the death of their loved ones as well as to remember those individuals. The majority of youth in the program had lost their loved ones 3 to 6 months prior to beginning the program. This passage of time may have affected variables such as emotional reactivity. Furthermore, it may be neither appropriate nor feasible to expect the limited number of variables that can be collected in a temporary setting in front of a camera to encompass the entirety of the complex process of grief.

Nonetheless, this technological intervention was a safe outlet for the participating children and adolescents to communicate feelings about their grief and loss; society provides many less optimal avenues for self-expression. Roberts (2004) said that adolescents used online social networking to communicate feelings that they would not have felt comfortable discussing in person. Cohen (2007) also suggested that some adolescents who are resistant to therapy might prefer the use of video therapy in order to receive help. Young people tend to use the Internet more heavily following the death of a loved one; however, some researchers have raised questions about the safety of this practice (Leung, 2007; Livingstone, 2008; Williams & Merton, 2009). The Confessional is a safe alternative to engage with technology, giving young people a means of verbal and emotional expression without parents or caregivers present (Scaletti & Hocking, 2010). The Confessional also provides youth with the freedom to choose how to use the technology (alone, with peers, or with the program director) and a place to express themselves that is not necessarily face to face.

GLOBAL EXPLANATION OF FINDINGS

While participating in the program, youth were told that all of their emotions were acceptable and were given the skills to manage them. Administrators told participants that they would not perform therapy; they designed the program to be an educational and supportive milieu, a validating and supportive environment for young people to share their stories verbally with others experiencing similar grief and loss (Cohen & Mannarino, 2004; Scaletti & Hocking, 2010). This study, with others, has shown that hope and a sense of mastery are significant factors related to grief (McNess, 2007). Participants found the Confessional to be helpful overall and in particular by offering ways to help remember deceased loved ones. This innovative tool might give youth the opportunity to share their experiences safely while interacting with an expressive and creative technology within a secure and trusted environment.

IMPLICATIONS

The data in this study show that the youth who used it found using the Confessional helpful as they worked their way through grief as depicted in Worden's (1996) model. Moreover, within the context of the program, hope and a sense of mastery changed significantly for this group of children and adolescents. These findings suggest that utilizing an intervention similar to the Confessional might yield similar effects for clients in other therapeutic settings.

Based on a review of the literature, therapists should consider the development of coping skills in addition to the provision of hope to children as a main goal of bereavement therapy. Interventions could include empowering children to create reasonable goals and ways to achieve them as a way of fostering self-efficacy, optimism, and hope. It also might be appropriate to refer families to grief and loss centers or camps for youth, or to work with them independently in more traditional therapeutic settings. Grieving children should be monitored long-term because of their tendencies to revisit bereavement, manifest symptoms extending beyond 1 or 2 years past the deaths of loved ones, and experience possible delayed or prolonged grief (Melhem, Porta, Payne, & Brent, 2013; Silverman & Worden, 1996).

LIMITATIONS AND FURTHER STUDY

Limitations of this study included a lack of standardization of the Confessional experience, in terms of time and selected activities, and the fact that ethnicity could not be investigated because of incomplete demographic information provided by parents or guardians. In addition, the various types of losses the children experienced might have caused variations in the intensity of the experience; closeness to deceased loved ones, the type of death, and presence at the time of death, for instance, all have possible effects on grief (Draper & Hancock, 2011). Another factor that would interfere with drawing conclusions from the data was that the children and adolescents in the program received different levels of professional help outside of the program. In addition, the Confessional Questionnaires were not linked to participants or to participants' other survey data. This precluded individual pre- and post-measure comparisons and analysis of how the Confessional related explicitly to hope and resilience measures. The Confessional was only part of a program with other tools available to participants, any of which could have affected the hope and resilience measures or even the efficacy of the Confessional itself. The study also had no control group; although it is therefore possible to identify areas for further study, it is not possible to draw definitive conclusions from these data.

Further studies may be enhanced by the use of a larger sample size, the inclusion of a control group, the expansion of demographics, and the inclusion of long-term follow-up. It also might be useful to conduct studies using a similar technological intervention in other settings such as a private practice office or a school in order to isolate the effects of the tool.

Having a more comprehensive understanding of specific instruments that can be used to evaluate the grief of children and adolescents will facilitate recognition of the changes in processes involved in grief recovery. A growing body of research indicates that bereaved children and adolescents benefit from timely therapeutic interventions that are sensitive to their developmental level and emerging cognitive complexity. In addition to more traditional psychotherapeutic models, innovative approaches, including multimedia therapy, and technological components, such as therapeutic filmmaking and the videotaped Confessional approach described in the current study, may provide youth with specialized opportunities to further process their grief. Researchers should continue to explore the effectiveness of novel technologically based interventions as ways to help bereaved children and adolescents adjust.

REFERENCES

Anderson, R.E., Spence, S.H., Donovan, C.L., March, S.P., & Kennedy, J. (2012). Working alliance in online cognitive behavior therapy for anxiety disorders in youth. *Journal of Medical Internet Research, 14*(3), 86–101.

Cohen, J. (2007). *The use of video therapy to treat depression in adolescent males* (Unpublished masters' thesis). Walden University, Minneapolis, MN.

Cohen, J. (2012). Film and soul: A theoretical exploration of the use of video and other film-based therapy to help transform identity in therapeutic practice (Doctoral dissertation). Available from ProQuest Dissertation and Theses database. (UMI No. 3551606)

Cohen, J.A., & Mannarino, A.P. (2004). Treatment of childhood traumatic grief. *Journal of Clinical Child and Adolescent Psychology, 33*(4), 819–831.

Currier, J.M., Neimeyer, R.A., & Berman, J.S. (2008). The effectiveness of psychotherapeutic interventions for the bereaved: A comprehensive quantitative review. *Psychological Bulletin, 134*(5), 648–661.

Cutcliffe, J.R. (2004). The inspiration of hope in bereavement counseling. *Issues in Mental Health Nursing, 25*(2), 165–190.

Dowdney, L. (2000). Childhood bereavement following parental death. *Journal of Child Psychology & Psychiatry & Allied Disciplines, 41*(7), 819–830.
Draper, A., & Hancock, M. (2011). Childhood parental bereavement: The risk of vulnerability to delinquency and factors that compromise resilience. *Mortality, 16*(4), 285–306.
Gilbert, K.R., & Horsley, G.C. (2011). Technology and grief support in the 21st century: A multimedia platform. In R.A. Neimeyer, D.L. Harris, H.R. Winokuer, & G.F. Thornton (Eds.), *Grief and bereavement in contemporary society: Bridging research and practice* (pp. 365–373). New York, NY: Routledge/Taylor & Francis Group.
Johnson, J.L., & Alderson, K.G. (2008). Therapeutic filmmaking: An exploratory pilot study. *The Arts in Psychotherapy, 35*(1), 11–19.
Jones, D.J. (2014). Future directions in the design, development, and investigation of technology as a service delivery vehicle. *Journal of Clinical Child & Adolescent Psychology, 43*(1), 128–142.
Kauer, S., Reid, S.C., Crooke, A.H., Khor, A., Hearps, S.J., Jorm, A.F., . . . Patton, G. (2012). Self-monitoring using mobile phones in the early stages of adolescent depression: Randomized controlled trial. *Journal of Medical Internet Research, 14*(3), 19–35.
Leung, L. (2007). Stressful life events, motives for internet use, and social support among digital kids. *CyberPsychology & Behavior, 10*(2), 204–214.
Livingstone, S. (2008). Taking risky opportunities in youthful content creation: Teenagers' use of social networking sites for intimacy, privacy, and self-expression. *New Media & Society, 10*(3), 393–411.
Marsick, E. (2010). Film selection in a Cinematherapy intervention with preadolescents experiencing parental divorce. *Journal of Creativity in Mental Health, 37*(4), 311–318.
McClatchey, I.S., & Wimmer, J.S. (2012). Healing components of a bereavement camp: Children and adolescents give voice to their experience. *Omega: Journal of Death and Dying, 65*(1), 11–32.
McMinn, M.R., Bearse, J., Heyne, L.K., Smithberger, A., & Erb, A.L. (2011). Technology and independent practice: Survey findings and implications. *Professional Psychology: Research and Practice, 41*(2), 160–168.
McNess, A. (2007). The social consequences of "how the sibling died" for bereaved young adults. *Youth Studies Australia, 26*(4), 12–20.
Melhem, N.M., Porta, G., Payne, M.W., & Brent, D.A. (2013). Identifying prolonged grief reactions in children: Dimensional and diagnostic approaches. *Journal of the American Academy of Child and Adolescent Psychiatry, 52*(6), 599–607.
Morgan, J.P., & Roberts, J.E. (2010). Helping bereaved children and adolescents: Strategies and implications for counselors. *Journal of Mental Health Counseling, 32*(3), 206–217.
Ortiz, C.D., Cozza, S.J., Fullerton, C.S., & Ursano, R.J. (2013). Feasibility of a multimedia program for parentally bereaved children. *Children & Youth Care Form, 42*(6), 489–506.
Prince-Embry, S. (2007). *Resiliency Scales for Children & Adolescents: A profile of personal strengths*. Minneapolis, MN: Pearson.
Roberts, P. (2004). The living and the dead: Community in the virtual cemetery. *OMEGA, 49*(1), 57–76.
Rosner, R., Kruse, J., & Hagl, M. (2010). A meta-analysis of interventions for bereaved children and adolescents. *Death Studies, 34*(2), 99–136.
Sandler, I. N., Ma, Y., Tein, J. Y., Ayers, T. S., Wolchik, S., Kennedy, C., Millsap, R. (2010). Long-term effects of the family bereavement program on multiple indicators of

grief in parentally bereaved children and adolescents. *Journal of Consulting and Clinical Psychology, 78*(2), 131–143.

Sapienza, J.K., & Masten, A.S. (2011). Understanding and promoting resilience in children and youth. *Current Opinion in Psychiatry, 24*(4), 267–273.

Scaletti, R., & Hocking, C. (2010). Healing through storytelling: An integrated approach for children experiencing grief and loss. *New Zealand Journal of Occupational Therapy, 57*(2), 66–71.

Silverman, P.R., & Worden, J.W. (1992). Children's reactions in the early months after the death of a parent. *American Journal of Orthopsychiatry, 62*(1), 93–104.

Silverman, P.R., & Worden, J.W. (1993). Children's reactions to the death of a parent. In M.S. Stroebe, W. Strobe, & R.P. Hansson (Eds.), *Handbook of bereavement: Theory, research, and intervention* (pp. 300–316). New York, NY: Cambridge University Press.

Silverman, P.R., & Worden, J.W. (1996). Parental death and the adjustment of school-age children. *OMEGA, 33*(2), 91–102.

Slyter, M. (2012). Creative counseling interventions for grieving adolescents. *Journal of Creativity in Mental Health, 7*(1), 17–34.

Snyder, C.R. (2000). *Handbook of hope: Theory, measures, and application.* San Diego, CA: Academic Press.

Snyder, C.R., Hoza, B., Pelham, W.E., Rapoff, M., Ware, L., Danovsky, M., . . . Stahl, K.J. (1997). The development and validation of the Children's Hope Scale. *Journal of Pediatric Psychology, 22*(3), 399–421.

Solomon, G. (2001). Reel therapy: How movies inspire you to overcome life's problems. New York, NY: Lebhar-Friedman Books.

Swank, J.M. (2013). Obstacles of grief: The experiences of children processing grief on the high ropes course. *Journal of Creativity in Mental Health, 8*(3), 235–248.

Van Allen, J., & Roberts, M. (2011). Critical incidents in the marriage of psychology and technology: A discussion of potential ethical issues in practice, education, and policy. *Professional Psychology: Research and Practice, 42*(6), 433–439.

Webb, N.B. (2011). *Helping bereaved children: A handbook for practitioners* (3rd ed.). New York, NY: Guilford Press.

Williams, A.L., & Merton, M.J. (2009). Adolescents' online social networking following the death of a peer. *Journal of Adolescent Research, 24*(1), 67–90.

Worden, J.W. (1996). *Children and grief: When a parent dies.* New York, NY: Guilford Press.

8 Digital Storytelling as a Trauma Narrative Intervention for Children Exposed to Domestic Violence

Kim Anderson and Beatriz Wallace

This chapter presents the use of digital storytelling (DS) as a trauma narrative intervention, in the context of trauma-focused cognitive behavioral therapy (TF-CBT), for children exposed to domestic violence (CEDV) who received mental health services at a rural domestic violence (DV) agency. The youth therapy program (YTP) was conducted by the first author as clinical coordinator, the second author as program coordinator, and a licensed professional counselor who was a registered play therapist. We wanted to understand the capacity of DS to accommodate the unique needs and circumstances of child witnesses of DV in telling their stories. Digital storytelling, as the term implies, combines storytelling with technology (Lambert, 2006).

The goals of our DS project were two-fold. One was to evaluate the potential mental health benefits of digital storytelling for processing trauma-related information and enhancing narrative integration. Another goal was to develop a DS curriculum to supplement the trauma narrative component of TF-CBT, an evidence-based intervention for children that focuses on the expression and discussion of traumatic experiences and memories along with their associated thoughts and feelings (Cohen, Mannarino, & Deblinger, 2006). YTP staff sought to understand the elements (i.e., digital images, text, audio narration, and music) of DS and their individual and collective benefits (Gubrium, 2009; Lambert, 2006). In doing so, we wanted to provide mental health clinicians with practical information on narrative development to use in their own practices. Our project findings indicated that this is a powerful tool to help children process their traumatic experiences.

EFFECTS OF CHILDHOOD EXPOSURE TO DOMESTIC VIOLENCE

Approximately 15 million children are exposed to DV each year, with 7 million living in families with severe partner violence (McDonald, Jouriles, Ramisetty-Mikler, Caetano, & Green, 2006). Traumatic responses vary for each individual, yet several studies show that children who are exposed to acts of violence between their parents or parental figures are less well-adjusted when compared to individuals from nonviolent families (Dehon & Weems, 2010; McFarlane, Groff, O'Brien, & Watson, 2003). Being exposed to violent acts and enduring a family environment characterized by control, fear, and powerlessness often negatively affects children's adaptive abilities, social functioning, emotional well-being, and physical health (Holt, Buckley, & Whelan, 2008). The impact of such adverse childhood experiences is well understood today; helping professionals know the harmful effects of such trauma, and understand the struggle to recover faced by many youth exposed to DV (Graham-Bermann, Gruber, Girz, & Howell, 2009).

Witnessing DV can cause children to split off one or more aspects related to the abusive experience, including their thoughts, memories, perceptions, or feelings. The resulting chaos of fragments is difficult to understand and may be associated with confounding emotions (e.g., terror, fear, shame, and anxiety), thus overwhelming children with experiences they cannot process and consequently inhibiting their ability to construct a coherent self-narrative (Anderson, 2012; Graham-Bermann, Howell, Lilly, & Devoe, 2010). Inadequate processing and integration of trauma-related information underlie psychological and physical problems, including posttraumatic stress disorder (PTSD) and other stress symptoms (Anderson & Bang, 2012; Margolin & Vickerman, 2011). Left untreated, PTSD in children exposed to DV can lead to difficulties that last into adulthood, such as increased suicide attempts, hospitalizations, substance abuse, depression, and victimization (Anderson, 2010; Becker, Stuewig, & McClosky, 2010; Davies, DiLillo, & Martinez, 2004). For child witnesses, these problems are associated with increased use of mental health and health care resources (Dube, Anda, Felitti, Edwards, & Williamson, 2002; Russell, Springer, & Greenfield, 2010). Thus, there is a clear imperative to identify, disseminate, and implement effective psychosocial treatments for children and families exposed to DV and to provide these in a timely manner.

NARRATIVE INTERVENTIONS FOR TRAUMA RECOVERY AND GROWTH

Research findings demonstrate how the ability to formulate an integrated and coherent story after experiencing traumatic events is positively correlated with better trauma recovery and growth (e.g., Anderson & Hiersteiner, 2008; van Minnen, Wessel, Dijkstra, & Roelofs, 2002). The organization of stressful memories, particularly in a narrative structure, may be critical to obtaining beneficial effects from processing one's story about stressful events. Traumatic memories are more disorganized than other memories, and therefore narrative interventions aimed at organizing memory may be particularly effective because more organized memories are easier to integrate into existing ones (Foa & Rauch, 2004). However, the professional literature is lacking regarding the range of ways narratives can be used during the therapeutic process to open stories to new possibilities, new meanings, and new information, thereby positively influencing trauma recovery and growth.

A problem with processing, organizing, and integrating traumatic memories seems to be that the latter lack verbal properties and therefore cannot be communicated or organized effectively (Niederhoffer & Pennebaker, 2009). Integrated functions such as cognition, memory, and emotion become disconnected, particularly in cases of prolonged exposure to trauma (Simon, Feiring, & McElroy, 2010). Children often do not speak or write plainly about their trauma (Hanney & Kozlowska, 2002). Therefore, many children may need to find another avenue, another mode of expression, to discover their voices. DS provides such a means, as it uses a multimedia approach to help tell one's story. DS embodies the narrative approach of *emplotment*, which involves arranging temporal elements into a whole by connecting them and directing them toward a conclusion or ending (Polkinghorne, 1991). In the process, traumatic reactions that youth might otherwise carry with them throughout their lives may be prevented, lessened, or ameliorated.

DIGITAL STORYTELLING AS A NARRATIVE INTERVENTION FOR TRAUMA RECOVERY

Typically, digital stories are created in intensive three-day workshops (see Center for Digital Storytelling [CDS], http://storycenter.org/). Six to eight participants, along with trained digital story facilitators, work on their personal stories and offer feedback to each other, often in the context of what we call a Story Circle. At the conclusion of the workshops, everyone views the completed stories (Lambert, 2006). Although healing may occur, the purpose of DS workshops is not to serve as a therapeutic intervention; instead, they provide consciousness-raising of social issues (e.g., poverty, violence, or racism) and a sense of empowerment for the storyteller. For instance, through DS foster-care, youth who have shared their experiences raise awareness about the need to improve care in the child welfare system (e.g., see National Resource Center for Permanency and Family Connections, http://www.nrcpfc.org/digital_stories/ and the Y.O.U.T.H Training Project, http://www.youthtrainingproject.org/?q=digital stories, also found at www.filmandvideobasedtherapy.com).

DS can involve a computer-based program (e.g., Moviemaker or Final Cut Express), iPad application (e.g., iMovie or Pinnacle Studio), or other digital media that integrate a mixture of digital images, text, audio narration, and music. Such modalities allow any element to interact with any other one. In addition, one can employ pan and zoom effects to make one's story more unique and personal. The process involves the author assessing and making decisions regarding how the story interacts with the images (e.g., photographs, drawings), narration (e.g., voiceovers, text on photographs), or music/sounds (original or commercial) (Gubrium & Turner, 2011). The technical process is user-friendly; both youth and adults often catch on quickly (Davis & Weinshenker, 2012). Once one's story is created and saved, one can view, edit, and add to it until the final version is complete. Upon saving the visual narrative, all the pictures, narrations, and music are compiled into a video file that one can view in increments or in its entirety. The result is a two- to five-minute film (Gubrium, 2009, Lambert, 2006).

A comprehensive literature search (including PsychINFO, PILOTS, Social Work Abstracts, Medline EMBASE, CINAHL, Google Scholar, and the Cochrane Library) did not yield any other clinical examples or research studies in which DS was used as a therapeutic intervention in trauma narrative development in general, or for child witnesses in particular. This innovative and multi-sensory narrative approach has the potential to significantly influence the trauma field for children exposed to DV and possibly survivors of family violence overall. DS was intuitively recognized by the YTP staff as fitting the needs of traumatized children, yet it was a novel intervention. Therefore, we chose not to use it as a stand-alone protocol but instead integrated it with an evidence-based intervention.

TRAUMA-FOCUSED COGNITIVE BEHAVIORAL THERAPY (TF-CBT)

Optimally, one would adapt existing effective treatments rather than continually develop new treatment models for children exposed to violence (Cohen, Mannarino, & Murray, 2011b; Feather & Ronan, 2009). For this project, YTP staff added DS to the trauma narrative phase of TF-CBT, an intervention for youth with emotional and behavioral difficulties associated with violence exposure and trauma (Cohen, Mannarino, & Deblinger, 2006). Randomized controlled trials have demonstrated the efficacy of TF-CBT over other treatment modalities in achieving and maintaining greater symptom reduction for traumatized children (Cohen, Mannarino, & Iyengar, 2011a; Cohen, Mannarino, Perel, & Staron, 2007). TF-CBT integrates trauma practice with cognitive behavioral therapy, and helps children and parents gain knowledge and skills in working through traumatic events and reminders, as well as improve parent-child communication and support.

Creating a written trauma narrative is a critical component of standard TF-CBT. The child creates a storybook with chapters using words, pictures, and/or drawings to tell the story of his or her trauma (see Cohen et al., 2006, pp. 119–146; Saxe, Ellis, & Kaplow, 2009, pp. 269–275). The core components of standard TF-CBT make up the acronym PRACTICE (Cohen et al., 2006) and consist of the following sequential components and phases, typically delivered in 12–16 weekly 90-minute sessions (60 minutes with the child, 30 minutes with the parent):

- Phase I (4–5 sessions): "PRAC" includes *p*sycho-education, *r*elaxation skills, *a*ffect expression and modulation, and *c*ognitive coping.
- Phase II (5–8 sessions): "T" includes *t*rauma narrative development.
- Phase III (3 sessions): "ICE" includes *i*n-session mastery of trauma reminders, *c*onjoint parent-child sessions, and *e*nhancing future safety and development.

Children who witness DV often face ongoing exposure to violence that presents unique challenges to the TF-CBT model. Cohen et al. (2011a) stated that, to their knowledge, their study was the only one in which TF-CBT had been tested and evaluated with children exposed to DV. Cohen et al. found that TF-CBT effectively improved children's intimate partner violence (IPV)-related PTSD and depression in 75% of youth who completed treatment. However, as evidenced by a 40% dropout rate, their findings also illustrate the challenge in keeping this population engaged in treatment. Additionally, effect sizes were modest and smaller than found in their other studies of TF-CBT with children who had been sexually abused. These authors highlighted that more research is necessary "to address optimal treatment for children traumatized by ongoing threat or reality of IPV" (Cohen et al., 2011a, p. 21).

DS Project at a Rural DV Agency

The DS project developed out of the TF-CBT services offered by the only victims' service provider for a rural county (population 43,464) in a Midwestern state. The goals of the YTP were to increase access to mental health services—particularly evidence-based intervention—and to promote healing and resilience for child witnesses and their non-abusing parents/guardians. To this end, the DV agency partnered with the first author, Kim Anderson, Ph.D., associate professor in the School of Social Work at the University of Missouri (MU). Dr. Anderson's clinical and research expertise in trauma and recovery, along with training in DS, provided the foundation for establishing the DV agency's TF-CBT services for children exposed to DV.

The second author, Beatriz Wallace, M.A., adjunct professor in the Reynolds School of Journalism at MU, was the agency's youth community outreach and education coordinator and became the YTP coordinator. Additionally, a licensed professional counselor (LPC), who was a registered play therapist and a well-respected child and adolescent therapist, was hired to provide TF-CBT services for youth aged 7–17 years. We met weekly to discuss issues related to the YTP program in general and TF-CBT services in particular. From this collaboration and with the support of the agency's executive director, we created a DS curriculum and made it a component of TF-CBT because youth were having difficulty constructing their trauma narratives. The DS curriculum added essential structure to the trauma narrative component, and it helped youth process and develop their stories of exposure to DV in a less threatening and more approachable manner.

Core participants (n = 16, 9 male and 7 female, all Caucasian) ranged in age from 7–16 years old (M = 12; SD = 3.28). Children were first exposed to DV at a young age (M = 2 years old, SD = 2.68, range 1–11) and were exposed for several years (M = 6 years, SD = 3.31, range 1–12). The majority of their mothers' abusers were their birthfathers (64%, n = 10). In addition to being exposed to DV, several (64%, n = 10) were also abused by the perpetrator.

Following approval from the DV agency and the university's Institutional Review Board, we initiated the DS project. Youth and their non-abusing parents/guardians who consented to TF-CBT services were also offered a written consent form to participate voluntarily in the research component related to DS (i.e., TF-CBT/DS). During the intake process, all parents/guardians received documents on their and their children's rights and responsibilities regarding treatment and research participation. After discussing any questions or concerns they had, parents/guardians were asked to sign documents confirming that they understood and were in agreement with consent procedures. They received a copy of such signed documents.

Participants were recruited through counseling referrals to the agency (e.g., child welfare, school district, civil/criminal court, medical care providers, etc.). Children were required to have at least five PTSD symptoms, including at least one symptom representing, respectively, avoidance, hyperarousal, and re-experiencing, as defined by the *Diagnostic Statistical Manual of Mental Disorders, IV-R* (APA, 2002). Of 41 referrals, 28 children met criteria for PTSD and 25 of those followed through after intake to begin DS within the context of TF-CBT. Of the 25 who started TF-CBT services, 16 completed treatment. Non-completion (n = 9) was most often due to life crises such as loss of housing, transportation, and/or employment. The average number of TF-CBT sessions per child was 12, and the range of completed sessions was 6–17.

We modified the protocol for DS from a three-day workshop model for individuals without PTSD to one integrated into an evidence-based therapeutic model (TF-CBT) for youth with PTSD. This adaptation resulted in a web-based DS curriculum for the trauma narrative component (see Digital Storytelling Therapy, http://digitalstorytherapy.com/) that provided direction and guidelines that were not sufficiently delineated in the professional literature regarding trauma story construction with children. DS was defined as stories that were three- to five-minute visual narratives synthesizing images, text, and audio recordings of voice and music to create compelling accounts of one's trauma experience. The DS curriculum consisted of three structured sessions covering the purpose, process, and technical tools of DS. These sessions were followed by two to three unstructured ones to allow for completion of the participants' digital stories. The clinician provided the youth with technical assistance and reminded and encouraged them to use the therapeutic skills they learned in TF-CBT. Throughout this process, all youth experienced varying degrees of mastery over challenging thoughts and emotions as they constructed their stories.

Our research aim was to develop and test the feasibility of DS as a trauma narrative intervention within the context of TF-CBT for treating post-trauma symptoms in CEDV. Specifically, we were interested in decreasing post-traumatic stress symptomatology, including depression, while increasing self-esteem and coping levels for 80% of children receiving TF-CBT/DS. To assess changes in psychosocial functioning, youth completed the following standardized instruments at pre- (intake session) and postintervention (exit interview). The rationale for selected measures included previous use with traumatized children/CEDV and good to excellent psychometric properties (Cohen's alpha coefficients for reliability).

1. PTSD Checklist—Child Form (Daviss et al., 2000; Ford et al., 1999), a 17-item instrument that assesses PTSD symptoms, including subscales of re-experiencing, avoidance, and arousal. Cronbach's alpha is in the range of .92/.80 for the total scale with subscale alphas of .88/.84 (re-experience), .80/.77 (avoid), and .79/.80 (arouse); it has good test-retest reliability (.92). Clinical cutoff score is ≥44.
2. The Mood and Feelings Questionnaire—Child Version (MFQ-C; Angold & Costello, 1987), a 33-item instrument that measures depression. It has good criterion validity and good reliability (Cohen's $\alpha = .95$). Clinical cutoff score is ≥8 for depression.
3. Hare Self-Esteem Scale (HSS, Hare, 1996), a 30-item instrument that measures the youth's overall self-esteem and subscales relating to peers, home, and school. Overall internal reliability (Cronbach's alpha) for the HSS is .85. Test-retest correlation = 0.74 for total, 0.56–0.65 for the subscales, and concurrent validity of 0.83 with similar instruments (Grizenko, Archambault, & Pawliuk, 1992). The norm average for the total is 99 (*SD* = 6.2). No clinical cutoff score; significant clinical differences pre- and post-treatment = 10 points.
4. Youth Coping Index (YCI; McCubbin, Thompson, & Elver, 1996), a 31-item scale designed to address psycho-social-spiritual coping displayed in the last month. Overall internal reliability (Cronbach's alpha) for the YCI is .86; test-retest reliability is .43. The norm average for the YCI is 94 (*SD* = 5.6). No clinical cutoff score; significant clinical differences pre-and post-treatment = 10 points.

During the exit interview, participants completed a Likert-type questionnaire pertaining to the process and outcome of DS in the framework of

TF-CBT. Additionally, open-ended questions were included to provide a further context for quantitative responses.

Quantitative data analysis included descriptive statistics to examine the demographic characteristics of the sample and to assess clinical significance regarding pre- and post-treatment changes. Because of the small sample size, nonparametric tests were used to assess statistical difference (Mann-Whitney U Test, Wilcoxon Signed-Rank Test). The qualitative method of thematic analysis was used for the open-ended statements gathered in the exit interviews to assess convergent content and themes (Braun & Clarke, 2006).

RESULTS OF THE DS PROJECT

Our findings indicated that creating a multi-sensory trauma narrative allowed for a reduction in post-trauma symptoms and an improved quality of life for CEDV. Comparing pre- and post-treatment scores, we noted that PTSD symptoms decreased by an average of 12 points (pre: $M = 54.60$, post: $M = 42.33$; clinical cutoff score ≥ 44) for 100% (16/16) of the sample. Of the 14 children who exhibited depression at pre-treatment, all ($n = 14$) showed a decrease in depression scores by 7 points at post-treatment (pre: $M = 11.35$, post: $M = 4.00$; clinical cutoff score ≥ 8). Eleven children showed an increase in self-esteem by an average of 17 points (pre: $M = 84.55$, post: $M = 101.75$); of the four who did not show significant clinical increases (i.e., ≥ 10 points) in self-esteem, at pre-treatment they were already at the average of 99. Thirteen showed an increase in coping by an average of 10 points (pre: $M = 88.17$, post: $M = 98.50$); of the three who did not show significant clinical increases (i.e., ≥ 10 points) in coping, at pre-treatment they were already at the average of 94. Wilcoxon Signed-Rank Tests also indicated a statistically significant difference in coping ($z = -1.99$, $p = .05$).

During the exit interviews, youth were asked to use the following Likert rating scale to assess the helpfulness of the skills learned during the DS process: 1 = *Not Helpful*, 2 = *Sometimes Helpful*, 3 = *Fairly Helpful*, 4 = *Often Helpful*, 5 = *Very Helpful*. In regard to the trauma narrative process, on average youth perceived all aspects of the trauma narrative ("story") process as helpful, including the highest rated items: selecting pictures for one's story ($M = 4.86$), writing one's story ($M = 4.67$), organizing pictures for one's story ($M = 4.42$), and recording and listening to one's voice ($M = 4.5$).

Responses to open-ended questions collected during the exit interviews indicated that developing their trauma narrative through digital storytelling was the most significant component of participants' treatment gains. As one stated, "I feel like I got *me* back." Youth found that creating a digital story that included their most difficult, along with their more positive experiences, was an enjoyable process even though the material was challenging. Hearing their own voice (reading their story aloud and recording their story) became an integral part of participants' trauma narrative process.

They reported valuing the creative process along with having control over the story they wanted to tell. As one participant summed up the DS process, "The story is fun because you can pick out your own music to go with the story, pick your own pictures, write your own words, you can make a title, you can make credits; it's *your* story." Thematic analysis indicated that, in addition to incorporating the traumatic events into one's ongoing life story, other major transformative aspects of narrative development were identity (e.g., "I've come to think that I'm my own hero."), mastery (e.g., "I think I can make things happen."), and a sense of relatedness (e.g., "I get along better with my mom. We communicate more.").

DISCUSSION/IMPLICATIONS

Narrative approaches such as DS can influence trauma recovery and resilience by offering a means of owning and telling one's story. For these youth, the opportunity to gain insight and understanding regarding a personally traumatic event enhanced their feelings of efficacy and control over the event, their emotions, and life in general, resulting in increased self-esteem and coping, and decreased PTSD and depression. Implementing the protocol specifically for the digital storytelling aspect of TF-CBT enabled youth to negotiate a balance between representing their traumatic experiences with their words, pictures, or music while simultaneously learning technological skills. Such balance allowed youth to shift between negative memories and mastery over the traumatic experience(s) and their portrayal in their narrative.

The clinician's role was to provide a safe environment for the youth to develop their digital stories, and to support the process. Participants had an intuitive sense of how they wanted their stories to develop. It did not always make sense to the clinician during story construction, but for the child it made perfect sense. The children knew how they wanted their stories portrayed in regard to the sequencing of images, music selected, and the use of their voice, even though they may not have been able to articulate the "why" and "how" of their process. Consequently, we learned that it is best not to ask about the construction process (for example, asking youth to talk about what the digital images represent). Instead, it was better to focus on the written script and ask questions regarding how selected images, songs, etc. helped to complete their stories.

Of the 25 participants who started TF-CBT treatment, 16 (63%) completed the program. Cohen et al. (2011a) noted the difficulty of offering effective TF-CBT to individuals who may continue to have contact with their abuser. They reported a 40% non-completion rate, showing how challenging it is to keep this population engaged in treatment (Cohen et al., 2011a). Cohen et al. underscored that continued research is necessary to address optimal treatment for those traumatized by an ongoing threat or the reality of IPV. Similar to Cohen et al.'s (2011a) study, our project experienced a 37% non-completion rate (9 of 25); however, those who did complete treatment demonstrated a 100% improvement in pre- and post-treatment changes in PTSD and depression in comparison to Cohen et al.'s findings of 75% who showed improvement. A difference between Cohen et al.'s work and ours is that they provided services in a large metropolitan area, whereas the DV agency in the current study focused on individuals residing in rural areas. We are not certain as to why there was a disparity between the findings. Perhaps it was because of differences in caseload size: the rural agency had a smaller caseload, allowing for more flexibility and availability to its clients.

Though the results of our study suggest that this intervention is effective, DS as an intervention for trauma narrative development was not assessed separately with respect to overall TF-CBT treatment changes. In our follow-up study regarding the relationship of DS to overall treatment changes, four data-collection points have been added: pre-treatment, initial session of trauma narrative, last session of trauma narrative, and post-treatment. In the study described in this chapter, there was no TF-CBT comparison group regarding trauma narrative development as usual (i.e., a written format, often in the form of a book). In our follow-up study, participants have been randomly assigned to experimental and comparison groups. In the experimental group, participants are receiving the narrative intervention of creating a digital story (TF-CBT/DS). In the comparison group, therefore, participants are receiving the narrative intervention of writing a story (TF-CBT/W). Because this study is in progress, the results are not yet conclusive, and thus will be forthcoming.

LIMITATIONS

Youth and their parents were committed to counseling, but often faced many barriers in following through, including the effects of the economic downturn on farming and small-town families. The rural county was located in an area comprising 847 square miles; thus, several clients travelled a distance to receive services, and the majority had problems with unreliable or unavailable transportation. Although the DV agency assisted in transportation (e.g., providing gas cards, picking children up for appointments), it could not meet this need on a weekly basis because of limited financial and staff resources. Consequently, a commitment of 12–16 weeks for many families with limited resources proved to be a significant barrier.

CONCLUSION

Digital storytelling for CEDV allowed for processing trauma-related information in an innovative and multi-sensory manner that enhanced narrative integration. Youth who use such narrative strategies, therefore, may develop skills to form adaptive meanings regarding their exposure to DV, both in its immediate aftermath and over time. In doing so, they may continue to construct their stories, and thus their lives, into ones of possibility, promise, and potential, thereby preventing continuation of the cycle of violence.

REFERENCES

American Psychiatric Association (APA). (2002). *Diagnostic and statistical manual of mental disorders*, 4th ed. (text rev.). Washington, DC: Author.

Anderson, K.M. (2010). *Enhancing resilience in survivors of family violence*. New York, NY: Springer.

Anderson, K.M. (2012). Fostering resilience in daughters of battered women. In D. Becvar (Ed.), *Handbook of family resilience* (pp. 495–514). New York, NY: Springer.

Anderson, K.M., & Bang, E. (2012). Assessing PTSD and resilience for females who during childhood were exposed to domestic violence. *Child & Family Social Work*, 17(1), 55–65.

Anderson, K.M., & Hiersteiner, C. (2008). Recovering from childhood sexual abuse: Is a storybook ending possible? *The American Journal of Family Therapy*, 36(5), 413–424.

Angold, A., & Costello, E.J. (1987). *Mood and Feelings Questionnaire*. Developmental Epidemiology Program, Duke University. Retrieved from devepi.mc.duke.edu/mfq.html

Becker, K.D., Stuewig, J., & McCloskey, L.A. (2010). Traumatic stress symptoms of women exposed to different forms of childhood victimization and intimate partner violence. *Journal of Interpersonal Violence, 25*(9), 1699–1715.

Braun, V. & Clarke, V. (2006). Using thematic analysis in psychology. *Qualitative Research in Psychology, 3*(2), 77–101.

Cohen, J.A., Mannarino, A.P., & Deblinger, E. (2006). *Treating trauma and traumatic grief in children and adolescents*. New York, NY: Guilford Press.

Cohen, J.A., Mannarino, A.P., & Iyengar, S. (2011a). Community treatment of posttraumatic stress disorder for children exposed to domestic violence: A randomized control trial. *Archives of Pediatrics and Adolescent Medicine, 165*(1), 16–21.

Cohen, J.A., Mannarino, A.P., & Murray, L.K. (2011b). Trauma-focused CBT for youth who experience ongoing traumas. *Child Abuse & Neglect, 35*(8), 637–646.

Cohen, J.A., Mannarino, A.P., Perel, J.M., & Staron, V. (2007). A pilot randomized controlled trial of combined trauma-focused CBT and Sertraline for childhood PTSD symptoms. *Journal of the American Academy of Child and Adolescent Psychiatry, 46*(7), 811–819.

Davies, C.A., DiLillo, D., & Martinez, I.G. (2004). Isolating adult psychological correlates of witnessing parental violence: Findings from a predominantly Latina sample. *Journal of Family Violence*, 19(6), 377–385.

Davis, A. & Weinshenker, D. (2012). Digital storytelling and authoring identity. In C.C. Ching & B. Foley (Eds.), *Technology and identity: Research on the development and exploration of selves in a digital world* (pp. 47–64). Cambridge, UK: Cambridge University Press.

Daviss, W.B., Mooney, D., Racusin, R., Ford, J.D., Fleischer, A., & McHugo, G.J. (2000). Predicting posttraumatic stress after hospitalization for pediatric injury. *Journal of the American Academy of Child and Adolescent Psychiatry, 39*(5), 576–583.

Dehon, C., & Weems, C.F. (2010). Emotional development in the context of conflict: The indirect effects of interparental violence on children. *Journal of Child and Family Studies, 19*(3), 287–297.

Dube, S.R., Anda, R.F., Felitti, V.J., Edwards, V.J., & Williamson, D.F. (2002). Exposure to abuse, neglect, and household dysfunction among adults who witnessed intimate partner violence as children: Implications for health and social services. *Violence and Victims, 17*(1), 3–17.

Feather, J.S. & Ronan, K.R. (2009). Trauma-focused CBT with maltreated children: A clinic-based evaluation of a new treatment manual. *Australian Psychologist, 44*(3), 174–194.

Foa, E.B., & Rauch, S.A. (2004). Cognitive changes during prolonged exposure versus prolonged exposure plus cognitive restructuring in female assault survivors with posttraumatic stress disorder. *Journal of Consulting Clinical Psychology, 72*(5), 879–884.

Ford, J.D., Racusin, R., Daviss, W.B., Ellis, C.G., Thomas, J., Rogers, K., . . . Sengupta, A. (1999). Trauma exposure among children with oppositional defiant disorder and attention deficit-hyperactivity disorder. *Journal of Consulting and Clinical Psychology, 67*(5), 786–789.

Graham-Bermann, S.A., Gruber, G., Girz, L., & Howell, K.H. (2009). Factors discriminating among profiles of resilient coping and psychopathology in children exposed to domestic violence. *Child Abuse & Neglect, 33*(9), 648–660.

Graham-Bermann, S.A., Howell, K.H., Lilly, M.M., & Devoe, E. (2010). Mediators and moderators of change in adjustment following intervention for children exposed to intimate partner violence (IPV). *Journal of Interpersonal Violence, 26*(9), 1815–1833.

Grizenko, N., Archambault, P., & Pawliuk, N. (1992). Level of disrupted peer relations and poor self-esteem in children with behavior problems and the effectiveness of day treatment. *International Journal of Partial Hospitalization, 8*(2), 97–106.

Gubrium, A. (2009). Digital storytelling: An emergent method for health promotion research and practice. *Health Promotion Practice, 10*(2), 186–191.

Gubrium, A., & Turner, K.C.N. (2011). Digital storytelling as an emergent method for social research and practice. In S.N. Hess-Biber (Ed.), *Handbook of emergent technologies in social research* (pp. 469–491). Oxford, UK: Oxford University Press.

Hanney, L., & Kozlowska, K. (2002). Healing traumatized children: Creating illustrated storybooks in family therapy. *Family Process, 41*(1), 37–65.

Hare, Bruce R. (1996). The Hare General and Area-specific Self-esteem Scale. In R.L. Jones (Ed.), *Handbook of tests and measurements for black populations* (Vol. 1). Hampton, VA: Cobb & Henry Publishers.

Holt, S., Buckley, H., & Whelan, S. (2008). The impact of exposure to domestic violence on children and young people: A review of the literature. *Child Abuse & Neglect, 32*(8), 797–810.

Lambert, J. (2006). *Digital storytelling: Capturing lives, creating community*. Berkeley, CA: Digital Diner Press.

Margolin, G., & Vickerman, K.A. (2011). Post-traumatic stress in children and adolescents exposed to family violence: I. Overview and issues. *Couple and Family Psychology: Research and Practice 1*(S), 63–73.

McCubbin, H.I., Thompson, A.I., & Elver, K.M. (1996). Youth Coping Index. In H.I. McCubbin, A.I. Thompson, & M.A. McCubbin (Eds.), *Family assessment, resiliency, coping and adaptation. Inventories for research and practice* (pp. 585–611). Madison, WI: University of Wisconsin Publishers.

McDonald R., Jouriles, E.N., Ramisetty-Mikler, S., Caetano, R., & Green, C.E. (2006). Estimating the number of American children living in partner-violent families. *Journal of Family Psychology, 20*(1), 137–142.

McFarlane, J. M., Groff, J. Y., O'Brien, J. A., & Watson, K. (2003). Behaviors of children who are exposed and not exposed to intimate partner violence: An analysis of 330 Black, White, and Hispanic children. *Pediatrics, 112*(3), 202–207.

Niederhoffer, K. G., & Pennebaker, J. W. (2009). Sharing one's story: On the benefits of writing or talking about emotional experience. In S. J. Lopez & C. R. Snyder (Eds.), *Oxford handbook of positive psychology* (2nd ed.) (pp. 621–632). New York, NY: Oxford University Press.

Polkinghorne, D. E. (1991). Narrative and self-concept. *Journal of Narrative and Life History, 1*(2 & 3), 135–153.

Russell, D., Springer, K. W., & Greenfield, E. A. (2010). Witnessing domestic abuse in childhood as an independent risk factor for depressive symptoms in adulthood. *Child Abuse & Neglect, 34*(6), 448–453.

Saxe, G. N., Ellis, B. H., & Kaplow, J. B. (2009). *Collaborative treatment of traumatized children and teens: The trauma systems therapy approach*. New York, NY: Guilford Press.

Simon, V. A., Feiring, C., & McElroy, S. K. (2010). Making meaning of traumatic events: Youths' strategies for processing childhood sexual abuse are associated with psychosocial adjustment. *Child Maltreatment, 15*(3), 229–241.

van Minnen, A., Wessel, I., Dijkstra, T., & Roelofs, K. (2002). Changes in PTSD patients' narratives during prolonged exposure therapy: A replication and extension. *Journal of Traumatic Stress, 15*(3), 255–258.

9 Special Education Students and Documentary Production

A Case Study

Penelope P. Orr

INTRODUCTION

Seiden (2001) wrote, "[When] approaching materials, [one] must first accept the significance of the nonliving object, matter transformed into some symbolic energy, which is capable of affecting human behavior" (p. 20). He stated that the concept that the art medium is the message implies that canvas, wood, stone, radio, and television are symbolic messages in and of themselves. When artists choose their art media, they must take into account the inherent qualities of the media, as well as the effect these qualities have on the artists and their audiences. Seiden stated that, when working with children, it is important that therapists consider which materials fit the goals for specific individuals, because the right choice of material can greatly enhance the therapeutic or educational process, whereas the wrong choice of material can hinder it. The inherent qualities of the media themselves become a third consideration in the therapeutic process.

FRAMEWORK OF SPECIFIC TECHNIQUES

Using a framework developed by Dunn-Snow and Joy-Smellie (2000) to teach students specific techniques during their art therapy training, I will explore the inherent qualities and possible uses for digital video with students with disabilities. According to Dunn-Snow and Joy-Smellie (2000), learning about a new media requires (a) conducting historical research about the techniques; (b) determining the populations that might most benefit from particular techniques; (c) identifying the issues, settings, and approaches where the techniques would be the most successful and suitable; and (d) experiencing the techniques. Dunn-Snow and Joy-Smellie specifically discussed teaching the technique of mask-making as an intervention in art therapy practice. The four aforementioned steps are applicable when analyzing other techniques, methods, or media used in any educational setting, but they have particular importance in the special needs community.

Historical Placement of Digital Video Technology in Art Education and Art Therapy Among Students With Special Needs

Photography was invented in 1839 and was seen primarily as a documentation tool, not an art medium. Brady used it to document the Civil War, and Muybridge used it to scientifically understand how a horse runs. It was not until 1879, 40 years after its invention, that Riss used photography in intentionally artistic and social ways and was recognized by society at large as having created art (Newhall, 1982). It took another 70 years for art therapists to pick up the camera to determine how to use it artistically and therapeutically in the practice setting.

Therapists were using traditional film and photography as creative technology tools within art therapy as early as 1972 (Arnott & Gushin, 1976; Fox & Wortman, 1975; McNiff & Cook, 1975; Muller & Bader, 1972; Nelson-Gee, 1976; Wolf, 1976; Zwick, 1978). Researchers studied and wrote about photography as an art therapy medium as early as 1975 (Hogan, 1981; Maciag, 1976; McNiff & Cook, 1975; Milford, Fryrear, & Swank, 1983; Nelson-Gee, 1976; Wolf, 1976; Zwick, 1978). Other, newer media, such as video and color photography, followed quickly (Canter, 1987; Fryrear & Stephens, 1988; Weinberg, 1985). When the expressive therapies continuum (ETC) was developed in the late 1970s, art therapists gained a systems approach framework for understanding and intentionally using media within art therapy (Kagin & Lusebrink, 1978; Lusebrink, 1990, 1992). By the 1980s, digital media in the form of computer art making, photography, and filmmaking were being explored (Canter, 1987).

Computers were invented in 1951, used to create art by 1963, and used by art therapists with clients by 1985. With the availability of digital cameras in the early 1980s and digital manipulation software in the early 1990s, access to digital media became easier and its use within therapeutic sessions more prevalent. At the same time, thanks to the invention of the Internet and its symbiotic relationship with digital media, the social and confidential aspects of using digital media beyond the therapeutic environment became a new issue that art therapists had to work through. The Internet allowed clients easy access to ways to share their work, and the social boundaries among clients, therapists, and the larger world suddenly became murky.

Art therapists continued to struggle to define the boundaries and reality of digital media and the Internet by exploring the use of these media within their own practices. Art therapists have written about the therapeutic elements of digital media (Barbee, 2002; Hartwich & Brandecker, 1997; Horovitz, 1999; Martin, 1997; McLeod, 1999; Orr, 2005; Parker-Bell, 1999; Rutherford, 2002; Seiden, 2001; Thong, 2007; Wolf, 2007); the non-therapeutic elements of digital media (Williams, Kramer, Henley, & Gerity, 1997); the ethics that might be involved in the use of digital media in art therapy practice (Alders, Beck, Allen, & Mosinski, 2011; Jacobs, 1994; Moon, 2006; Orr, 2011a, 2011b, 2011c); digital media's social implications (Belkofer & McNutt, 2011; Kapitan, 2011; Orr, 2011a, 2011b, 2011c); and the training needed by future art therapists to address the complicated theoretical and ethical aspects of digital media (Moon, 2006; Orr, 2012). Many of these research projects have dealt with using digital media with a variety of populations with special needs.

Since the advent of digital technology and computers, the opportunities for special needs populations to create art with technology have increased substantially. Weinberg (1985) wrote about the use of computers to create art by clients who have physical limitations. Weinberg found that using the computer as an art-making tool stimulated curiosity and motivation and increased clients' access to the art-making process, which clients' disabilities would otherwise have prevented or limited. Canter (1989) argued that children and adolescents work well with computers because of their prior knowledge and comfort level with them. She found that creating art with computers increased the concentration skills and improved the self-esteem of this population. Parker-Bell (1999) and McLeod (1999) studied the use of specific software programs as interactive and creative tools in art therapy practice with children and adults. Riner (2005) wrote a case study in which inner-city at-risk youth participated in a digital photography project. In regular art education, many art teachers have written about the use of digital media in the art room (Fionda, 2000; Garcia, 2000; Gerrish, 2000; Hunter-Doniger, 2005; Mollhagen, 2004).

The filmmaking process involves many arts beyond the arts of photography, digital graphics, and visual imagery. Cohen (2013) pointed out that a film also uses the arts of narrative writing, journaling, acting, drama, music, and movement. He stated that the expressive art therapies that use these media also have a rich history, and that these therapies can come together with visual art therapy in the filmmaking process.

Determining Populations, Issues, Settings, and Approaches

To address Dunn-Snow and Joy-Smellie's (2000) second and third requisites for learning about a new method or medium, Orr (2012) sent out a preliminary survey to practicing art therapists to determine how, when, and with whom they used digital media, including video, with their clients. Based upon the populations, issues, settings, and approaches that the participants identified, it became apparent that the use of digital media can have benefits and drawbacks and can be a good choice with some students, but not with others. The survey showed that, of the 85 art therapists surveyed, 17.6%, or 15 therapists, had clients work on film projects.

When the survey participants described what they thought was detrimental about using technology within art therapy sessions (total of 81 answers), the top answers were safety issues (27), personal connection issues (25), and creativity/sensual issues (16). When the survey participants described what they thought was therapeutic about using technology within art therapy sessions (total of 82 answers), the top answers were comfort/lowering resistance (29), mastery/creativity (24), and adaptive qualities (11). Under the category of comfort/lowering resistance, the survey participants felt that youth and adults under the age of 40 years are already comfortable with this medium, that technology use is helping to lower clients' resistance to therapy and art making, and that technology use can improve therapeutic rapport.

As with other therapeutic medium choices, artists and educators should choose to use technology-based media only when it benefits the client or student. When educators choose to use technology, they must take into account not only its inherent qualities, but also its potential effect on the educational and therapeutic process and its relationship with students. As Seiden (2001) indicated, when working with students, it is important to consider which materials fit the goals for specific individuals. The right choice of material can greatly enhance the therapeutic or educational process, whereas the wrong choice of material can hinder it. For instance, asking a person with tactile resistance to work in papier-mâché without gloves during the first session could hinder the process of building a therapeutic relationship. However, the therapist could use the same medium with the same client after many sessions, during which the client has worked through the tactile resistance, so that the medium becomes therapeutic. With film and video, therapists should consider the following qualities in deciding whether to use the medium with clients: its tactile sensual interaction; the potential ethical implications regarding how and when it is used; its ability to lower resistance to therapy, owing to the client's or student's comfort with the medium; the potential for a sense of mastery when the client or student completes a project; and the ability to adapt the medium to meet physical and intellectual limitations of the client or student.

Experiencing Technology Media

The last step suggested by Dunn-Snow and Joy-Smellie (2000) for students learning about new media is to experience working with those techniques and media. This last step is represented in the following case study, in which digital video was used with a group of students with special needs.

THE CASE STUDY

I chose the case study format for this action research, the purpose of which was an in-depth analysis of using portable technology within a program for students with special needs who had little access to technology. The results of this case study do not have strong generalizability to other art education or therapy programs, but they provide insight into the implementation and process of a digital video project among small groups with little access to technology. The focus of this case study was on teaching a digital video unit, which comprised the study of documentary films, the filming and editing of documentary films, and the exhibition and critique of the films. The purpose of focusing on documentary film was to help the students experience narrative as a form of truth and to find and express their own narratives. In addition to conducting this study, I am also an art educator and an art therapist who worked in both capacities with the participants of the study.

Participants

The students with special needs participating in this project attended a school where a computer lab existed but was not used for art production. A single computer was available in the art education classroom, but the school's art teacher mainly used it for administrative tasks and research. Eight high-school students with different emotional, learning, and behavioral disabilities participated in the study. The three boys and five girls in grades 9 to 11 worked in two groups of four. This sample was a sample of convenience. The participants were volunteers from a contained classroom. Each group of four students worked as a collective learning community to develop their narrative and then film, edit, and produce their own documentary. The students signed assent forms, their parents signed consent forms, and the principal of the school approved their video topics. Students, teachers, and school personnel who appeared in the videos signed forms providing creative product consent to use their images or words in the videos.

Media Used in the Case Study

Participants used one laptop computer with a DVD burner, one digital video camera, and one video editing program in this project. The computer, the camera, and the DVD burner all fit into one over-the-shoulder carrying case that I transported to and from the school for each session. The students edited the films on a laptop using a standard video editing program. The students burned the final films to DVD format and showed the films on DVD players that were available at the school.

The Lesson Plan Process

The eight participants worked for 30 to 40 minutes per session for 18 sessions over two months. In determining the goals for this project, I used Jordan's (2005) *Art/Technology Performance Standards* as a guiding framework. I gave students the goals of learning about the technology as well as the editing and filming processes. I asked them to write and create their own narratives, create storyboards, gain the requisite permissions, and complete the filming.

Sessions 1–2: Art history and aesthetics. The first two sessions included an introduction to documentary film history and digital movie making, as well as a discussion of ethics and social responsibility in the film industry as compared to personal filmmaking or filmmaking as a part of therapy and education. I introduced students to documentaries. As visual introductions to the documentary genre, I used clips from films such as *Frida* (Kahlo), *Supersize Me*, and *The Endless Summer*.

Sessions 3–4: Planning and brainstorming. Students worked in groups to develop their narratives, storyboards, and script ideas; music lists; and logistical lists (e.g., getting permission forms from the individuals whom they videotaped). Students identified the knowledge that they would need to gain in order to complete the videos that they had designed. Students wrote project proposals for their documentaries; the principal and the participants' parents then approved. The chosen narratives for the films dealt with a spiritual presence felt at the school and the history of the school from the students' perspectives.

Sessions 5–15. Students worked in two groups that alternated the use of technology devices each session. One group would concentrate on filming or finding imagery or appropriate music, while the other group would work on the laptop to learn the editing program, capture clips and music from the Internet, or edit their documentary. Students in both groups could use their time to search in the library or computer lab for information that the group had deemed necessary to complete the project. Each group also worked to obtain permission from the participants in the documentaries and investigate ethical issues, such as gaining copyright permission to use music. During the next session, the groups would change tasks and exchange devices.

Sessions 16–17. Students focused primarily on fine-tuning their editing and getting feedback from the other group and from me. Students continued to take turns on the laptop. The students approached the editing process with great seriousness and intragroup negotiation. Students had to determine how to emphasize their chosen narratives and manipulate them through decisions made during the editing process. As Cohen (2013) wrote in his dissertation:

> In the film industry, professionals in postproduction understand that editing is actually part of the writing process, not just "where you take out the bad bits" (Murch, 2001, p. 10). Walter Murch, a film editor, director, and writer, described the editing process as similar to the creative writing process in the revising stages. Editing is different from writing because it can require collaboration with others, which helps to develop one's interpersonal skills. Murch commented that "there are frequent times when two or more editors are working simultaneously, sometimes with equal authority." (p. 29)

Session 18. On the last day, the students showed their documentaries to the larger student body. Participants then separated from the larger group and critiqued the works, discussed what was and was not accomplished, filled out a departing survey, and received copies of their films on DVD to use for their portfolios for college and advanced placement art credits.

Case Study Data Collection and Analysis

Throughout the filming and editing process, I observed the students at work and during discussions. I participated in guiding the students through the learning process while allowing them to make all of their creative decisions, follow their own learning plans, and do their own technical troubleshooting. I collected the final surveys, finished videos, and extra footage and coded them for themes.

Findings

Based upon this case study, I determined that one laptop, one video camera, and one video editing program was sufficient for every eight students. Working in groups of four was appropriate for the students with special needs in grades 9 to 11 who participated in this study. With this number of students, members of the learning community were able to share roles based upon individual strengths. For instance, each group found that one student in that group was more comfortable and better at actually filming with the video camera, whereas others were better suited to handling the various administrative, planning, editing, or creative input phases of the project. In each learning community, the students took on several tasks and contributed the information and raw media that the group needed to complete its film.

The main unexpected difficulty that arose during this study was that the session lengths were too short to optimize learning. The individual sessions lasted only 30 to 40 minutes, which was just enough time for students to learn a new technique or process before they had to close down the computer and camera. The short sessions meant that the students would have to remind themselves what they did in the last session before beginning to use this new technique or process. It increased the learning time necessary because they had to repeat some steps; it also increased the amount of time needed to finish the project. The original plan was for this project to take 12 sessions, but, because of this issue, the project took 18 sessions total. This suggests that students could complete similar projects more efficiently using 1–2-hour sessions.

On the final surveys, the students discussed learning about working in groups, time management, the filming process, and the slowness and detail needed during the editing process. They listed learning about legalities, such as obtaining copyright and gaining permission for filming individuals, as one of the important concepts learned during this project.

Overall, the students felt that this was a valuable project for their personal use of technology as well as their future professional lives. The students verbally expressed feelings of accomplishment, pride, and enthusiasm about this project and potential future projects with this medium. Students who were not part of the video project were curious about what the students with special needs were doing and approached them about wanting to participate in future sessions. This expression of interest from peers gave the students with special needs, who had reputations for making trouble, pride in their new positive status in the student community. Students showed their final videos to the entire student population, and administrators placed one on the school website because they felt that it was a good advertisement for the school. The students benefited personally from the creation of the film, the viewing of the film, and then the affirmation of peers and authority figures upon viewing the film.

The participants reported experiencing positive outcomes as a result of the project, including increased feelings of competence and self-esteem, greater interest in school, better social and peer interactions, and academic learning of digital video production. Students expressed pride in being able to tell their narratives in ways that they chose. This project also had unexpected positive effects for the art program and the special education program by increasing the programs' visibility and by demonstrating the important role that these programs could play in the school.

The limiting qualities of the video medium, such as the amount of time it took to edit the films, the sharing of cameras and editing decisions, and the ethical and risk-taking aspects of creating a film that others would view, also contributed to the positive outcomes for the students. The slow process of editing and the shared use of limited materials slowed students down, enabled them to discuss with peers how they wanted to represent their narratives, allowed time for building and mastering new skills on the computer, and provided framing for the project. The risk-taking and ethical aspects of creating art for public consumption allowed students to process and discuss what they wanted to leave in the film, what was appropriate to show the world, and what they wanted to remain private. The limitations of the medium, such as the slow pace of the work, also led students to experience frustration and loss of interest in their work at times. The limitation of creating a film for public viewing could have led students to create a film different from that which they might have created for a more private or limited audience.

Directly involving the principal, the instructional technology specialist, and the parents of the participating students and of students in the film brought greater respect to, support for, and interest in both the art and special education programs. Administrators viewed the project as beneficial because they were able to see its public relations value and usefulness in increasing students' skills, positive behaviors, and interest in school. The project also led several special needs and nontraditional students to express, for the first time, an interest in gaining college entrance. The project helped students to see potential next steps and a positive direction for their lives.

Digital video has benefits and drawbacks for use with students with special needs, so it is the responsibility of artists, educators, and therapists to determine when it is appropriate to use this medium. Students benefit from working with digital video in many ways: they build group work skills, technical skills, communication skills, creative expression, and self-esteem. Digital video can give minority populations, such as the students with special needs in this project, a voice within a larger organization or culture. Through the process of creating the film, these students learned to deal with frustration, identify their own strengths, and practice social skills. Some drawbacks to using digital media include the lack of tactile qualities, the amount of time needed for therapists or teachers to learn the media prior to use, and the amount of time needed for the editing process. This study demonstrated that these drawbacks can have a positive or negative impact, depending on the goals of the filmmaking project and the needs of the creators. Slowing down in the editing process gave participants time to reflect, but sometimes slowing down caused too much frustration and hindered the process.

Digital video's inherent qualities include empowering students or clients to create narratives told from particular points of view; to express creativity and imagination; and to creatively edit, slowing down or speeding up time. It is a malleable medium, but obtaining worthwhile results requires patience and adherence to step-by-step procedures. These qualities made digital video the ideal medium for the students with special needs who participated in this research. If the medium is the message, as Seiden (2001) said, then the message here is that students with special needs have narratives full of emotion, thought, and concern that they can translate into motion, sound, and light, yielding a form of creative holistic expression.

REFERENCES

Alders, A., Beck, L., & Allen, P. & Mosinski, B. (2011). Technology and art therapy: Ethical challenges. *Art Therapy: The Journal of the American Art Therapy Association, 28*(4), 165–170.

Arnott, B., & Gushin, J. (1976). Film making as a therapeutic tool. *Art Therapy: The Journal of the American Art Therapy Association, 16*(1), 29–33.

Barbee, M. (2002). A visual-narrative approach to understanding transsexual identity. *Art Therapy: The Journal of the American Art Therapy Association, 19*(2), 53–61.

Belkofer, C., & McNutt, J. (2011). Understanding social media culture and its ethical challenges for art therapists. *Art Therapy: The Journal of the American Art Therapy Association, 28*(4), 159–164.

Canter, D. (1987). The therapeutic effects of combining Apple Macintosh computers and creativity software in art therapy sessions. *Art Therapy: The Journal of the American Art Therapy Association, 4*(1), 17–26.

Canter, D. (1989). Art therapy and computers. In H. Wadeson, J. Durkin, & D. Perach (Eds.), *Advances in Art Therapy* (pp. 296–316). New York, NY: Wiley.

Cohen, J. (2013) *Film and soul: A theoretical exploration of the use of video and other film-based therapy to help transform identity in the therapeutic practice* (Doctoral dissertation). Pacifica University, Carpinteria, CA, USA. ProQuest UMI 3551606

Dunn-Snow, P., & Joy-Smellie, S. (2000). Teaching art therapy techniques: Mask-making, a case in point. *Art Therapy: The American Art Therapy Association, 17*(2), 125–131.

Fionda, R. (2000). Digital evolution: Pixel palette. *Arts & Activities, 128*(3), 38–41.

Fox, C., & Wortman, C. (1975). A therapeutic use of film with university students. *Art Therapy: The Journal of the American Art Therapy Association, 15*(1), 19–21.

Fryrear, J., & Stephens, B. (1988). Group psychotherapy using masks and video to facilitate intrapersonal communication. *Arts in Psychotherapy, 15*(3), 227–234.

Garcia, L. (2000). Technology as a crayon box. *School Administrator, 57*(4), 38–51.

Gerrish, M. (2000). Digital artistry: Technology infused projects created in the art room. *MultiMedia Schools, 7*(5), 34–36, 38–39.

Hartwich, P., & Brandecker, R. (1997). Computer-based art therapy with inpatients: Acute and chronic schizophrenics and borderline cases. *Arts in Psychotherapy, 24*(4), 367–373.

Hogan, P. (1981). Phototherapy in the educational setting. *Arts in Psychotherapy, 8*(3/4), 193–199.

Horovitz, E. (1999). *A leap of faith: The call to art*. Springfield, IL: Charles C. Thomas.

Hunter-Doniger, T. (2005). Digital masterpieces. *School Arts: Art Education Magazine for Teachers, 104*(7), 28.

Jacobs, L. (1994). Photography and confidentiality. *Art Therapy: The Journal of the American Art Therapy Association, 11*(4), 296–297.

Jordan, A. (2005). Dancing across the digital divide: The story of digital arts. In G. Szekely (Ed.), *Video art for the classroom* (pp. 159–164). Reston, VA: National Art Education Association.

Kagin, S., & Lusebrink V.L. (1978). The expressive therapies continuum. *Art Psychotherapy, 5*(4), 171–179.

Kapitan, L. (2011). "But is it ethical?" Articulating an art therapy ethos. *Art Therapy: The Journal of the American Art Therapy Association, 28*(4), 150–151.

Lusebrink, V. (1990). *Imagery and visual expression in therapy*. New York, NY: Plenum.

Lusebrink, V. (1992). A systems oriented approach to expressive therapies: The expressive therapies continuum. *Arts in Psychotherapy, 18*(5), 395–403.

Maciag, B. (1976). The use of film, photography and art with ghetto adolescents. In A. Robbins & L. Sibley (Eds.), *Creative art therapy* (pp. 154–173). New York, NY: Brunner/Mazel.

Martin, R. (1997). Looking and reflecting: Returning the gaze, re-enacting memories and imagining the future through phototherapy. In S. Hogan (Ed.), *Feminist approaches to art therapy* (pp. 150–176). London, UK: Routledge.

McLeod, C. (1999). Empowering creativity with computer-assisted art therapy: An introduction to available programs and techniques. *Art Therapy: The Journal of the American Art Therapy Association, 16*(4), 201–205.

McNiff, S., & Cook, C. (1975). Video art therapy. *Art Psychotherapy, 2*(1), 55–63.

Milford, S., Fryrear, J., & Swank, P. (1983). Phototherapy with disadvantaged boys. *Arts in Psychotherapy, 10*(4), 221–228.

Mollhagen, N. (2004). Inner image. *School Arts: The Art Education Magazine for Teachers, 104*(1), 26.

Moon, B. (2006). *Ethical issues in art therapy*. Springfield, IL: Charles C. Thomas.

Muller, C., & Bader, A. (1972). Therapeutic art programs around the world—IX: Film making in a Swiss psychiatric hospital. *Art Therapy: The Journal of the American Art Therapy Association, 11*(4), 185–189.

Murch, W. (2001). *In the blink of an eye*. Los Angeles, CA: Silman-James Press.

Nelson-Gee, E. (1976). Play, art and photography in a therapeutic nursery school. In A. Robbins & L. Sibley (Eds.), *Creative art therapy* (pp. 103–127). New York, NY: Brunner/Mazel.
Newhall, B. (1982). *The history of photography: From 1839 to the present*. New York, NY: Museum of Modern Art.
Orr, P. (2005). Technology media: An exploration for "inherent qualities." *Arts in Psychotherapy, 32*(1), 1–11.
Orr, P. (2011a). Ethics in the age of social media: Confidentiality. *Art Therapy Credential Board Review, 18*(2), 3–5.
Orr, P. (2011b). Ethics in the age of social media: Electronic means. *Art Therapy Credential Board Review, 18*(3), 4–7.
Orr, P. (2011c). Ethics in the age of social media: Multiple relationships. *Art Therapy Credentials Board Review, 18*(1), 7–9.
Orr, P. (2012). Technology use in art therapy practice: 2004–2011 comparisons. *Arts in Psychotherapy, 39*(4), 234–238.
Parker-Bell, B. (1999). Embracing a future with computers and art therapy. *Art Therapy: The Journal of the American Art Therapy Association, 16*(4), 16–19.
Riner, P. (2005). Digital photography in an inner-city fifth grade, part 1. *Phi Delta Kappan, 86*(8), 567–635.
Rutherford. (2002). The shadow of the photographer: Using photographic snapshots in our search for meaning and fulfillment. *Canadian Art Therapy Association Journal, 15*(2), 14–32.
Seiden, D. (2001). *Mind over matter: The uses of materials in art, education, and therapy*. Chicago, IL: Magnolia Street.
Thong, S. (2007). Redfining the tools of art therapy. *Art Therapy: The Journal of the American Art Therapy Association, 24*(2), 52–58.
Weinberg, D. (1985). The potential of rehabilitative computer art therapy for the quadriplegic, cerebral vascular accident and brain trauma patient. *Art Therapy: The Journal of the American Art Therapy Association,* 2(2), 66–72.
Williams, K., Kramer, E., Henley, D., & Gerity, L. (1997). Art, art therapy, and the seductive environment. *Art Therapy: The Journal of the American Art Therapy Association, 35*(4), 106–117.
Wolf, R. (1976). The polaroid technique: Spontaneous dialogues from the unconscious. *Art Psychotherapy, 3*(3), 197–201.
Wolf, R. (2007). Advances in phototherapy training. *Arts in Psychotherapy, 34*(2), 124–133.
Zwick, D. (1978). Photography as a tool toward increased awareness of the aging self. *Art Psychotherapy, 5*(3), 135–141.

10 Digital Storytelling

Using Videos to Increase Social Wellness

Marty Otañez and Wanda Lakota

Visual stories, especially those that involve wellness and personal change, are widely popular. Digital video is a method and process for individuals to narrate, share, and archive health experiences using accessible video editing applications and social media platforms. Wanda Lakota participated in a digital storytelling research project in Denver, Colorado, in 2010 and produced *Betsy Bug*, a video about Wanda's struggle with her brother, who had suffered from paranoid schizophrenia. She revealed her brother's story for the first time in a public setting. *Betsy Bug* is a prototypical digital story with elements that draw viewers in, such as an encounter with an individual who had a family member with a mental health issue and personal imagery that the storyteller used to communicate her own health narrative. In the process of creating and sharing *Betsy Bug*, Wanda underwent a transformation that was akin to a personal renewal. Individuals who engage in the digital storytelling process experience such a transformation to varying degrees. The renewal also extended to Wanda's family members, who, after viewing *Betsy Bug*, started talking about her brother's disease for the first time. In addition to engaging in therapeutic dialogue, Wanda and her family members had an opportunity to seek mental health services, which Wanda's brother was unable to access.

Two years after the workshop, Wanda started her doctoral studies in human communication and completed courses in video editing, film production, and documentary filmmaking at the University of Denver (UCD). The skill set Wanda obtained partly mirrored the expertise I (Otañez) developed as a doctoral student in cultural anthropology in the early 2000s. Prior to completing my studies and with virtually no formal training in videography, I turned my dissertation about tobacco farm workers in Malawi into a documentary video. Witnessing the power of my scholarly video to influence policymaking regarding the global control of tobacco and increase public awareness of how tobacco industry behavior harms rural communities, I was determined to work with others so that they could create the stories that they wanted to share. In the fall of 2008, a colleague introduced me to digital storytelling. The colleague had been the videographer on a documentary I had produced on nursing in California. Through our discussions, I learned that digital storytelling was ideally suited for my interests in using video to increase health equities and develop visually based research strategies. Drawing on my own skills and contacts as a professional filmmaker since the early 2000s, I have, since 2009, supervised the production of more than 50 digital stories by community members in research projects and more than 250 by students in university courses with themes of health equity, cultural change, and social justice. In addition, I oversaw the research project where Wanda crafted *Betsy Bug* and, through a relationship that developed during and after the workshop, we agreed to coauthor this case study to explain the therapeutic qualities of digital wellness stories. Wanda and *Betsy Bug* appealed to me because, like many, I felt unsettled by the silence in society associated with mental health. As Wanda indicated to me in the process of writing this chapter, "No, it's OK to talk about it. There is healing in talking about [it]." Our goal was to examine the production of *Betsy Bug* and explore the agency of a digital story in personal healing projects.

Health care providers, community groups, and other organizations that serve marginalized populations have embraced the digital storytelling process to portray in a compelling way the link between individuals' lived experiences and factors that undermine mental health. The dominant model of personal video making in this context is a facilitator-run, three-day workshop pioneered by the Center for Digital Storytelling in Berkeley, California, in 1994 (Lambert 2013). In this model, individuals who are in a workshop setting prepare to share their stories and receive instruction on script writing, image and music selection, video editing, and the value of narrating one's own stories. In the universe of visual storytelling, important strides have been made in understanding the steps required to create first-person narrative videos (Gubrium & Harper, 2013; Lambert, 2013; Worcester, 2012) and participatory videos with community members (Thompson & Lozecznik, 2012; Wheeler, 2012; Yonas et al., 2013), as well as understanding the ethical praxes associated with story making and story sharing (Gubrium, Hill, & Flicker, 2013; Sandercock & Attili, 2010).

Researchers and community leaders have come to recognize that digital storytelling is not about making videos about other people or creating a documentary report on neighborhood concerns. Rather, this type of storytelling is a method and process in which co-facilitators with psychological knowledge and expert knowledge of narrative making and story sharing construct a platform for individuals and groups to publicly disseminate their personal experiences through video. Individuals are drawn to video storytelling because the process is fun and can be therapeutic, providing a fresh outlet for sharing an old memory. The difference between digital storytelling and ethnographic and documentary film is the production process; individual storytellers in a group setting make their own videos on the stories that they wish to share, and in this setting they have greater control over their story and the sharing of their story. Anthropologists engaged in digital storytelling and kindred researchers in psychology share an interest in the convergence of culture and imagery and in building hope for families and raising awareness for other families, so that tragedies like the one discussed in our analysis can be prevented.

The rise of digital storytelling in neighborhoods and health-related organizations is encouraging collaboration between universities and communities, and is leading health care providers to be more open and aware of local interests. Community members involved in studies that use visual strategies prefer this research to be disseminated through personal videos and social media tools over the peer-reviewed papers that traditionally emerge from collaborative efforts. As health researchers and community leaders tackle accountability issues, digital storytellers move on with their lives, which have taken on new meaning because they openly narrated a private moment in a workshop.

Wanda and I continued to keep in touch with each other after the digital storytelling workshop was over. Wanda was one of the founding members of the Coalition for Excellence in Digital Storytelling, an informal group of community members, university students, and instructors interested in innovative approaches to digital storytelling that I cofounded in 2010 (dscoalition.org). She was a guest lecturer in my course "Video and Social Change" in the Anthropology Department of UCD during the summer of 2011, and she accompanied me to my invited presentation, "Listening to the Telling and Telling about the Listening: Digital Storytelling in Research," at the Qualitative Research Methods Forum sponsored by the Colorado Health Outcomes Program at the University of Colorado, Anschutz Medical Campus, in December, 2012.

Betsy Bug was screened at these events, which included an informal discussion with Wanda and audience members. I integrated screenings of *Betsy Bug* as a sample digital story in six invited lectures on digital storytelling as a research method, five undergraduate and graduate level university courses, and four community-based digital storytelling workshops. Multiple interactions with Wanda—and public screenings of *Betsy Bug* that included discussions with audience members about the narrative elements and visual features—presented opportunities for me to get to know Wanda and her story in a different way than I had during the workshop alone.

In addition, my own knowledge of digital storytelling and my career trajectory as a cultural anthropologist in a tenure track professorial position changed in ways that I never expected owing to my interaction with Wanda and others who were willing to share wellness stories in visually based academic projects. *Betsy Bug* taught me that in order for students of anthropology and social scientists in general to tell other people's stories, we need to first learn to share our own stories. Periodic face-to-face meetings and personal correspondences with Wanda in May 2010 and June 2014 contributed to our wish to examine digital story agency by using *Betsy Bug* as a prototypical example of personal video crafted in a workshop setting that can influence the personal and professional transformation of storytellers and workshop facilitators.

In March 2014, as part of our work pertaining to the creation of this chapter, I gave Wanda a number of questions about *Betsy Bug* and her activities related to the video during and after the workshop, which took place in May 2010. I have integrated some of her exemplary responses into the analysis. Additional data used in the case study include ethnographic visual material obtained in the workshop through participant observation, informal interviews, and pre- and posttests with workshop participants. Our project builds on ethnographic film strategies that comprise the visual documentation of culture and a research approach to collecting ethnographic data. In the past two decades, ethnographic film researchers and practitioners have started to address the politics of representation and the West's obsession with visual imagery of nondominant cultures (Rony, 1994). Digital storytelling is an approach that seeks to make ethnographic film methods transparent and to place greater control over image production and dissemination in the hands of research participants. Pre- and posttests included questions about knowledge of digital storytelling skills and health disparities and satisfaction with digital storytelling workshop activities.

Key activities in the workshop were audio- and videotaped, and then transcribed. Major themes and statements were identified and integrated into the case study based upon the need to present an informative analysis and narrative synthesis of the storyteller-facilitator experience with social change. We drew upon research literature (Gubrium & Harper, 2013; Willox et al., 2012; Worcester, 2012) and upon our engaged practice as video makers and researchers, as well as upon ethnographic data obtained by Otañez in two additional workshops that were part of this same research project. Wanda and other project participants completed consent and media release forms required by the Colorado Multiple Institutional Review Board at UCD, which provided approval for the use of human subjects for the project. We present this case study on the creation and circulation of a visual health narrative to broaden discourse on the therapeutic value of digital storytelling and the context in which personal videos are produced and shared (Edwards, 2012).

THE CREATION OF *BETSY BUG*

In May 2010, Wanda and nine other individuals joined my two-day workshop, the final workshop in a series of three in a research project spanning 2009–2010. A two-day instead of a three-day workshop format was necessary to accommodate individuals' schedules and optimize recruitment. The project focused on the theme of health disparities, which included topics of tobacco use and cancer. I administered this project through a postdoctoral training fellowship from the Education, Training and Career Development

Core of the Colorado Clinical and Translational Sciences Institute at the University of Colorado, Anschutz Medical Campus. Two facilitators with the Center for Digital Storytelling, a graduate student in visual anthropology, and I (Otañez) ran the final workshop. The same facilitators (except for the student) had administered the first two workshops with me and had benefitted from these by learning about the influence of facilitators on story development, script length, and recruitment of participants. Gift cards valued at $100 were provided to the workshop participants; lunch was also provided. A local community media center near downtown Denver provided a convenient venue for the two-day workshop.

Despite the incentives and about 30 days of recruitment strategies that included informational flyers using new and existing contacts and list-serves, finding participants was a challenge. Nearly all of the 10 participant slots were filled two days prior to the beginning of the workshop. For the first two workshops, the three-day model had presented a recruitment problem, as community members found it difficult to devote three eight-hour days to a workshop. With these challenges in mind, I designed the event in May 2010 as a workshop held over two consecutive days with 16 hours of instruction, compared to the 24 hours typical of the first two workshops. Using four co-facilitators in the workshop (a three-day workshop usually has two facilitators) helped to ensure that Wanda and other digital storytellers received digital storytelling instruction in a supportive but fast-paced environment.

After brief introductions, an overview of the workshop, and completion of the consent forms, we started a story circle. The story circle is a performance in which individuals are given 15 minutes each to verbally share their script ideas in a group setting and receive and provide feedback. In essence, the story circle is the epicenter of the digital storytelling process. Bonds of solidarity emerge in the story circle as individuals listen to and observe each other narrating personal experiences. Storytellers develop their voices and begin to create scripts while in the story circle. More than one storyteller has described the story circle to me as akin to a group therapy session, with individuals discussing wellness issues that had been private up to that time. For anthropologists and psychologists interested in video-based mental health and therapy, the story circle is a key entry point to therapy that requires more systematic analysis. For the purposes of this study, we defined the story circle as a moment in time when a storyteller conceptualizes a digital story and the story begins to exercise agency and contribute to wellness.

In the story circle, co-facilitators lay out the ground rules for providing and receiving suggestions on draft narratives. The ground rules include allowing speakers to complete their ideas without interruption, making appreciative comments about the speaker's story before providing suggestions, and remembering that what speakers say in the circle stays in the circle. Privacy is self-enforced, and I believe this fact encourages individuals to censor themselves when sharing stories in a group setting. Individuals receive additional information about privacy in the consent forms, with statements that the workshop setting is "not private and we cannot guarantee confidentiality." Options for story sharing include reading from a printed script, reading from a computer, or speaking with little or no preparation. In the moment, the participants are encouraged to listen thoughtfully and share insights into story themes and details. Some participants might appear to be listening as they replay in their minds their own stories and how they fit or do not fit with the project themes. Feedback and discussion of draft stories can help the participants uncover deeper meanings and identify imagery for their videos. In principle, all members of the circle are encouraged to contribute to the discussion about script ideas as a way to cultivate storytelling skills. In practice, storytellers offered input and tended to defer to co-facilitators, who present a particular kind of digital storytelling model that prioritizes first-person encounters. After the story circle, individuals are encouraged to process the feedback received in the circle, develop their stories, and work with co-facilitators to finalize scripts.

Wanda agreed to be the second person to share her draft story in the story circle. She had shortened the script based upon feedback from a facilitator who was concerned about the excessive length of the first draft. In her comments to the group before reading her story, Wanda said,

> I have some questions that I'll tell you up front so that you can help me. I need help with any visuals that pop up for you as you are hearing my words. That would be helpful for me. I'm the one that wrote on and on and on. So, tell me if it's too long. I can cut a lot. Another question is, Are you going to get enough examples of the schizophrenia? So, if you don't, that's fine. And my last question is, Is there too much set up [in the draft script]?

Wanda's reading of the draft script about her brother's schizophrenia was compelling, owing to her measured cadences and steady, audibly emotional speech. She completed her reading and glanced at the faces around the table, ready for input. Part of the discussion that followed focused on her voice. According to one facilitator, "You have a really nice voice, or I think that you gave it the time and the care in your reading that informed me that it was definitely a lot at stake for you as a sister. I can feel that." Wanda had no formal voice coaching or theatre training. Her voice is easy to listen to, setting her apart from other storytellers, who have voices that participants often perceived as flat, disengaged, or low in energy. Wanda's literary voice is a characteristic of *Betsy Bug* that contributes to its status as a prototypical digital story.

After reading her draft script, Wanda declared, "It's hard. It's very hard, but it's a story I have to say. I had to say this story a long time ago. So, now I am just thrilled to say this story. I got this story out. But now I need to fix it."

For the next 10 minutes, the workshop participants and co-facilitators discussed Wanda's story. Conversation themes included suggestions about imagery. One of the storytellers suggested imagery that evokes a "lonely garden" and "nooks and crannies." Participants raised the issue about story length, and I stated that, based upon my estimate, the story as Wanda read it was about six minutes long. A stated goal of the workshop was for individuals to produce videos about three minutes long. After reviewing transcripts of the audio obtained in the story circle several months later, I realized that the story length was actually around three minutes. My miscalculation could have been the result of a number of several issues, including my preoccupation with the limited time that we had in the workshop, knowledge of Wanda's first script, which was excessively long, and the discomfort that I might have experienced by listening to the intense narrative about a person who was suffering from paranoid schizophrenia. The time issue is significant because Wanda received feedback to cut parts of the script, as well as suggestions to add more about her role in the story.

On the second day, the group focused on creative work and the sharing of videos. While in a group setting, the storytellers received a basic tutorial on video editing with Final Cut or an equivalent software application. Audio files and other media assets, such as imagery, sound effects, and background music, were organized in folders on the computers. Participants learned to import media assets into the video editing program and place those assets in the program's timeline. The timeline is the digital space where storytellers perform about 90% of the visual creative work involved in digital storytelling. The storytellers adjusted audio levels, assembled images to enhance the audio, and added dissolves and other transitions. Wanda and the other participants added the titles and credits to their projects.

In preparation for the group screening of the videos at the end of day two of the workshop, the storytellers worked with the co-facilitators on an as-needed basis to make last-minute changes. The time to create video in a two-day workshop was limited, and the energy in the room was hectic, with the co-facilitators frequently checking in with each other about the status of individual projects, technology problems waiting to be solved, and the availability of sufficient time to export video files from the editing program for screening. The co-facilitators acknowledged that time deficits are always an issue and that last-minute adjustments in the production process make a tremendous difference to the pacing or emotive impact of digital stories.

In the 2010 workshop where Wanda created *Betsy Bug*, a co-facilitator introduced the group viewing of digital stories as a celebratory affair. Laptops were turned off, lights were turned low, and storytellers and co-facilitators prepared to watch the videos. Excitement and nervousness were apparent among the group of amateur moviemakers who, 32 hours earlier, had met each other for the first time. A co-facilitator congratulated the storytellers and encouraged them to share some brief thoughts about their videos before screening them. Co-facilitators informed storytellers that digital stories produced by new moviemakers in a two-day period vary widely in terms of quality, and that apologizing for the aesthetic look or any aspect of their work was unnecessary. The internal screening of the videos contributed to a sense of exhaustion by signifying the end of the workshop but also to a sense of accomplishment by making visible formerly private experiences.

Betsy Bug was the final video previewed in the group screening. After the video was over, the room remained quiet, not only because of Wanda's video but also because the closing credits signified the accomplishments of the storytellers at the end of the intensive two-day workshop. Wanda spoke first, saying, "Wow. For someone who talked the whole time now I can't say a word." The group laughed. I mentioned that the music fit nicely with the story. A few others praised Wanda and *Betsy Bug*, but it was evident that the story's content was intense and contributed to an awkward silence in the room. Wanda said, "Quick. Somebody say something funny." By invoking humor to break the awkward silence, Wanda revealed the potential healing power of laughter in a group setting (Cousins, 1979) and demonstrated that the group therapy experienced among workshop participants in the story circle extended to the video screening process.

One of the co-facilitators offered a summary statement about expectations and uncertainties that participants may encounter when sharing the workshop videos with their family and friends:

> When you share these with people, be conscious that sometimes when you share these, people's reactions might not be what you might expect. I've had people come back [after a workshop] and tell me that it was really hard sharing them. Some people might prefer to share them . . . because people get hit pretty hard by a lot of these, and a lot of audiences, they just can't react immediately. It's almost better to just send it to someone and wait for them to like . . . instead of like showing it to them in person and you're like, "I just made this thing and what do you think?" And, you know, they're like, "A, a . . . Wow, wow. I just need to think." Just be aware of that when you are showing it, especially with some of these heavy pieces.

As a co-facilitator, I understood that the digital storytelling model used in the workshop often produced emotionally charged and sometimes traumatic stories. Informing individuals at the beginning of and throughout the workshop that screening stories can be a powerful and intense experience is required to prepare storytellers for publicly sharing videos. In the workshop, access to counseling services was not provided. We believe that in future workshops it would be worthwhile to provide on-site or ongoing support to project participants to address adverse reactions that may occur during digital storytelling projects.

STORYTELLER'S REFLECTION ON BETSY *BUG*

The consequences of producing *Betsy Bug* and other issues associated with Wanda's experience as a digital storyteller are illuminated in her exemplary responses to follow-up questions provided in the spring of 2014, four years after the workshop. The responses are presented to showcase some of Wanda's experiences of making *Betsy Bug* and her reflection on the digital storytelling process as a cathartic one.

Q: What does Betsy Bug *mean to you?*

Wanda: The fact that my father called mentally ill people "crazy as Betsy bugs" when his own son suffered from schizophrenia speaks to one of the many layers that took place within my family. As I created *Betsy Bug*, I was able to somehow break through a memory shield and could actually "smell" my brother's home. The images of his home flashed before me—many images that I had not photographed. These memories created a type of dance, and that dance helped to create the story. After I created *Betsy Bug*, I realized my own positionality in the story that I thought was about my brother. I was wrong. The story was also about me. As an example, one of the many things that families of schizophrenics experience is how others wonder if other family members are also mentally ill. I spoke to that experience at the end of my digital story, when I said, "In honor of my brother, don't call me crazy." This sentence spoke to a layer within me and my family that I was not fully conscious of until after I completed the story.

Q: Can you tell me about the creation of the script—what one memory of the process stands out as something that was hard or surprised you? Do you like the script? Which line in the script is your favorite?

Wanda: The line in my story that is my favorite is, "My brother died alone in his home . . . from complications from heart disease." As I am stating this line, a sepia image of a single shirt on a clothesline is seen. This is my favorite line because although family surrounded my brother, I envision him now as being quite alone—just like that shirt on the clothesline. I envision patients of heart disease and many other illnesses also just like that single shirt—caught up by the wind, alone, and desperately sad. These feelings would just be left there if it were not for digital storytelling's ability to make sense of them.

Betsy Bug was a story that I NEVER spoke about to anyone—not even within my immediate family. When the workshop was complete, I loved my script. As a child, I grew up with stories of tortoises, flying carpets, and evil stepmothers. These thinly veiled moral stories are wonderful for the imagination, but risk very little. Conversely, my digital story risked it all. In fact, I believe most digital stories have a commonality in terms of their tremendous risk factor. They risk breaking through previously established norms. They risk sharing a rarely seen/heard point of view.

Q: Can you share a personal and/or wider social experience that directly reveals one or more norms that you have in mind?

Wanda: After my brother died, we hired some help to clear out his home. It was a chaotic mess! A real visual picture of what it must have been like to live inside of his mind. When the workers arrived, they stood in his doorway with their mouths flopped open. My mother explained that my brother had been "sick." Just sick. That struck me as odd. We can easily say, "My sister had heart disease," or "My brother had high blood pressure." Those are the norms of the way we talk about illness. The norms of the way we share our pain about that illness. Somehow, talking about schizophrenia falls into another category where it is normal *not* to talk about it. And, it is normal *not* to share our pain about mental illness. Instead, silence is normal. Digital stories turn that kind of thinking on its head and say, "No, it's ok to talk about it. There is healing in talking about [it]."

Q: Can you share anything about how you felt screening your piece with others and speaking publicly about your video and the story?

Wanda: In the workshop, hearing everyone else's digital stories made me feel quite welcome and considerably less alone. We've all had the feeling of being alone in a crowd, but screening my digital story had the opposite effect. As I viewed the other stories, I discovered there was no one way to create a digital story, and yet they are not a one-size-fits-all endeavor. They are personal, individual, yet somehow the stories strike a universal chord. After creating my story, I shared it with my family. That resulted in a dialogue that had never taken place before, and our family was enriched because of it. Sharing our truth is the only thing that really connects us to each other and is a missing ingredient in much of our world today. Using the digital stories as a type of kindling, to keep ourselves and others warm and visible, is important work.

Q: How long after the workshop did you screen your video with your family?

Wanda: I shared my video with most of the family in my home the weekend after our workshop ended. After I showed those family members the video, I remember how quiet the room was. Everyone was sitting very still, and no one said a word, which in itself is a shocker in my family. I looked over and saw that a few family members were crying. Wow—members of my family openly acknowledging my brother and his illness! Amazing! After a while, a conversation about my brother and his illness took place. It was incredible, because up until that digital story, the entire issue was NEVER discussed! The other day, my sister called me after hearing an old song on the radio. It was a song that my brother liked. We had a nice conversation about him.

The anecdote about Wanda's conversation with her sister is an example of the power of digital storytelling as a communicative medium to address issues that are difficult to put into words. Wanda agreed to share for the first time a narrative about her brother's struggle with a mental health issue rather than keep private a personal issue that influenced her identity as a sibling of a mentally ill family member. She produced *Betsy Bug* in a workshop, representing a safe space co-constructed by project participants and facilitators. Wanda's story is unscripted in the sense that it is not a story she shared multiple times in a rehearsed fashion. Imagery such as a bowl of cherries used to tell the story represents Wanda's visual interpretation of her brother's debilitating wellness issue and an important step in finding comfort to narrate a story that had remained hidden prior to engagement in the digital storytelling process. At the center of this process is the workshop, where individuals develop basic proficiency in video editing and participate in an intervention through video to reduce hardship associated with wellness issues. Reflecting on story sharing, Wanda discussed feelings of loss and grief: "During the workshop, I felt the undertow of the story of my brother's mental illness start to loosen. It was as though, in making the digital story, I somehow gained power over it; as opposed to the power to silence it had held over me."

CONCLUSION

Betsy Bug was a prototypical digital wellness story that exercised agency through its production in a research workshop, screening in diverse venues, and a focused revisit in which the storyteller and the co-facilitator presented this reflective analysis to try to makes sense of the video's therapeutic qualities. Wanda had never openly shared the story of her brother and his paranoid schizophrenia until she participated in a story circle and other activities in a workshop designed to express personal experiences as video documents. In the process, *Betsy Bug* emerged with a well-modulated voice, a conventionally interesting story about mental health, and amalgam imagery that enhanced the emotional intensity of the once-buried story.

In presenting this information, our intention is not to showcase *Betsy Bug* as a standard for digital storytellers to achieve, but merely to assert that Wanda's video and its moving parts are change agents in the process of an individual making visible formerly private experiences. The changes that Wanda experienced included an enhanced identity, which came about through publicly acknowledging her brother's mental illness, a new sense of understanding of her brother's condition, and greater self-worth, which came about through contributing to a positive family dynamic by denormalizing her brother's struggle with paranoid schizophrenia.

REFERENCES

Cousins, N. (1979). *Anatomy of an illness as perceived by the patient: Reflections on healing and regeneration*. New York, NY: Norton.

Edwards, E. (2012). Objects of affect: Photography beyond the image. *Annual Review of Anthropology, 41*, 221–234.

Gubrium, A., & Harper, K. (2013). *Participatory visual and digital methods*. Walnut Creek, CA: Left Coast Press.

Gubrium, A.C., Hill, A.L., & Flicker, S. (2013). A situated practice of ethics for participatory visual and digital methods in public health research and practice: A focus on digital storytelling. *American Journal of Public Health, 103*(10), e1–e9.

Lambert, J. (2013). *Digital storytelling: Capturing lives, creating community* (4th ed.). New York, NY: Routledge.

Rony, F. (1994). The quick and the dead: Surrealism and the found ethnographic footage films of *Bontoc Eulogy* and *Mother Dao: The Turtlelike. Camera Obscura 52, 18*(1), 128–155.

Sandercock, L., & Attili, G. (2010). Digital ethnography as planning praxis: An experiment with film as social research, community engagement and policy dialogue. *Planning Theory and Practice, 11*(1), 23–45.

Thompson, S., & Lozecznik, V. (2012, Fall/Winter). Harvesting hope in northern Manitoba: Can participatory video help rebuild aboriginal food sovereignty? *Women and Environments, 88/89*, 10–13.

Wheeler, J. (2012). Using participatory video to engage in policy processes: Representation, power and knowledge in public screenings. In E. Milne, C. Mitchell, & N. De Lange (Eds.), *Handbook of participatory video* (pp. 365–379). Lanham, MD: AltaMira Press.

Willox, A., Harper, S., Edge, V., My Word: Storytelling and Digital Media Lab, & Rigolet Inuit Community Government (2012). Storytelling in a digital age: Digital storytelling as an emerging narrative method for preserving and promoting indigenous oral wisdom. *Qualitative Research, 13*(2), 1–21.

Worcester, L. (2012). Reframing digital storytelling as co-creative. *Institute of Development Studies Bulletin, 43*(5), 91–97.

Yonas, M.A., Burke, J.G., & Miller, E. (2013). Visual voices: A participatory method for engaging adolescents in research and knowledge transfer. *Clinical and Translational Science, 6*(1), 72–77.

Part IV

Tools for Practice Through Didactic Instruction

11 Video Art and Activism

Applications in Art Therapy

Basia Mosinski

The use of video as a medium in art therapy provides a contemporary form of expression that includes the moving image and sound. The process of making a video in art therapy includes two distinct phases. Phase 1 is the preproduction phase, which includes brainstorming ideas, planning, gathering source materials, and scouting locations. Phase 2, the production phase, includes directing, shooting, logging, screening, reshooting, rescreening, editing, and adding titles and effects. As with other art forms, therapists can use video to encourage personal growth, self-discovery, and insight, as well as to assist in emotional reparation (Malchiodi, 2003; Rogers, 2001). Video is uniquely suited as a medium to offer clients a chance to observe themselves.

This chapter presents a person-centered art therapy approach to using video art for learning, image making, processing life experiences, self-discovery, and empowerment. A brief discussion of video art and activism is presented in order to provide a context for the use of video in art therapy. The anecdotal experiences of adults with little or no previous video training provide examples of practical applications for group art therapy.

VIDEO ART, ACTIVISM, AND ACCESS

In the 1970s and 1980s, because of the high cost of portable video equipment and the underrepresentation in the media of some sectors of society, artists and interested citizens formed small collectives for the purpose of increasing public access and fostering social change. These collectives included groups such as Free Speech TV, AIDS Coalition to Unleash Power (ACTUP), and the Guerilla Girls (Mason, 1992). Universities and art schools provided equipment for student and faculty experimentation. Simultaneously, protests about underrepresentation of women and minorities in art galleries and museums (Halter, 2007) caused representatives of arts funding and educational institutions to acknowledge the disparity that existed and to create opportunities for women and minorities in the arts and education. Female artists brought portable video cameras into their studios and turned the cameras on themselves, thereby becoming the subject of their work rather than the object of the male gaze (Halter, 2007). They documented, performed, and told their stories about body image, family discord, and shifting paradigms. They made art videos that crossed narrative boundaries, broke linear structures, created abstractions, and critiqued the content of popular television (Bard, 2007).

At the same time, informed citizens lobbied to preserve access to representation on noncommercial television for the general public, as the government sold airwaves to giant media conglomerates whose interests were in commercial television programming, not in providing diverse perspectives, talents, and cultural representation. Today, individuals experiencing poverty, mental illness, or chronic disease are hampered by the bond that media has with capitalism (Cubitt, 1993). In a capitalist society, anyone with access to technology can produce media; however, those who profit politically and financially from media also control its production. While technology in the form of computers, televisions, recording devices, and communication platforms has become easier to use and is commonplace in middle- and upper-class households, the need for continual upgrades makes it cost prohibitive for poor and working-class families. Citizens without access to technology miss out on the dissemination of crucial information and the social exchange that takes place through electronic means. The exclusion of the poor and other minority groups, including those who have mental illness, from social dialogue reinforces their disenfranchisement.

VIDEO ART THERAPY GROUP STRUCTURE AND APPROACH

This chapter contains anecdotal information gathered from two video art therapy groups that took place from 2006 to 2007 at Housing Works, a community-based, minority-controlled, nonprofit corporation in New York City that provides vital services to homeless men and women living with HIV/AIDS (Housing Works, 2002). The Women with Cameras group was a mental health group for women between the ages of 35 and 60, and the 50 & Over Club was a group for men over 50 years of age. Both groups obtained funding through a grant from the Medical and Health Research Association, which sought to provide services to underfunded segments of the population living with HIV/AIDS, including women of any age and elderly men.

The video art therapy groups met twice weekly for 90 minutes per session, and clients had the opportunity to participate in two consecutive eight-week modules. Module 1 consisted of video production activities, and Module 2 consisted of video editing activities. The group members shared and discussed current feelings and experiences, learned new technical skills, brainstormed ideas, created personal project plans, gathered footage from various sources or recorded new footage, and edited media clips into final video projects of no more than 20 minutes in length.

The video groups incorporated a person-centered approach to art therapy. Each client constructed his or her video through a series of personal choices related to content, visuals, audio, and the look of the finished product. The resulting video became an external expression of an internal psychological landscape. My therapeutic role was to support the participants in trusting their own inner guidance systems, with the underlying belief that their innate impulses were to seek the direction of self-growth and well-being (Rogers, 2001). In a safe, therapeutic setting, the participants learned, experimented, shared experiences, examined personal issues, and created individual video projects. They also collaborated with each other by providing technical and emotional support.

In general, art therapy groups employ selected art materials in a series of processes directed toward the creation of an art product (Pizarro, 2004). In the Housing Works video art therapy groups, the art product was the resulting videotape or DVD. The clients' styles of engagement in their video projects varied according to previous video experience, interest in subject matter, willingness to self-disclose, and degree of trust in other group members and the art therapist. While clients with little or no video experience relied on assistance that I or other group participants provided, the completed videos reflected each client's content and aesthetic choices. When the groups concluded, each person received a DVD copy of his or her project.

METHODS

Participants

The participants were all U.S. citizens who identified as people of color and volunteered to take part in the video art therapy groups. Many of them had experienced a loss of occupational functioning; most were economically constrained and had inadequate housing; some had experienced reduced autonomy because of frequent medical interventions; and some felt emotionally depleted. Most of them also suffered from the stigma associated with HIV/AIDS. They often lived with the fear of becoming ill, of passing the illness onto others, and of end-of-life issues. All of these internal and external experiences are common for persons living with HIV/AIDS (Hrenko, 2005; Piccirillo, 2000). In addition, most of them were carrying unresolved childhood grief, loss, and trauma exacerbated by their ongoing physical concerns. Consequently, many clients were in a chronic state of crisis.

Access to Technology

Most of the clients in the video groups had a history of learning challenges due to previous traumas or learning disabilities; some found traditional learning methods intimidating. They came from low-income households where, according to research, only a small percentage of them were likely to have had access to the Internet and technology (Lamb, 2005). Most of them had not learned the vital language of universal icons and user-friendly software that is critical to functioning in a consumer society dependent on media information.

In the video art therapy groups, learning happened in a nonjudgmental, hands-on environment characterized by creative play, socializing, group activity, and personal expression. For some clients, the video groups provided an initial introduction to technology; they learned everything from how to power up a computer to how to troubleshoot when confronted with a technical problem. Their individual projects held their interest and provided the structure through which to learn technical skills. In turn, many of them seemed to experience an enhanced sense of self-efficacy.

The Video Art Therapy Groups

Initially, the clients expressed skepticism about joining a video art therapy group, based on their exposure to television news videos that depicted low-income people and their communities in a stereotyped and degrading fashion. It became apparent to me that the clients assumed they would be the subjects of the camera, their stories interpreted by someone else. They did not trust that they would have the final say about the content of the videos and about who would see the finished products. They also said they were fearful about disclosing their HIV status publicly. To allay some of their fears, I held several informational sessions before the groups began.

Eventually, five participants joined the Women with Cameras group, and four men joined the 50 & Over group. The groups had at their disposal video cameras, tripods, a monopod, a digital still camera, wireless microphone sets, a laptop computer, a printer/scanner, and miscellaneous reflectors, clamps, and surge protectors. This equipment created flexible choices for shooting footage and provided opportunities for group members to share both equipment and expertise.

Before each session began, the clients often walked into the group room with concerns and distractions from the outside world. I encouraged them to make a simple, quick *feeling drawing* to help them transition from outside stressors into the present moment (Mosinski, 2007; Ryan, 2007). A brief discussion of the drawings served as a way for me to check in with each person in the group and for members to create a common awareness of each other at an emotional level. At the close of the sessions, the clients each made another feeling drawing and briefly discussed it. This activity appeared to be an important part of the session, as evidenced by the care some of the clients used in writing their names and dating the drawings before handing them to me for safekeeping.

Each session, after the check-in, the clients talked about what they wanted to accomplish that day. I created an agenda that reflected the group's intentions and the status of each project, based on the previous week's activities. The agenda allowed the group to prioritize goals and tasks as well as provided clients with opportunities for group decision making. I also made available a binder with video log sheets, editing plans, and organizing notes from previous sessions.

In the women's group, the clients worked in pairs with one shared video camera between them; the goals of this structure were to foster peer learning and reliance and to make the best use of limited resources. Some of the participants had trust issues stemming from early childhood traumas and dysfunctional intimate relationships; they found it difficult to involve other participants in their planning or to ask for assistance. In the men's group, the participants initially tended to work independently or to seek a great deal of time and attention from me.

Over time, an atmosphere of sharing, bonding, and collective group identity developed. The sessions were active, with many opportunities for clients to try out new behaviors. For example, Demitra, who said she was afraid she could not learn and would not be able to help anyone, initially participated marginally in the group, arriving late and making few voluntary contributions to the group process. When asked about her project and what she would like to do, she usually shrugged her shoulders and said she did not know. On the days I introduced new equipment, she viewed the demonstrations from a distance, saying she could see from where she was sitting. In the first few group sessions, the other women prodded Demitra to become more involved. One day, while some group members were sorting out role assignments for the session's videotaping and others were logging their footage, Demitra stood up, walked over to the camera, and offered to record for someone else. The other women all stopped what they were doing, looked in her direction, and applauded. She had risked changing her behavior and, as a result, received the active and enthusiastic support of her peers. De Petrillo and Winner (2005) described the active group as sometimes providing distraction from feelings of low self-worth, depression, grief, loss, and trauma. This seemed to be true for Demitra as well as for other participants in the video art therapy groups.

Each client had control over which stories to tell, how much to tell, and what artifacts, if any, to bring in for recording. The video project provided the clients with a structure for experimenting with ideas, tolerating doses of frustration and uncertainty, and slowly building trust in their own decision-making abilities. A few clients expressed some frustration about their lack of experience with creative endeavors. I made myself available to such clients and judiciously offered suggestions without impinging on their sense of efficacy.

The clients edited their projects during weekly individual sessions with me and shared their works in progress with the group. Sometimes aesthetic considerations overlapped with therapeutic concerns. For example, Chardelle was a client with neuropathy, which caused weakness and shakiness in her hands. She had difficulty holding the video camera steady, even with the steady shot feature engaged. She videotaped images of African American authors and artists from book cover posters because she viewed the images as empowering to her and to other African Americans. During playback of the shaky footage, the group members sensed her discomfort at seeing a visual representation of the effects of her illness. Someone offered to reshoot the footage for her. After a pause to consider this offer, she commented with a sigh, "Oh well, that's me." Through the video project, Chardelle seemed to begin to come to terms with her shaky hand and to claim it as part of her identity. She integrated it with other aspects of her identity, including being a poet and an artist. She became interested in outtakes, the extraneous parts of clips that revealed behind-the-scenes activities, and edited these images over her recited poetry and songs. The finished video project, which she titled *Invisible Women*, is about her HIV/AIDS status and about sharing her identity (Video Clip 11.1 can be found at www.filmandvideobasedtherapy.com).

Personal investment in the projects helped clients maintain their interest. Some of them did outside homework for their projects by collecting published writings and previously recorded video and audio from a variety of sources. One client, Cheryl, decided she wanted to make a family video to share with her children and sisters. She included over 50 photos, which she narrated one by one. Many of the photos were of family members who had died of drug-related violence. She chose *Family Reunion* as the sound track that wove in and out of the video.

My style of providing therapy was to be active, compassionate, practical, and attentive to the opportunities for therapeutic group interaction. I used humor whenever possible, which allowed for a release of tension in the groups. When the clients were working on emotional content, I encouraged them to reflect on feelings related to the imagery. When group members encountered technical difficulties, I provided guidance with troubleshooting strategies, beginning with the most obvious reason equipment might not be working before moving on to the next potential solution.

Module 1. The goals of Module 1 were to brainstorm ideas; identify a subject for each video project; make a plan; gather previously recorded audio, video, or photos; and record new video footage. I designed Module 1 to be self-contained so that a client could end group participation when the module was completed. If a client chose not to go on to Module 2, the editing phase, the client received a DVD of his or her raw footage. The module structure gave clients the ability to make a short-term commitment and see the results of their efforts in a relatively short amount of time. Clients who wanted to proceed to the editing phase could move on to Module 2.

I discussed releases, contracts, privacy issues, and confidentiality with the clients before handing out the cameras. I instructed them to ask for permission prior to videotaping anyone, except when recording outdoors in public spaces. Each group member determined whether he or she wanted to be included in the recordings of the other group members.

Many tasks associated with creating individual videos required the assistance of group members. Clients set up and operated the equipment, tested microphones, monitored audio recordings, kept track of time, paid attention to continuity, and scouted locations for the shooting of footage. Each week, I introduced or reviewed previously introduced equipment and operating instructions, we discussed project ideas, and clients made and discussed video recordings. Each client was the director of his or her video project, and clients took turns being in charge of activities. Clients could ask for help with videotaping or sound capturing, but they were responsible for the overall content of their individual projects.

I introduced the filmmaking language, hand signals, and commands we used during recording sessions. The clients rehearsed terms like "quiet on the set," "rolling," and "cut." They communicated their discomfort with taking charge, as evidenced by their laughter at themselves and each other as they tried these new roles. It took time for them to gain confidence in using this new language. However, most of the clients not only learned to use voice commands and hand signals, but they also appeared to gain self-confidence by doing so.

When the group developed an agenda that included outdoor shooting, clients worked in pairs, with one camera between them. Before leaving the building, we discussed safety issues related to the narrowing of the cameraperson's peripheral vision while looking through the lens. Shooting in pairs allowed one person the freedom to videotape while the other person provided an extra set of eyes to protect the cameraperson from dangers such as obstructions, approaching cars, and collisions with other pedestrians. When shooting outdoors, the video crew tended to attract the attention of people on the street, and most of the clients appeared to enjoy this.

Once shot, we screened the video footage at least twice. During the first screening, the group members provided a supportive structure by witnessing in silence while the director talked about what he or she had experienced during shooting and viewing the footage. After the director spoke, I invited group members to share their emotional responses to the content of the recording.

We used the second screening to discuss the artistic and technical aspects of the recordings. Clients shared ideas with each other, which helped them develop and refine their projects. Multiple screenings helped clients acknowledge successes, build skills, and experience the impact of collective involvement. Sometimes we screened audio and video separately so that issues related to each were not lost. We briefly critiqued existing examples of footage, which enhanced discussions about shooting styles and shot compositions. Sometimes during screenings, we paused the footage or played it back frame-by-frame to examine what actually took place on screen and to identify how the shooting style contributed to the emotional tone of the video.

The projects served as an organizing factor that helped clients shift from emotional content into structural elements of the videos. For example, if a client became distressed while being recorded telling a personal story, I gently asked how much of the information he or she wanted to share in the video, and sometimes asked if the client wanted the camera to stop rolling. This shift in focus often provided the necessary psychological space to interrupt potential (re)traumatizing effects of the story on the person telling it, as well as on the other participants listening to it. Later, while screening material from a recording session, the client could experience the content with some reflective distance. Each screening provided further detachment from the emotional intensity of the story, which made it possible for the participant to integrate his or her trauma narratives into a developing sense of self.

I gave instructions to each group member about logging video footage, a process of recording the content of a tape. The clients noted the beginning and ending of clips, as well as their duration, and wrote a brief description about each. Clients did this before editing so that when they looked for a specific clip on their tape, the paper log pointed them to the exact location of the footage. Logging brought order to what otherwise would have been loose, random segments of video footage.

Some clients found logging difficult and gave up trying to do it. However, as a group, they recognized each other's differing strengths, talents, and accomplishments. The clients who became proficient in logging helped others, which strengthened their sense of achievement and self-confidence. The video projects presented many opportunities for clients to experience mastery, communication, enjoyment, belonging, and the creation of a personal legacy (Piccirillo, 2000).

Module 2. Computer editing is a nondestructive process (Brenneis, 2004) in which the editor copies original media footage onto a computer. This process preserves the footage without altering it. Once in the computer, all footage is accessible and brought into a timeline; the client can then edit and order component parts into the desired sequence. Video editing requires organization, planning, and an intuitive sense of where to make edits and place transitions (Brenneis, 2004).

I worked closely with each client during the editing process. Some clients gained technical proficiency and worked independently, while others relied on my technical skills to implement editing decisions. Some clients chose to cut out redundant material and refine what they were trying to communicate. Some of them imported sound recordings from other sources, such as CDs and downloaded audio files, as well as prerecorded video, television, or film footage. Postproduction additions and alterations such as titles, transitions between clips, and credits, gave the videos a professional look.

Once the projects were completed, I showed each client how to export his or her video to DVD. Overall, when reviewing their projects in the timeline, most of the clients expressed satisfaction with the look of their videos. Some of them expressed excitement about sharing their work with people outside the group.

CLIENT STORIES

Sonya

Sonya, a woman in her 30s, initially planned to make a pleasant video about her life, using optimistic imagery contained in some of her initial drawings from early in the group's formation. Rainbows, butterflies, and images of an idealized family with two children, two parents, a house with a yard, and a white picket fence surfaced. The images represented a wish she had about reunification with her children who, because of neglect, were in foster care.

During one group session, Sonya shared feelings and experiences that were in stark contrast to the images she wanted to use in her video. As a child, raised by her grandparents, she had experienced sexual abuse, denial of her basic needs, a reward system that contributed to her obesity, and exposure to a worldview that supported machismo and tolerated violence from men toward women and children. As an adult, she had been involved in a series of abusive relationships. While in one such relationship, she depended on her drug-addicted partner to care for her young children while she went to work. Her partner either took the children with him to drug houses or left them home alone. At the time, Sonya thought she could not live without her partner, and she was in denial about the danger her children were in and the abuse she was experiencing. The state eventually removed her children and put them into foster care.

Sonya was devastated, although she understood that placing her children in foster care was in their best interest. She left the abusive relationship and became very depressed. After several years of psychotherapy, her depression turned to anger, and then to rage. In the video art therapy group, rage frequently appeared to be under the surface of her otherwise depressed demeanor, including when she heard of injustices other women in the group had experienced or were experiencing. Strong protective behaviors directed toward other group members seemed to be indicative of her sense of powerlessness in her own life.

Several weeks into the women's group, another participant shared that she was currently in an abusive relationship, which was causing her tension and stress. Sonya said, under her breath, "I should make a video about domestic violence." The room fell quiet. It was an idea that touched deeply on Sonya's experiences. In that moment of inspiration, an observable shift took place in Sonya. As she entertained the idea of making such a video, she leaned forward in her chair and then sat taller. Her eyes became clear and engaged. Her presentation as a sluggish, helpless victim gave way to enthusiasm for her idea and a plan of action.

Sonya decided to make a video so that other women might break through their denial sooner than she had. The theme motivated the group members, who discussed the warning signs of the domestic violence some of them had experienced. Their stories confirmed Sonya's idea and provided direction for the project. Sonya decided to make several recordings of herself and another woman in the group who had also been abused. Through the process of making the video, Sonya transformed her rage into art. *The Early Warning Signs of Domestic Violence* (Video Clip 11.2, images blurred to protect privacy) is a moving piece about how denial, shame, guilt, and conditioning kept Sonya in one abusive relationship after another (Video Clip 11.2 can be found at www.filmandvideobasedtherapy.com).

The video was emotionally difficult for Sonya; however, the process proved to be cathartic for her. She was able to identify points of denial in her life, such as when she ignored her inner knowledge that the abuse was wrong and that it was escalating. As she worked on making, viewing, and editing recordings, she redirected her trauma story's content into the video project. Consequently, she seemed to experience a helpful reflective distance between herself and her life story. Bits of her personal narrative surfaced, and she integrated them into the larger context of her life. The healing that occurred allowed her to have some newfound compassion for herself and for women in similar situations. She showed signs of resilience and hope throughout the course of the group and reported that her depression had lifted. A few weeks prior to termination of the group, Sonya had the strength and conviction to re-establish contact with her children.

Andre

Andre, a member of the 50 & Over Club men's group, reported that he did not know what he wanted to do for his video project. As the weeks passed, he expressed his frustration. During one outdoor practice session, Andre's perspective shifted. He began to use the camera to zoom in and out of billboards near our SoHo facility and found that he could isolate the segments of the billboard he found most interesting. His mood changed from frustration to mild curiosity as he developed an idea related to the intention of billboard advertisers: to sell products. He discovered images of seduction and desire in the billboard that he framed with the camera lens, and he decided to work on these themes in his video. As Andre's interest deepened, he took notice of surroundings of which he had been oblivious for most of his life.

During the next session, the group members screened the images Andre had collected in the field. His tape showed that he had been recording at times when he thought the camera was turned off. Viewing the imagery was unsettling for him. He expressed embarrassment at not knowing when the camera was recording and when it was not. Some of the other group members remarked that the unintended footage, taken while the camera was swinging at his side, was interesting. At times, the imagery was completely upside down. He had inadvertently captured images of people, snippets of conversations, street noises, the sidewalk, and the sky in the same clip. Andre said it made him feel sick to watch the imagery.

Andre's mother had abandoned him during infancy, and he grew up in an orphanage where he experienced neglect, physical abuse, and violence. As a result, Andre reported having difficulty trusting others. He appeared hypervigilant and rarely spoke directly to other participants. During group sessions, he anxiously stood close to the door instead of sitting with the other group members. When it was pointed out to him that the other men tolerated his antisocial behaviors, he said he sensed that others cared for him, but felt incapable of genuinely caring for anyone in return.

One day, during check-in, Andre began talking about a childhood abuse experience that occurred while he was living in the orphanage. One of the group members interrupted Andre and asked if Andre wanted him to record the story on videotape. Andre agreed to this suggestion, and the other group member attached a wireless microphone to Andre's shirt. Andre went on to relate personal experiences of profound abuse, neglect, and torture in the orphanage. Afterward, the men in the group, who had previously known little about Andre, said that his story moved them and that they felt a stronger bond with him.

Later, while screening his personal narrative, a group member reminded Andre of the accidental video footage he had recorded on the street. Andre decided to match the accidentally recorded images with the audio portion of the recording about the abuse he had experienced in the orphanage. The imagery conveyed the frightening, chaotic feeling of the story as it might have been experienced from a child's perspective (Video Clip 11.3, image blurred to protect privacy, can be found at www.filmandvideobasedtherapy.com).

There were multiple opportunities during playback and editing for the clients to engage with their recorded footage. Once part of Andre's trauma story was recorded, the story existed outside him, which provided him with objective distance and a new perspective. Multiple screenings of the same footage allowed him to slowly incorporate his trauma narrative into his life story, with the hope of reducing its overall impact as a life-defining memory.

CONCLUSION

Video is an art medium with a rich history of art, storytelling, activism, and documentation. Yet it also has a history as a public medium in which the dominant culture has often presented popular opinions, stereotypes, and monocultural perspectives. Today, video production and consumption are accessible to many people through relatively inexpensive technologies, though the medium remains less accessible to those marginalized by poverty and mental and physical disabilities. Instead, the dominant culture often produces media interpreting underrepresented people's experiences. By providing video technology as an art-making tool, art therapists offer clients an opportunity to reclaim the camera's lens and become the authors of their self-representations.

The clients discussed in this chapter often talked about their personal identities in relation to the culture at large. While making their videos, they addressed the social implications of disclosing their HIV status. Many of them expressed a sense of empowerment that came from making the videos because they were able to focus on issues of interest to them and to record in their own voices. They became interested in video as a vehicle for effecting social change through the inclusion of their perspectives in the general pool of public videos. Many of the clients were motivated to share their videos with others and to use them as teaching tools in the hope of helping other members of their communities avoid self-harmful behaviors, particularly those behaviors that had contributed to the clients' contracting HIV.

As art therapists integrate technology into their practices, new questions arise concerning the individualized, confidential emphasis that characterizes traditional therapeutic practice. The potential for easy distribution of videos via the Internet has implications relative to the blurring of boundaries between private and public, as well as between personal and political. As the relationship between art therapy and technology develops and the conversation surrounding it becomes more sophisticated, theorists and practitioners need to address the merits and dangers of this blurring.

The images and voices of people marginalized by poverty and disability have largely been confined to group therapy rooms, hospital wards, clinics, prisons, and, on occasion, public art exhibitions. By gaining access to video-making equipment and knowledge, people from underrepresented groups have the opportunity to become producers of their self-representations and collective identities, and to convey content that is of significance and import to them. Video technology provides those who are marginalized with a chance to accurately represent and share their life experiences, inner worlds, and alternate perspectives, thus enriching those on the outside of that experience who are willing to look and listen.

REFERENCES

Bard, P. (2007). Art and the moving image: An interview with Berta Sichel. *Afterimage: The Journal of Media Arts and Cultural Criticism, 34*(6), 12–15.

Brenneis, L. (2004). *Final Cut Pro: For OS X*. Berkeley, CA: Peachpit Press.

Cubitt, S. (1993). *Videography*. New York, NY: St. Martin's Press.

De Petrillo, L., & Winner, E. (2005). Does art improve mood? A test of a key assumption underlying art therapy. *Art Therapy: Journal of the American Art Therapy Association, 22*(4), 205–212.

Halter, E. (2007, January 23). Before YouTube: Plunge into the archives of the Video Data Bank. *Village Voice*. Retrieved August 5, 2007, from http://www.villagevoice.com/film/0704,halter,75625,20.html

Housing Works, Inc. (2002). *About us. Introduction* (para. 1). Retrieved August 5, 2007, from http://www.housingworks.org/aboutus/index_more.html

Hrenko, K. (2005). Remembering Camp Dreamcatcher: Art therapy with children whose lives have been touched by HIV/AIDS. *Art Therapy: Journal of the American Art Therapy Association, 22*(1), 39–43.

Lamb, P. (2005). Technology and the new class divide. Retrieved August 5, 2007, from http://news.cnet.com/2100-1028_3-5924758.html

Malchiodi, C. (2003). The art and science of art therapy. In C. Malchiodi (Ed.), *Handbook of art therapy* (pp. 1–3). London, UK: Jessica Kingsley.

Mason, C. (1992). ACT UP women speak up. *ACT UP San Francisco, 2*(4), 2. Retrieved August 5, 2007, from http://www.queerculturalcenter.org/Pages/Mills/crystal.html

Mosinski, B. (2007). A tool for healing. *Afterimage: The Journal of Media Arts and Cultural Criticism, 34*(6), 5–7.

Piccirillo, E. (2000). Beyond words: The art of living with AIDS. In C. Malchiodi (Ed.), *Medical art therapy with adults* (pp. 163–188). London, UK: Jessica Kingsley.

Pizarro, J. (2004). The efficacy of art and writing therapy: Increasing positive mental health outcomes and participant retention after exposure to trauma. *Art Therapy: Journal of the American Art Therapy Association*, 21(1), 5–12.

Rogers, N. (2001). Person-centered expressive arts therapy: A path to wholeness. In J. Rubin (Ed.), *Approaches to art therapy: Theory and technique* (2nd ed.) (pp. 163–177). Ann Arbor, MI: Sheridan Books.

Ryan, B. (2007, March/April). A special approach to therapy aims to help a group of women overcome tortured memories of the past. *HIV Plus Magazine, 57*, 28–31.

12 Digital Storytelling

Healing for the YouTube Generation of Veterans

Rivka Tuval-Mashiach and Benjamin Patton

> Narrative is central to recovery from severe trauma. It's not simply the telling of the story; it is the whole social process. The first steps in the communalization of trauma—what I call this process—is to be empowered to tell the story. You have to be empowered to hear and to believe and to remember it. The final step that closes the loop is to retell the story to others.
>
> —Shay, 2010, Kindle location 726

The purpose of this chapter is to present and discuss a new therapeutic intervention developed for traumatized veterans and those exposed to military-related adversities. This intervention is a filmmaking workshop that gives veterans coping with service-related stress the opportunity to work together over several days to produce short films. This intentional, collaborative process enables them to creatively address experiences that they might be unable to express in more traditional ways. We begin this chapter with a short discussion of the psychological harm caused by trauma and briefly describe the principal therapeutic interventions to treat it. We then explain the theoretical framework that guides our work in the filmmaking workshops. Next, we present the I Was There (IWT) film workshop model. Finally, we discuss the model's therapeutic value to participants and potential application to nonmilitary populations.

THEORETICAL BACKGROUND

Harm of Exposure to Trauma

Exposure to traumatic and life-threatening events is common to the human experience in all societies. Kessler, Chiu, Demler, Merikangas, and Walters (2005) estimated that most Americans (60% of men and 51% of women) experience trauma at some point in their lives. The harmful psychological impact of exposure to traumatic events on many of those who have been exposed has been documented extensively (Breslau, 2009; Norris et al.,

2002). The most studied response is posttraumatic stress disorder (PTSD), which develops in 10% to 15% of exposed individuals and creates major challenges for them (Brewin, Andrews, & Valentine, 2000; Kessler, 2000; Shalev, Tuval-Mashiach, Frenkiel-Fishman, Hadar, & Eth, 2006).

PTSD is a clinically significant stress response that causes distress or impairment in social, occupational, or other important areas of functioning. Patients with PTSD might exhibit persistent reexperiencing of the traumatic event(s), persistent avoidance of stimuli associated with the traumatic event(s), numbing of previously normal responsiveness, and persistent symptoms of increased arousal (American Psychiatric Association [APA], 2000). Other responses to trauma include depressive symptoms, adjustment problems, grief responses, compromised physical health, other anxiety disorders, and possibly suicide (National Center for Injury Prevention and Control, 2011; Shalev et al., 1998).

Military Trauma

Military service involves a unique context of exposure to trauma. Service personnel can be exposed to several traumatic events that can be far more intensive than in civilian contexts (Richardson, Frueh, & Acierno, 2010). In many countries, including the United States, military service can involve extended tours of deployment that often approach or exceed one year in locations that are far from home and the soldiers' natural support networks (e.g., family, friends, churches, community organizations), as well as ongoing exposure to the risk of death, injury, or sexual trauma (Bowling & Sherman, 2008). Therefore, the reintegration of veterans with their families requires an extended process of adjustment. Factors that can complicate this adjustment process include long periods of separation, exigencies of leaving the military and finding new jobs, existence of injuries or disabling medical conditions, disruptions in family routines, and potentially compromised parenting stemming from injuries or exposure to traumatic events and subsequent health problems. In addition, exacerbation of mental disorders, particularly PTSD, traumatic brain injury (TBI), anxiety disorders, and depression, can hinder veterans' readjustment.

Military Service-Related Stress in the United States

Over the past 12 years, about 2.5 million military service personnel have served in Operation Enduring Freedom (OEF), Operation Iraqi Freedom (OIF), and Operation New Dawn, for a total of more than 3.3 million deployments (Siegel & Davis, 2013). Updated estimates have shown that about 20%, or some 500,000 returning veterans, meet the criteria for PTSD (Peterson, Luethke, Borah, Borah, & Young-McCaughan, 2011). When veterans cope with reintegration issues or stress related to their military service, the potential ripple effect can be enormous, affecting millions of other people at least indirectly (Richardson et al., 2010). The following statistics provide some background information supporting this contention:

- The unemployment rate for Gulf War II veterans is currently 7.9%, whereas the national average is 6.6% (U.S. Department of Labor, 2014).
- One of every eight homeless adults is a veteran (Henry, Cortes, Morris, Khadduri, & Culhane, 2013).
- Every day, 22 American veterans of all wars take their own lives. The suicide rate is particularly high among veterans under 30 years of age, a 44% increase over the past 3 years in this age group (Kuehn, 2009; Shane, 2014).
- More than half of all service members are married, and there are nearly 2 million children in military families (Paley, Lester, & Mogil, 2013).

The U.S. Department of Veterans Affairs (VA) offers various services to veterans, including evidence-based psychological and psychiatric interventions, for the treatment of trauma and PTSD. These interventions include medications, cognitive behavioral therapy, cognitive processing therapy, and prolonged exposure therapy, all of which are directed toward changing traumatic memories and cognitions until they are less troubling.

Why Another Intervention?

A new and different intervention might be necessary because many veterans in need choose not to seek the medical help that they are entitled to. There is a significant underuse of mental health care among military personnel (American Psychological Association, 2008; Hoge, Auchterlonie, & Milliken, 2006; Hoge et al., 2004). Some reasons for not seeking treatment are related to the stigma associated with treatment; institutional barriers (e.g., staff skill and sensitivity); and/or logistical barriers (e.g., accessibility of service) (Ouimette et al., 2011). PTSD symptoms have been positively associated with perceived barriers to care, with the most consistent results observed for PTSD avoidance symptoms (Ouimette et al., 2011). Given these barriers, we developed our model for working with veterans to address the issues of stigma and avoidance.

A RAND study in 2008 of veterans of the wars in Iraq and Afghanistan indicated that only half of the veterans surveyed who manifested symptoms of depression or PTSD sought mental health treatment in the following year (Tanielian & Jaycox, 2008). Although the reasons are unclear, VA clinicians have confirmed that OIF/OEF veterans are more difficult to engage in treatment than veterans of previous wars (Najavits, Norman, Kivlahan, & Kosten, 2010). The average age of veterans deployed to Iraq or Afghanistan was 27, and digital video was the preferred communication medium of what many consider the YouTube generation of warriors (Vaughn, 2009). According to Hoge (2010), who previously ran the top U.S. research program at the Walter Reed Army Institute of Research on the psychological and neurological consequences of the Iraq and Afghanistan wars, we need to "meet the warrior where they are, and do whatever is necessary to ensure that the warrior feels understood and supported while telling their story" (p. 121). It is our assertion that the written word is simply no longer the principal way younger veterans generally communicate.

Theories and Mechanisms of Traumatic Responses: The Narrative Approach

One of the core challenges in the study of responses to traumatic event(s) is to identify the mechanisms responsible for the way in which survivors respond to exposure. Cognitive models of PTSD have suggested that avoidance plays an important role in the development and maintenance of the disorder (Brewin, Dalgleish, & Joseph, 1996; Foa, Steketee, & Rothbaum, 1989). These models have indicated that avoidance of traumatic memories limits the processing of these memories and their associated emotional reactions, with the result being the maintenance of PTSD (Kenny et al., 2009).

Because responses to trauma involve the issue of memory, we chose to use the narrative approach to guide our thinking in the development of our workshop (Tuval-Mashiach et al., 2004). The narrative theory proposes that autobiographical memories are strongly related to one's sense of identity because they serve as the building blocks of past experiences, plans, and self-perceptions. The theory holds that people infuse meaning into their lives and the events that they have experienced through the narratives that they share with others about themselves (Berntsen & Rubin, 2004, 2006, 2007; Lieblich, Tuval-Mashiach, & Zilber, 1998; McAdams, 2008).

During their daily routines, people maintain the ability to construct coherent, meaningful, and dynamic life stories. Trauma, by its very nature, shatters this sense of continuity and flow of daily life (Janoff-Bulman, 1992; Tuval-Mashiach et al., 2004; Wigren, 1994). This break is expressed in stories that trauma survivors tell about themselves and their lives. Wigren (1994) asserted that trauma disrupts narrative processing on two levels: At a specific level, there is disruption of the narrative of the traumatic event; on a more general level, there is disruption of the whole life story of the individual.

When a traumatic event occurs, the traumatic memory is particularly impaired "with respect to oneself and . . . other autobiographical information" (Halligan, Michael, Clark, & Ehlers, 2003, p. 422). Therefore, memories of trauma are isolated from and incompatible with the rest of autobiographical memory and sometimes result in maladaptive self-evaluations (Ehlers, Mayou, & Bryant, 1998); a loss of meaning; or a sense of loss of autonomy and effectiveness (Stiles, Honos-Webb, & Lani, 1999). Narrative therapy focuses on a client's life story as the main tool for a therapeutic change. By locating those parts in the story that hinder continuity and coherence while jointly creating an alternative story, a richer construction of one's life and identity is promoted (Omer & Alon, 1997; Schafer, 1981; White & Epston, 1990). Research has shown that the narration of trauma, be it in written or verbal form, has many physical and psychological health benefits, and decreases PTSD symptom levels. This finding has been replicated by researchers across age, gender, culture, social class, and personality type (Castillo, C'de Baca, Qualls, & Bornovalova, 2012; Gidron et al., 2002; O'Kearney & Perrott, 2006; Pennebaker & Seagal, 1999; Richards, Beal, Seagal, & Pennebaker, 2000).

These findings bear important implications for therapeutic interventions for the victims of traumatic events because the creation of coherent verbal narratives is the focus of treatment (Brewin, 1996; Resick, 2001; Van Minnen, Wessel, Dijkstra, & Roelofs, 2002). Indeed, several researchers have identified the relationship between narrative organization and PTSD in therapeutic situations, where narrative changes during and following treatment might be correlated with a decrease in PTSD symptomatology. In these cases, such as in narrative exposure therapy (Schauer, Neuner, & Elbert, 2005) or narrative reconstruction (Peri & Gofman, 2014), the therapeutic intervention involves telling the whole life story with a repeated recounting of the trauma narrative.

Video Therapy

Video has been used as an element in therapy in recent years for different populations and in the treatment of various psychological issues (Wedding & Niemiec, 2003). Cohen (2013) referred to video therapy as a component of art therapy and discussed several uses of video in therapy, such as watching films (Cinematherapy) or producing films as part of another type of therapy. However, although various mechanisms of change contributing to the efficacy of this type of therapy have been identified, the field is in the early stages of development, so no consensus has yet been reached regarding what precisely constitutes video or filmmaking therapy or how it works to alleviate patients' suffering (Johnson & Alderson, 2008). Consequently, many definitions and uses exist, and evidence of its effectiveness is slowly beginning to emerge (Cohen, 2013). For this reason, we consider it important to offer our theoretical and operational understanding of the way we use video as an intervention.

In line with the narrative approach to therapy, we view filmmaking much like storytelling. The production of films is essentially a narrative process, wherein directors and their teams use digital video and audio to convey their messages. However, filmmaking is different from oral narration in several important ways that make it potentially more attractive and engaging for military veterans, especially younger ones. First, although writing and talking often are solitary activities, video production is inherently collaborative: It is very difficult to make a film alone. Second, PTSD is primarily a visual disorder because the memories of traumatic experiences are vivid and visual, and often cannot be expressed in words. The more traditional verbal approach to therapy can be enhanced by adding a multisensory and more synoptic and concise visual means of creating a narrative.

THE IWT FILM WORKSHOP MODEL

The IWT film workshop, which had its genesis in 2011, was designed as a practical implementation of video-based therapy for veterans coping with service-related stress. The first of its kind, this innovative multiday filmmaking workshop combined the proven therapeutic value of storytelling or narrative with the immense power of digital media.

Background

The initiative was the result of a confluence of several factors. First, its creator, coauthor Benjamin Patton, has had a long association with the military through his family on both sides, most notably, his grandfather and father, General George S. Patton, Jr., and Major General George Patton IV, respectively. As a professional filmmaker and film instructor, Mr. Patton had worked extensively with adolescents through a summer film camp to use filmmaking as a way to explore adolescent identity issues.

A seminal conversation in 2011 between Patton and network news anchor Bob Woodruff was the final piece leading to the founding of the IWT film workshop. Woodruff is an ABC television journalist and anchor who was severely wounded by an improvised explosive device while embedded with the American 4th Infantry Division in Iraq in January of 2006. He suffered a serious TBI that required major reconstructive surgery and several years of extensive physical therapy. In a conversation with Ben Patton in 2011, the journalist noted that in regard to his own TBI and dealings with veterans coping with PTSD, there was the expressed need to "unpack" and "repack" the daunting and often overwhelming memories of an experienced trauma to make that memory more manageable. This conversation was an epiphany. Organizing material in this way is the essence of filmmaking: shooting footage, recording audio, taking photographs, composing music and adding sound effects, and placing them in a video project time line in an effort to communicate something in a specific and intentional way.

The first IWT film workshop was held in May of 2011 at Fort Carson, CO. As of mid-2014, nearly 20 IWT workshops have been held in the United States and Israel with more than 300 participants and more than 150 films produced. Most of the workshops have been conducted at warrior transition units (WTUs), located on all major army bases, in order to reach these veterans as soon as possible following their return home from deployment and to help with their reintegration. Moreover, it is easier for them if we meet them where they work, live, and presumably are the most comfortable rather than require them to come to us and acclimate to a strange place. As the current military drawdown continues, however, fewer and fewer veterans are passing through WTUs, so our recruitment and hosting model is evolving. We are now beginning to organize these workshops in direct partnership with behavioral health departments and Ready and Resilient Campaigns located at military hospitals because these are more permanent programs.

Concept

The IWT concept was based upon three basic principles—namely, listening, collaboration, and empowerment—that helped to inform the design of the program. Following is a brief description of each principle.

Listening. Based upon our personal experience of working in therapeutic settings at military bases, a frequent complaint by the veterans whom we have encountered is that "no one understands me" or "no one cares." Keeping this assertion in mind, our first goal at a workshop is to convince the participating veterans that we do care about their stories and that we are listening.

Shay (1994) emphasized the importance of the listener's role:

> To be trustworthy, a listener must be ready to experience some of the terror, grief, and rage that the victim did. This is one meaning, after all, of the word *compassion*. Once the veteran sees that the listener authentically experiences these emotions, even though with less intensity than in combat, the veteran often loses the desire to shout in the listener's face, "You weren't there, so shut the fuck up!" (p. 189)

Affirming a veteran's story is critical to this program's effectiveness. Many veterans returning from deployment have conditioned themselves not to share their service-related traumatic experiences with friends and family. The collegial setting of our workshops encourages veterans to share their experiences not only with one another but also with our instructors, not as in an intervention or a therapy per se, but rather as colleagues considering working together to produce a film.

Collaboration. This is perhaps the most important element of a successful workshop. The brainstorming process, combined with film exercises designed to break down barriers between veterans, as well as between veterans and civilian instructors, lays the foundation for veterans working together with the shared objective of completing a film. Our emphasis on collaboration is a direct response to the tendency among far too many veterans, as already noted, to keep their experiences to themselves. It is extremely difficult to make a film alone: The filmmaking process requires dialogue among all members of the production team.

Empowerment. This is the third key concept on which the IWT model is based. We want the veterans participating in our workshops to have a thoroughly positive experience during their four days with us. Empowerment is the hoped for and not atypical result of the parts of a workshop successfully blending together: being listened to; being invited to form or participate in a team (not unlike, say, a cohesive squad of soldiers); having a greater degree of control over one's personal narrative and "new norm"; and acquiring new technical skills associated with video production. Similar mechanisms such as skills mastery and changed perspectives of oneself and others have been used in previous studies (Johnson & Alderson, 2008).

Procedure. Typically, we insist that the WTU or hosting entity at a particular base vet and approve the workshop registrants based upon their team members' assessment of diagnosis, need, interest, and availability. It is important to note, however, that even though supervising therapists and health care personnel often must urge suitable candidates to register for the workshop, no one is required to participate. The veterans' willingness to take part in the workshop is an important element of its success.

The program consists of four half-day (3.5-hour) sessions for each participant, meaning that each participant comes for either four mornings or four afternoons. A team of five professional video editors/filmmakers supervise both sessions each day, with up to 15 participants per session, resulting in a 3:1 participant-instructor ratio. This low number of participants induces collaboration while still ensuring that each participant receives sufficient individual attention. It should be noted that even though such incidents happen rarely, we insist that a social worker or other qualified clinician from the hosting facility be on hand or immediately available to assist any participants who become aroused or visibly affected negatively during the workshop.

A Typical Workshop

The words "listen, collaborate, empower" also help to inform the practical flow of an IWT film workshop. What follows is a brief description of a typical workshop.

Day 1: Introductions and film exercise. This session is mostly about listening in both directions. After completing a short pre-workshop survey containing questions from the PTSD Checklist for the Military (PCL-M; APA, 2000) to assess their PTSD symptoms, the participants listen to us as we, the instructors, introduce ourselves in an effort to gain their trust, without which little or no productive work is possible. They need to understand that we instructors are sympathetic without being pandering and are technically qualified without talking down to them.

When holding a workshop at a base where we have worked previously, we usually have a veteran from a previous workshop share his or her experience and impart a few words of encouragement to the group. Then we listen to the veterans as they introduce themselves to us and to each other. An early revelation for us was that many of these veterans do not know one another, despite often residing in the same complex. Their introductions tend to reveal important details about their histories and personal circumstances, and how they came to attend the workshop, as well as how open they are to the experience ahead of them. Many recently deployed veterans, for instance, insist on sitting in the back row with their backs to the wall to avoid being startled by someone approaching them from behind. On average, 10% to 15% of the participants drop out of the workshop during or after Day 1.

Day 1 concludes with a simple group filmmaking exercise, which gives the participants an understanding of filmmaking basics, including storyboarding; video camera operation; production deadlines; how video allows one to "show" rather than "tell" a story; and the importance of teamwork, a concept that they all know well from their service. At the end of the session, we screen the films and happily inform the participating veterans that they are all now filmmakers! In our role as instructors, we then convene brief and private postmortem sessions immediately following the Day 1 sessions. This is a critical opportunity for us to share our impressions of the participants in regard to what we learned, whom we want to encourage to work together, and which instructor seems to connect the best with which group of veterans.

Day 2: Group brainstorming. At the start of Day 2, we screen a few carefully selected short films, including at least one produced at a previous workshop, to help the participants to understand that they can actually complete a coherent and meaningful film in just a few days. We also emphasize to the group that all of us are now filmmakers and that from here on, we should view ourselves as collaborators working together to make movies.

The rest of the session is spent brainstorming together and then in smaller groups of veterans and instructors to begin generating ideas that could actually lead to films. Each workshop session has room for 15 participants and five instructors. With five camera/editing packages per session, participants can form up to five production teams per session, each with a dedicated instructor. Participants start this session thinking about broad, relevant topics; ideally, they end it with a solid short film concept in mind and selection of the members of their production team.

With one production package (i.e., camera/laptop) per instructor (assuming five instructors), we encourage the participants to self-select into groups of two to four participants based upon their interest in the same film theme, shared histories or expertise, or any other criteria of their choosing. This group size induces collaboration without being so large as to leave some members without enough to do during postproduction. Production teams exchange contact information; develop a production schedule; determine props, wardrobe, and locations for the shoot day; and assign tasks. For many of the participants, this process draws directly on their experience as veterans working in teams.

By the end of Day 2, broad, often nonvisual, ideas must be distilled down to visual concepts that can realistically be transformed into finished films within two more sessions. In addition, the instructors' role in the conceptual process is critical in that an idea must be broad and relevant enough to each member of a group so that it is not considered the vision of only one person. We like to describe it this way: If three participants make a film that speaks to each of their experiences in some way, chances are that others beyond that group also will be able to relate to it. Once again, at the end of Day 2, the instructors convene privately to share and discuss observations, issues, or concerns about how the groups are coalescing and working together, and what changes, if any, should be made prior to the next session.

Day 3: Shoot day. This is the day when the groups normally shoot their films. We begin this session by screening a feature film scene that demonstrates shooting techniques that they might wish to use in their own short films (e.g., passage of time, pacing, establishment of shots, point-of-view shots, close-ups, etc.). By the end of Day 3, the groups have completed principal shooting of their films and have loaded them with assistance from their instructors onto their assigned laptops. This outcome enables the participants to finish the session feeling satisfied that they have the beginnings of a film in place. Collaboration now begins to give way to empowerment. Immediately following the session, the instructors meet again to discuss how things are going with the groups and to determine roles and responsibilities for the following day.

Day 4: Editing and reflection. Day 4 is the busiest day of the workshop for the participating veterans and the instructors. The groups that have completed shooting begin editing and selecting music to score their films. They title their films and add end credits or commemorations. They also are invited to participate in brief interviews conducted by the instructors to contextualize their films and reflect on the workshop experience. Although participation in these interviews is entirely voluntary, most of the veterans enjoy taking part in them because by then, they are invested in their films and are eager to share their reflections while the filmmaking experience is still fresh in their memories. Meanwhile, the members of each group do whatever is needed to finish, with the instructors doing everything to ensure that all participants complete their films and have the opportunity to screen them for all of the groups immediately following this session. All participants also complete a post-workshop survey to record any change in PTSD symptoms and answer a few more qualitative questions about the workshop experience. On the final day, we also invite, but never require, the participants to sign a written release granting us permission to share their films with the leadership, post them on our website, and publicize them at our discretion. To date, every participant in our workshops has signed this release, and no one has ever contacted us afterward to rescind this permission.

Immediately following the afternoon session on Day 4, we organize an informal screening of all of the films for all participants from the morning and afternoon sessions. Attendance at the screening is strictly voluntary. The opportunity for filmmakers to be present while having their work seen by others can validate the experience for these veterans while giving them the opportunity to see and affirm the work of the other participants. Many participants bring family members and friends to the screening. Usually, a general officer and members of the WTU or hospital leadership also will attend. We have found that most of the participants are eager to have their films seen by as broad an audience as possible.

Kinds of Films Made at IWT Workshops

The main advantage of the digital video medium is that it encompasses many other media, in addition to the verbal medium. Our participants have produced films with an array of styles and content using all manner of metaphor, symbol, and subtext. In terms of design and style, the films have represented a variety of media and genres, including spoken word/poetry, stop-action animation, music videos, public service announcements, marketing/promotions, comedy, documentaries, and narrative fiction. In terms of content, the films produced at the IWT film workshops generally center on themes relevant to the experiences of the attending veterans, including combat, physical or psychological injury, personal loss, stigma, suicide, military sexual trauma, domestic abuse, medical retirement, transition to civilian life, parenthood and family, and spirituality.

Impact of the Workshops

We are in the process of evaluating the impact and effectiveness of the workshops in alleviating PTSD symptoms and improving the participants' well-being. In our quantitative evaluation of more than 11 workshops, we tracked the changes in 10 symptoms of PTSD, as listed on the PCL-M (APA, 2000), and found an overall average symptom reduction of 17%. Notably, we found a 20% reduction in the following symptoms:

- Having difficulty concentrating.
- Being "super alert" or watchful or on guard.
- Feeling irritable or having angry outbursts.
- Avoiding thinking about or talking about a stressful experience or avoiding having feelings related to it.

This last symptom is particularly interesting, in that avoidance, as noted previously, is a primary reason why veterans who need and are entitled to treatment for mental health issues such as PTSD do not seek it. Because of our impression and that of others (e.g., Cohen, 2013; Johnson & Alderson, 2008) that merely tracking PTSD symptoms does not capture the full therapeutic value of this process, we qualitatively explored the participants' feedback about filmmaking and their workshop experience. Cohen (2013) noted that in video therapy sessions, the process is more important than the product.

Following are a few examples of the responses that the participants provided in written or oral testimonials immediately following the four-day workshop:

- "It was refreshing to interact with veterans in an artistic space rather than a clinical setting. The dialogue has no choice but to be different."
- "[Collaboration] was beneficial because it reinforced I'm not alone."
- "When I finally had a chance to show [the film] to my wife, she simply said,
- 'I finally get it.' She could finally come to terms and understand what I couldn't put into words."
- Female army noncommissioned officer (NCO) and multiple military sexual trauma (MST) survivor:

> Day 1, someone like me comes in unsure, not feeling at ease at all, and not sure how things are going to turn out. To Day 4, I'm coming in here with a smile on my face [and] feeling like I have a purpose in life.

- African American female NCO and MST survivor:

> This assault is what's really been haunting me in the worst dreams. It felt like the second day that I had a voice, a voice that I didn't have for so long, and everything in this movie is so symbolic of my life. And it really feels like I am empowered. I haven't been empowered in so long. I've been holding my head down. I was ready just to be a trooper through this whole thing. I wasn't trying to get anything out of it, just to check the [box], but I feel like it's changed my life because I get to tell how I feel and how it feels to not have a voice and just go along with everything. It feels good.
>
> After you get out of the military, it's very much an individual experience. You're thrown back into the world. You're no longer with your unit. You're doing on your own to readjust to civilian life. There's just something about slipping back into that fire team, that platoon, that section feel where you're with a bunch of people that had similar experiences and you're working towards a goal together. There's something beautiful about that.

Military spouses' responses to the films also have been sought as often as possible. Some examples are as follows:

- Wife of an army NCO who attended the workshop:

> This week, he's come home, and he's open and happy and talkative, and we have sat in the living room and talked. . . . It's refreshing. It's

special. . . . He was visually walking taller . . . happy. He had a smile on his face. He came home and accomplished other things at the house, finished projects. It was so uplifting to see him dealing, just dealing, and happy.

- Wife of an army NCO who had suffered a TBI, following the couple's completion of a film at our workshop: "I thought the filmmaking process was cathartic because we were able to express our individual roles that we actually lived as witness."

CONCLUSION

In this chapter, we described a new mode of working with military veterans through the creation of short films to help them to cope with some of the adversities that they experienced during their service. It is by now well documented and accepted that hundreds of thousands of American veterans are in need of mental health services and continue to struggle after returning from the combat zones of Afghanistan, Iraq, and elsewhere. Despite a wealth of therapeutic interventions targeted at this population, many veterans are not being helped by existing therapies for a variety of reasons, some of which we described in this chapter.

Our claim is that for many veterans, the IWT film workshop model offers a promising new treatment pathway, partly because of its collaborative nature and also because it is a stigma-free activity unencumbered by the formats or procedures associated with more traditional interventions. Theoretically speaking, our model is different from therapies that require full and repeated disclosure of traumatic events as part of therapy (e.g., Peri & Gofman, 2014). Because we view trauma as shattering the veterans' sense of agency and control, we argue that regaining self-confidence and control in their lives is even more critical for recovering veterans than their reexposure to the trauma. Our workshop participants always make the decision either to disclose their trauma narratives or to keep them private. We ask the participants to direct their own films so that they become the authors of their own narratives and can choose how to present them.

Because the workshops and their evaluation are quite new, we are still left with several open questions:

- Who benefits from this process, or to put it differently, for whom might this tool/intervention be the most effective?
- Which mechanisms are responsible for improvements in PTSD symptoms?
- Does the workshop have a long-term impact on the participants' general well-being?
- Is it the collaboration, the listening, the ability to share, the empowerment, or all of them together? Which is most effective?

We plan to study these questions as we continue to complete workshops. For example, we have already begun to evaluate participants' responses to the workshop over a longer period. We also are adding other measures of mental well-being to our toolkit.

Another consideration is that the workshop facilitators must have a high level of sensitivity to such ethical issues as decisions about who can participate and the ways in which they can be kept safe when listening to other participants' narratives about the trauma of war and combat. With this responsibility in mind, we insist that a clinician always be on site during a workshop and available for immediate consultation. This ethical sensitivity also must extend to the instructors, typically young professional producer-editors in their 20s or 30s who seldom have a military background. We are keenly aware that their cumulative exposure to the veterans' trauma over several workshops might prove harmful to them, so we insist that the instructors meet each day during a workshop to share and discuss their experiences. Follow-up instructor surveys and post-workshop discussions also are routine.

Two of the most important questions are these: (a) What is the long-term impact of these workshops on the participants' well-being? and (b) Does the workshop open the way to other types of interventions? Whether the workshop is considered an intervention or simply an "ice breaker" that can motivate a participating veteran to seek further care, we believe that based upon our initial findings, the process is therapeutic.

For the participants' positive shifts and achievements to endure, the workshop should be more than just a standalone event; rather, it must be used as an early element of a multistep recovery process. Subsequent steps can include taking the film to a therapist, an art therapist, or a social worker and processing it there with that professional or taking part in a subsequent IWT film workshop as a mentor who supports new participants in their creative process.

It is our hope and intention to broaden the target population for the IWT film workshop sessions. We believe that a similar process can benefit military families in general by helping them to cope with the challenges associated with reintegration issues. We further believe that this model can be applied successfully to nonmilitary populations and families coping with the effects of trauma in their lives.

REFERENCES

American Psychiatric Association. (2000). *Diagnostic and statistical manual of mental disorders* (4th ed.). Washington, DC: Author.

American Psychological Association and Presidential Task Force on Military Deployment Services for Youth, Families and Service Members (2007). *The psychological needs of US military service members and their families: A preliminary report.* Washington, DC: American Psychological Association.

Berntsen, D., & Rubin, D.C. (2004). Cultural life scripts structure recall from autobiographical memory. *Memory & Cognition, 32*(3), 427–442.

Berntsen, D., & Rubin, D.C. (2006). Centrality of Event Scale: A measure of integrating a trauma into one's identity and its relation to post-traumatic stress disorder symptoms. *Behavior Research and Therapy, 44*(2), 219–231.

Berntsen, D., & Rubin, D.C. (2007). When a trauma becomes a key to identity: Enhanced integration of trauma memories predicts posttraumatic stress disorder symptoms. *Applied Cognitive Psychology, 21*(4), 417–431.

Bowling, U.B., & Sherman, M.D. (2008). Welcoming them home: Supporting service members and their families in navigating the tasks of reintegration. *Professional Psychology: Research and Practice, 39*(4), 451–458. doi:10.1037/0735-7028.39.4.451

Breslau, N. (2009). The epidemiology of trauma, PTSD, and other posttrauma disorders. *Trauma, Violence, & Abuse, 10*(3), 198–210. doi:10.1177/1524838009334448

Brewin, C. (1996). Theoretical foundations of cognitive-behavior therapy for anxiety and depression. *Annual Review of Psychology, 47*, 33–57.

Brewin, C., Andrews, B., & Valentine, J. (2000). Meta-analysis of risk factors for posttraumatic stress disorder in trauma-exposed adults. *Journal of Consulting and Clinical Psychology, 68*(5), 748–766.

Brewin, C., Dalgleish, T., & Joseph, S. (1996). A dual representation theory of posttraumatic stress disorder. *Psychological Review, 103*(4), 670–686.

Castillo, D.T., C'de Baca, J., Qualls, C., & Bornovalova, M.A. (2012). Group exposure therapy treatment for post-traumatic stress disorder in female veterans. *Military Medicine, 177*(12), 1486–1491.

Cohen, J.L. (2013). *Film and soul: A theoretical exploration of the use of video and other film-based therapy to help transform identity in therapeutic practice* (Doctoral dissertation). Available from ProQuest Dissertations and Theses database. (UMI No. 3551606)

Ehlers, A., Mayou, R.A., & Bryant, B. (1998). Psychological predictors of chronic posttraumatic stress disorder after motor vehicle accidents. *Journal of Abnormal Psychology, 107*(3), 508–519.

Foa, E.B., Steketee, G., & Rothbaum, B.O. (1989). Behavioral/cognitive conceptualisation of post-traumatic stress disorder. *Behavior Therapy, 20*(2), 155–176.

Gidron, Y., Duncan, E., Lazar, A., Biderman, A., Tandeter, H., & Schvartzman, P. (2002). Effects of guided written disclosure of stressful experiences on clinic visits and symptoms in frequent clinic attenders. *Family Practice, 19*(2), 161–166.

Halligan, S.L., Michael, T., Clark, D.M., & Ehlers, A. (2003). Posttraumatic stress disorder following assault: The role of cognitive processing, trauma memory and appraisals. *Journal of Consulting and Clinical Psychology, 71*(3), 419–431.

Henry, M., Cortes, A., Morris, S., Khadduri, J., & Culhane, D.P. (2013). *The 2013 Annual Homelessness Assessment Report (AHAR) to Congress: Part 1, Point-in-Time Estimates of Homelessness*. Retrieved from https://www.hudexchange.info/resources/documents/AHAR-2013-Part1.pdf

Hoge, C. (2010). *Once a warrior: Navigating the transition from combat to home, including combat stress, PTSD and MTBI*. Guilford, CT: Globe Pequot PressLife.

Hoge, C., Auchterlonie, J.L., & Milliken, C.S. (2006). Mental health problems, use of mental health services, and attrition from military service after returning from deployment to Iraq or Afghanistan. *Journal of the American Medical Association*, 295(9), 1023–1032. doi:10.1001/jama.295.9.1023

Hoge, C., Castro, C.A., Messer, S.C., McGurk, D., Cotting, D.I., & Koffman, R.L. (2004). Combat duty in Iraq and Afghanistan, mental health problems, and barriers to care. *New England Journal of Medicine*, 351(1), 13–22. doi:10.1056/NEJMoa040603

Janoff-Bulman, R. (1992). *Shattered assumptions: Towards a new psychology of trauma*. New York, NY: Free Press.

Johnson, J. L., & Alderson, K. G. (2008). Therapeutic filmmaking: An exploratory pilot study. *Arts in Psychotherapy, 35*(1), 11–19.

Kenny, L. M., Bryant, R. A., Silove, D., Creamer, M., O'Donnell, M., & McFarlane, A. C. (2009). Distant memories: A prospective study of vantage point of trauma memories. *Psychological Science, 20*(9), 1049–1052. doi:10.1111/j.1467-9280.2009.02393.x

Kessler, R. C. (2000). Posttraumatic stress disorder: The burden to the individual and to society. *Journal of Clinical Psychiatry, 61*(5), 4–12.

Kessler, R. C., Chiu, W. T., Demler, O., Merikangas, K. R., & Walters, E. E. (2005). Prevalence, severity, and comorbidity of 12-month *DSM-IV* disorders in the National Comorbidity Survey replication. *Archives of General Psychiatry, 62*(6), 617–627.

Kuehn, B. M. (2009). Soldier suicide rates continue to rise: Medical news & perspectives. *Journal of the American Medical Association, 301*(11), 1111–1113. doi:10.1001/jama.2009.342

Lieblich, A., Tuval-Mashiach, R., & Zilber, T. (1998). *Narrative research: Reading, analysis and interpretation*. Thousand Oaks, CA: Sage.

McAdams, D. P. (2008). Personal narratives and the life story. In O. John, R. Robins, & L. A. Pervin (Eds.), *Handbook of personality: Theory and research* (pp. 241–261). New York, NY: Guilford Press.

Najavits, L. M., Norman, S. B., Kivlahan, D., & Kosten, T. R. (2010). Improving PTSD/substance abuse treatment in the VA: A survey of providers. *American Journal on Addictions, 19*, 257–263. doi:10.1111/j.1521-0391.2010.00039.x

National Center for Injury Prevention and Control. (2011). Web-based injury statistics query and reporting system (WIQARS). Retrieved from http://www.cdc.gov/

Norris, F. H., Friedman, M. J., Watson, P. J., Byrne, C. M., Diaz, E., & Kaniasty, K. (2002). 60,000 disaster victims speak: Part I. An empirical review of the empirical literature, 1981–2001. *Psychiatry: Interpersonal and Biological Processes, 65*(3), 207–239.

O'Kearney, R., & Perrott, K. (2006). Trauma narratives in posttraumatic stress disorder: A review. *Journal of Traumatic Stress, 19*(1), 81–93.

Omer, A., & Alon, N. (1997). *Constructing therapeutic narratives*. Lanham, MD: Jason Aronson.

Ouimette, P., Vogt, D., Wade, M., Tirone, V., Greenbaum, M. A., Kimerling, R., . . . Rosen, C. S. (2011). Perceived barriers to care among veterans health administration patients with posttraumatic stress disorder. *Psychological Services*, 8(3), 212–223. doi:10.1037/a0024360

Paley, B., Lester, P., & Mogil, C. (2013). Family systems and ecological perspectives on the impact of deployment on military families. *Clinical Child and Family Psychology Review, 16*(3), 245–265.

Pennebaker, J. W., & Seagal J. D. (1999). Forming a story: The health benefits of narrative. *Journal of Clinical Psychology, 55*(10), 1243–1254.

Peri, T., & Gofman, M. (2014). Narrative reconstruction: An integrative intervention module for intrusive symptoms in PTSD patients. *Psychological Trauma: Theory, Research, Practice, and Policy, 6*(2), 176–183. doi:10.1037/a0031965

Peterson, A. L., Luethke, C. A., Borah, E., Borah, A., & Young-McCaughan, S. (2011). Assessment and treatment of combat related PTSD. *Journal of Clinical Psychology in Medical Settings, 18*(2), 164–175. doi:10.1007/s10880-011-9238-3

Resick, P. A. (2001). Cognitive therapy for post traumatic stress disorder. *Journal of Cognitive Psychotherapy, 15*(4), 321–329.

Richards, J. M., Beal, W. E., Seagal, J. D., & Pennebaker, J. W. (2000). Effects of disclosure of traumatic events on illness behavior among psychiatric prison inmates. *Journal of Abnormal Psychology, 109*(1), 156–160.

Richardson, L. K., Frueh, B. C., & Acierno, R. (2010). Prevalence estimates of combat-related post-traumatic stress disorder: Critical review. *Australian and New Zealand Journal of Psychiatry, 44*(1), 4–19. doi:10.3109/00048670903393597

Schafer, R. (1981). Narration in the psychoanalytic dialogue. *Critical Inquiry, 7*, 29–53.

Schauer, M., Neuner, F., & Elbert, T. (2005). Narrative exposure therapy (NET): A short-term intervention for traumatic stress disorders after war, terror or torture. Seattle, WA: Hogrefe.

Shalev, A. Y., Freedman, S., Peri, T., Brandes, D., Sahar, T., Orr, S. P., & Pitman, R. K. (1998). Prospective study of posttraumatic stress disorder and depression following trauma. *American Journal of Psychiatry, 155*(5), 630–637.

Shalev, A. Y., Tuval-Mashiach, R., Frenkiel-Fishman, S., Hadar, H., & Eth, S. (2006). Psychological responses to continuous terror: A study of two communities in Israel. *American Journal of Psychiatry, 163*(4), 667–673.

Shane, L., III. (2014, January 9). Report: Suicide rate spikes among young veterans. *Stars and Stripes*. Retrieved from http://www.stripes.com/

Shay, J. (1994). *Achilles in Viet Nam: Combat trauma and the undoing of character*. New York, NY: Scribner.

Shay, J. (2010). The trauma of war. In A. Himes (Ed.), *Voices in wartime: The anthology* (Kindle Edition version). Retrieved from Amazon.com

Siegel, B. S., & Davis, B. E. (2013). Health and mental health needs of children in US military families. *Pediatrics, 131*(6), e2002–e2015.

Stiles, W. B., Honos-Webb, L., & Lani, J. A. (1999). Some functions of narrative in the assimilation of problematic experiences. *Journal of Clinical Psychology, 55*(10), 1–14.

Tanielian, T., & Jaycox, L. H. (Eds.). (2008). Invisible wounds of war psychological and cognitive injuries, their consequences, and services to assist recovery. Retrieved from http://www.rand.org/

Tuval-Mashiach, R., Freedman, S., Bargay, N., Boker, R., Hadar, H., & Shalev, A. Y. (2004). Coping with trauma—Narrative and cognitive perspectives. *Psychiatry: Interpersonal and Biological Processes, 67*(3), 280–293.

U.S. Department of Labor (2014). Employment situation summary news release. Retrieved from http://www.bls.gov/news.release/empsit.nr0.htm

van Minnen, A., Wessel, I., Dijkstra, T., & Roelofs, K. (2002). Changes in PTSD patients' narratives during prolonged exposure therapy: A replication and extension. *Journal of Traumatic Stress, 15*(3), 225–258.

Vaughn, J. R. (2009). Invisible wounds: Serving service members and veterans with PTSD and TBI. Retrieved from www.ncd.gov/

Wedding, D., & Niemiec, R. M. (2003). The clinical use of films in psychotherapy [Special issue]. *Journal of Clinical Psychology, 59*(2), 207–215. doi:10.1002/jclp.10142

White, M., & Epston, D. (1990). *Narrative means to therapeutic ends*. New York, NY: W. W. Norton.

Wigren, J. (1994). Narrative completion in the treatment of trauma. *Psychotherapy: Theory, Research, Practice, Training, 31*(3), 415–423.

13 Felt Sensing Video Art Therapy

Yarden Kerem

In this chapter, I present a unique and exciting therapy approach: a combination of video art therapy and the natural ability to find and feel the felt sense of situations as they are presented in the focusing method and the somatic experiencing method. Both approaches deal with the person's natural ability to sense the body and find the bodily sensation of the topic brought to therapy. The *felt sense* is a bodily sensation of a given situation, and it includes an understanding and meaning of that situation. In the felt sensing video art therapy model, the symbolization of the felt sense is visual or auditory, or both. The *focusing method* teaches that if the person experiences the felt sense and finds a symbolization for it, an inner movement toward change and relief takes place. The *somatic experiencing* method, which is used to treat people who have suffered trauma, teaches that traumas exist in the body because of the high level of energy that is present in the body when facing painful or threatening situations. This energy remains in the body. The goal of somatic experiencing is to teach clients how to release the energy from traumatic events that has accumulated in their bodies. This therapeutic model, which I developed, combines art therapy with the focusing method developed by Dr. Eugene T. Gendlin (2001) and somatic experiencing, the method developed by Dr. Peter A. Levine (1997), to treat trauma. Both approaches begin with inner work on clients' issues, what Gendlin called finding the "felt sense" (2000, [1996], p. 22). Clients learn to pay attention to their inner selves, so that they can recognize the feelings that come up inside them before each exercise, and to find the symbols that describe these feelings. In this model, therapists work with clients as the latter create videos with abstract characters and sound. In this chapter, I describe the connection between video art and focusing and then explain the connection between video art and somatic experiencing. The photos in this chapter are works of students in the Department of Therapy through Video in the Ma'ale Film School in Jerusalem. The photos in this article are works of students in the Department of Therapy through Video in the Ma'ale Film School in Jerusalem.

Figure 13.1 Image of a woman's face behind broken glass
Keren Hakak, by Daniel Clastornik

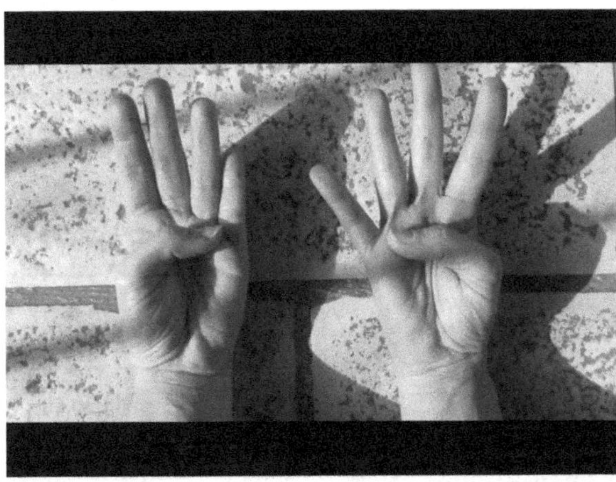

Figure 13.2 Two hands holding up 4 fingers each
By Keren Hakak

VIDEO ART

In video art, images are placed alongside one another, with or without a soundtrack, to express an idea. Most works of video art are short, sometimes only several minutes long, and do not necessarily have protagonists, conflicts, stories, or plots. The characters might even be abstract. Through the images, the video camera can express or symbolize emotional states, moods, ideas, reflections, or negative feelings that cannot be expressed in words. Video art, the filming of abstract images with a soundtrack, opens a new horizon of expression for clients.

Focusing

Focusing means spending time with something bodily sensed but unclear, until it comes "into focus" (Gendlin, 1996, p. 1). Gendlin (1996), a philosopher and psychologist at the University of Chicago, conceived the focusing method. He asserted that the human body contains information about all the situations that individuals encounter in their lives. When people pay attention to their bodies and their sensations, they receive information that had been hidden within the body:

> focusing is a mode of inward bodily attention that is not yet known to most people. . . . It differs from the usual attention we pay to feelings because it begins with the body and occurs in the zone between the conscious and the unconscious. Most people don't know that a bodily sense of any topic can be invited to come in that zone, and that one can enter into such a sense. At first it is only a vague discomfort, but soon it becomes a distinct sense with which one can work, and in which one can sort out many strands.
>
> (Gendlin, 1996, p. 1)

When individuals stay with and pay attention to the bodily sensations that happen regarding certain subjects, they allow the information contained implicitly within their bodies to emerge and be explicit. Focusing is the act of contemplating, that is, of paying attention within to recognize the bodily feelings created regarding the topics being addressed in therapy. It involves the symbolization of these feelings using words or other methods, such as movement or artistic expression. Symbolization of inner feeling brings people closer to themselves and their own authentic feelings. Symbolization of the inner world is a process that leads to psychological change and growth.

When people pay attention to their sensations regarding the topics being addressed in therapy, they learn how their bodies are carrying and holding on to past situations. In this way, the human body is like a monument to human problems (Gendlin, 2001), taking on the form of whatever is causing it distress. It contracts and responds to disruptions in life. When individuals become aware of the ways in which their bodies are experiencing problems and describe them, they give symbolization to the experience. A felt shift is created, enabling the individuals' bodies to change the ways they hold the situations and giving the individuals a chance to learn new ways to live with the problem. More details are provided later.

Experience

Gendlin (1962) studied the concept of experiencing to emphasize its reference to events that are happening at the present moment, together with the place of experience in human existence. Gendlin wrote about the major role of experience in human life, claiming that, together with a logical-rational dimension and the operational dimension of knowledge, human lives also hold a dimension of sensation that can be felt and experienced directly. Gendlin explained that although earlier philosophers recognized the presence of experience, along with the creation of meaning within it, they understood experience as logical schemes that organized the perception of feeling. The modern philosophers who have written about the role of experience in human life treat experience as something vague, the importance of which is recognized only at significant junctures in life.

Gendlin (1962) treated experience as something that is always present and has power. He asserted that some dimension of experience precedes logic and has a major role in the world of thought, understanding, and behavior. The dimension of feeling has decisive significance for all human behavior, be it healthy or unhealthy, which is why Gendlin studied it. He sought to bring clients to prelogical and preconceptual dimensions because the meaning of experience cannot be understood if individuals stay within the logical dimension exclusively. The dimension of feeling must be addressed directly. Experience is real and tangible. Experience is what people feel when they say, "I feel such-and-such." Human beings have the ability to direct their awareness to that "such-and-such," and they can direct their attention to this feeling at any given moment (Rice, 2008).

The Felt Sense

Gendlin described the felt sense as being greater than the sum of its parts, an implied feeling the body has about complex situations:

> A felt sense is a bodily sensation, but it is not merely a physical sensation like a tickle or a pain. Rather, it is a physical sense of something, of meaning, of implicit intricacy. It is a sense of a whole situation or problem or concern, or perhaps a point one wants to convey. It is not just a bodily sense, but rather a bodily sense of. (1996, p. 63)

In later work, Gendlin (2001) asserted that every event has its own physical feeling. Focusing allows individuals to come into contact with a special kind of inner body awareness, namely, the felt sense, or the physical feeling associated with the specific experience (Gendlin, 1996; Perl, 2004). Although the felt sense refers to physical feeling, it refers not only to such physical responses as a lump in the throat or a clenching in the belly, but also to a physical sense of significance. The felt sense is "a body sense of meaning" (Gendlin, 1996, p. 56) and is a major tenet of Gendlin's philosophy.

The concept of felt sense is complex because it refers to a physical feeling that contains emotions, imagery, thoughts, memories, and desires. The felt sense is a description of the way that the human body registers an experience and holds on to that experience. Although the felt sense is mostly the answer to the question, "How does my body feel right now?" it is highly complex. People have a felt sense for every situation that they encounter, and the body creates a felt sense for every life issue that people encounter.

The felt sense is very difficult to notice or pay attention to at first because it is not obvious or clear (Gendlin, 1996). Sometimes, the feeling is not comfortable or pleasant because it invites individuals to experience what lies at the edge of the mind, the edge of perception, in places or situations that cannot yet be expressed in words. Felt sense is not merely an emotion, a physical sensation, or a thought. It is a sensation with profound significance that gradually becomes clear in a systematic process of deep listening. According to Gendlin, that feeling, which is so difficult to notice initially, has significance.

When people are present and pay attention to this felt sense, they receive more information and knowledge about the situations and issues that they are dealing with in the form of thoughts, insights, images, emotions, desires, memories, and additional physical sensations. Words or sentences connected to the situations might emerge as well. When people pay attention to the felt sense, it shares the body's information about situations. Only our bodies know our problems and know where their roots are (Gendlin, 2001).

The felt sense is not something that exists. It is something that takes form, is created, and arises. It contains the past, senses the present, and acts toward the future. People can allow the body to experience the felt sense by

Figure 13.3 Image of a woman (whole body) under mattress
Keren Hakak, by Daniel Clastornik

creating a space for it. They cannot make it come by force or by will; rather, it will come if people make room for it. If people pay attention to the felt sense, it will offer images; bring ideas, memories, and emotions; and express what lies within the issues currently at hand (Perl, 2004). Gendlin (1962) believed that the felt sense must receive symbolization. Human life contains the infinite passage between feeling and symbolization, as I discuss in detail in the next section.

Symbol

Gendlin (1997) believed that although the life situations and events that people experience are always more delicate and complex than can be expressed in words, much of human life takes place in symbolic space. Human beings use speech and thought to turn the feelings that they experience in their bodies from implicit to explicit. Every word and idea starts with a feeling.

Gendlin (as cited in Rice, 2008) believed that people first experience meaning through feeling sense. Human life is a reciprocal relationship between the rich, full, and complex experiences that form and exist within events and the concepts that people use to express those situations. Human life is an interaction between the immediacy of what people are feeling and experiencing in the present and the forms or concepts that they use to express these feelings. A feeling that does not receive symbolization is blind in the sense that it cannot explain itself (Gendlin, 1962). The relationship between experience and symbolization is complex. These are not two different things that adhere together.

Gendlin said that the person becomes acquainted with the world through his body. In other words, a newborn infant is not a *tabula rasa*. The infant knows human history and culture. This means that there is no pure experience without symbolization; symbolization is already present within the experience itself. The moment a person feels a sensation, there is already meaning and understanding to that sensation. The meaning or understanding is the symbolization that the person gives to the experience. The opposite also is true: A sensation exists in every symbolization. But experiencing and concepts (or symbols) are surely not two separated things that have to become *related*. Each is always already implicit in the other. There is no *unsymbolized experiencing* any more than there is *pure logic*. Gendlin's (1962) philosophy discussed the various relationships that exist between experience and the verbal symbolization of experience. Although his philosophy on that topic is interesting, it is beyond the scope of this chapter. As stated earlier, most symbolization occurs through the use of words, but this chapter is a discussion of symbolization using images and sound.

Other philosophers have spoken of the interaction between an experience and symbolization. The discussion is mostly about the verbal symbolization of the feeling. One example is Lacan's theory of the three registers: the real, the symbolic, and the imaginary (as cited in Bowie, 2005). Lacan claimed that the word is on a symbolic plane and that a space exists between the word and the Thing itself, to the point where the Thing disappears. Words are the death of the Thing. Human beings use language to express themselves in a way that is almost taken for granted. Despite the supposed consensus that language transmits everything that human beings wish to transmit, many people feel that this is not so and that language is limited. Words cannot express the entire spectrum of emotions that a person feels. Language fails to represent or symbolize what a human being feels.

In the same vein, Ronen (2010) wrote:

> The symbolic is an indication that language does not conceptualize. On the contrary, it creates an obstacle, preventing the possibility of reaching the object itself, the thing for which it was created. In this sense, speech, unlike imagery, is by its very nature the absence of the object, while imagery pretends to convey and even reflect the object. (p. 11)

This is where video art therapy enters the picture. I propose that, through video art therapy, symbolization takes place in visual or auditory images rather than in words. In the process of video art therapy, therapists suggest that clients pay attention to the issues that they have brought to therapy. The therapist encourages the client to enter a space of focusing that invites the client to pay attention to his or her body and sensations so that the client can identify feelings, recognize them, and give them symbolization. The client gives these identified feelings symbolization through creating a video; recording sound; or using prerecorded sound such as music, sound effects, or any other existing audio. The use of video and sound gives clients more ways to give symbolization to their feelings. Focusing teaches clients the technique of paying attention to the experiences taking place in their bodies that happen at every moment and to find symbols for them.

Figure 13.4 Image of a woman's head and arm under mattress

Keren Hakak, by Daniel Clastornik

Video art therapy allows clients to symbolize images by using video. Therapists support their clients throughout the process in the following ways:

- Choosing the subject (either by using focusing to find what is bothering the clients at that moment of their lives or by engaging in traditional therapy conversation).
- Directing clients' attention inward to allow the felt sense to surface.
- Staying with the felt sense to allow visual images that express the topic to arrive.
- Using editing software to edit the resulting video.

The next section is a discussion of the therapeutic significance of editing the images.

VIDEO ART SOUND THERAPY

After this work model was developed, I met with Gittit Pearlmutter, a musician and sound editor. We added to the existing model a deeper approach to working with a soundtrack, which takes the form of working with three major channels: speech, sound effects, and music. Because most people focus on visual elements and do not pay attention to the sounds that are constantly around them, I felt that it would be appropriate to concentrate on working with sound. The request to create sound effects leads to fascinating inner work and new avenues of expression. For many clients, working with sound opens up a new channel of inner listening and symbolization of feeling. This model offers clients the ability to work in stages on symbolization through sound: Once clients have chosen the subjects and images to express them, they are asked to create their own sound effects. Then, once the sound effects have been uploaded with the images to the editing software, and after talking about them, clients are asked to create a speech channel that expresses the subjects. Finally, clients are asked to add music.

The second stage is that of recording speech, such as a monologue, a dialogue, or a conversation, whatever the clients feel is appropriate. Pearlmutter and I chose recording speech as the second stage of the work because speech remains an option for highly private self-expression. In the third stage, music is taken mostly from excerpts that are available and well known, unless the clients happen to be musicians. Pearlmutter noted that the choice of sound and images creates nonverbal substance for clients that develops as the sessions continue.

The Work Model

In the work model of felt sensing video art therapy, therapists give clients time to pay attention to their felt sense about particular issues and to see whether audiovisual images that describe the feeling come to consciousness. Although old materials from photographic or sound archives might be used, I prefer the model in which clients photograph and record material from the present (or a combination of both options). In other words, therapists and clients might go outside the clinic so that clients can find images or symbols that symbolize feelings. Clients also can search for images or create them during the week or between sessions, or bring in older materials. Therapists can suggest subjects for the clients to work on, or they can work on specific issues that the clients bring to therapy. Any subjects that the clients bring in can be subject to audiovisual symbolization.

When Gittit Pearlmutter and I teach the course in the videotherapy track at the Ma'aleh School in Jerusalem, we suggest to our students that they submit exercises according to the following list:

- My wound—work on the wound/trauma, pain, difficulty.
- The image that heals the wound—what makes me healthy, what heals me.
- A self-portrait.
- How I want to see myself in the future—in 5 years, in 10 years.
- The humanity within me.
- The godliness within me—my religion/faith.
- My image of myself.
- How other people see me (the image I believe that others have of me).
- An important moment, event, or year in my life.
- Difficulty with a certain person.
- Choosing a significant place and filming the way there or back.
- A journey between two significant points in life. A student might choose two significant physical places. The purpose of the sound work (described next) is to express the feeling of the journey between them.

This model offers clients the opportunity to work with editing software. Just as plastic arts therapy involves working with paint, paper, or clay for sculpture, and music therapy involves working with musical instruments kept in the treatment room, video art therapy requires a video camera and editing software. The therapeutic space should contain, maintain, and enable creative experimentation.

When focusing accompanies the therapeutic/artistic process, therapists take the position of acceptance. Clients are invited to meet what is within themselves, and therapists sit at their clients' side to accompany them throughout the process, making the focusing space available to the clients and inviting them to be in touch with the issues that are important to the therapy. The therapists also invite clients to bring audiovisual material to the sessions and edit it as they sit side by side.

Clients upload the material to the editing program for viewing and editing during the sessions. This model advises that therapists be close to clients when the material is being edited because the therapeutic process also takes place there, that is, during contemplation of the material on the time line in the editing software and in the clients' responses to the material. As clients respond, therapeutic conversations take place that can be either traditional therapeutic dialogues or, more precisely, conversations typical of art therapy that fluctuate between talking about the artwork and about the problems or subjects that the clients have brought to therapy. An alternative could be focusing therapy, a process in which therapists echo back to clients what the clients have brought to therapy.

During the editing process, therapists can ask their clients questions about the artwork, as well as their feelings and thoughts about it, such as:

- Response to the visual or audio material—What do you feel about this? Does it remind you of anything?
- What do you wish to express through the image and the sound? What do you want to say?
- Is there something specific that you want to emphasize?
- What do you choose to put in the beginning, the middle, and the end?
- What items do you choose to put next to each other in the work? An image next to an image, and sound next to sound? What is the meaning of the link between the image and the sound?
- What is difficult or painful for you during the process?
- What did you choose to cut from the final product? What was filmed or recorded that did not become part of the work?

In some cases, the material omitted is actually the most important.

The questions are an invitation to clients to observe and study the self. There are no correct answers; rather, the important thing is the clients' observations of self and the artwork being created. The questions can be asked at times when the clients pause and are engaging in inner contemplation and contemplation of the artwork. Silence is an acceptable response. Therapists mirror the clients' answers to give the thing a name, give the feeling a presence, and confirm that there is room and validity in the world for the clients' feelings, thoughts, and images.

Therapists who use the focusing approach allow clients time to focus. Clients might take the questions into themselves and see what comes up in their bodies following the questions, but they are not obliged to answer any questions. In the world of focusing, it is preferable to call these questions *invitations*, by which therapists solicit clients to pay attention to themselves deep within. This invitation does not require an answer. Even if clients describe what is happening inside themselves, thus supposedly answering the question, they can answer using new images, such as by describing bodily sensations or memories, or creating via photography, recording, or editing.

Therapists guiding the process according to focusing principles should give clients time to examine their artwork after every change (large or small) in editing so that they can see whether the work (visual symbolization, auditory symbolization, and the connection between them) appropriately expresses their inner feelings. Clients should feel that the audiovisual symbolization describes their feelings accurately and precisely. The goal of the work is not to create what art critics would consider good works of video art; instead, the goal is to create works that express and give symbolization to the clients' inner worlds. This is why the work is called felt sensing video art therapy.

The issue of precision in the way the video art work expresses the sensation calls to mind the concept of the *punctum* as laid out by literary theorist and cultural critic Roland Barthes. In his work *Camera Lucida: Reflections on Photography* (1981), Barthes described the feelings of a person viewing a photograph as two distinct sensations, the *studium* and the *punctum*. The studium is the cultural, linguistic, and political significance of a photograph to the viewer, while the punctum, "that which pierces," is the viewer's purely personal response to a specific detail of the image. Barthes, who wrote about photography before the age of Photoshop, described the feeling of the punctum as a sensation that says, "That's it!" This is something in the image that draws attention, awakening a desire in the viewer to become acquainted with the figure in the image. The model of therapy via creating video art does not require that the image be a character. Rather, it allows the unique meeting that takes place between the image and the viewer to become something that pierces the heart, even if the viewer is the one who created the image. That is the moment of the unique meeting between the person and a powerful inner sensation—the symbolization touches something deep within the person, and something within the person changes.

If therapists work according to the principles of focusing, they do not interpret what clients bring in, be it audiovisual material, the video artwork in progress, or what the clients say. The basic assumption of the focusing approach is that if people pay attention to themselves, the information about their situations will come from the body: "Nothing is more important than the person inside. Therapy exists for the person inside; it has no other purpose. When the inner being comes alive, or even stirs just a little, it is more important than any diagnosis or evaluation" (Gendlin, 1996, p. 23). The focusing approach suggests that therapists echo to clients what the clients have brought to therapy. In other words, the therapists can repeat the clients' words or reflect what they see in the work, not as interpretation, but as a description that attempts to be as faithful as possible to the facts. The therapists describe what they see and hear. I discuss the therapeutic significance of echoing later in this chapter.

If therapists are not guiding the focusing processes, then one must consider the place of the therapists' interpretations. Flusser wrote that "images are significant surface" (2014, p. 11). If we wish to deepen the significance, we must allow the eye to travel over the surface. Flusser wrote that the eye traveled a complex path outlined by the visual structure on the one hand and by the viewer's intentions on the other. In other words, images are not denotative complexes of symbols, like numbers, but connotative complexes of symbols that allow room for interpretation. Therapists who interpret the images from what they see within their own world may be interpreting wrongly.

I believe that it is difficult for us as therapists to avoid falling into the trap of expressing ourselves and our inner worlds when we view abstract material. On the other hand, because much of the material is very powerful, it is not right to not respond in some way. I suggest that therapists respond to the material with general statements such as, "The work is very powerful," or share their personal experience on viewing the material. The therapeutic process happens during the creation of the artwork itself and in the

Figure 13.5 Image of man looking at computer
Ziv Shiloach looking at his work

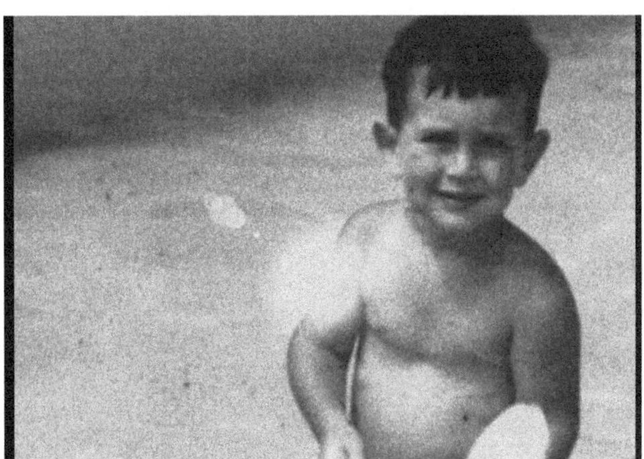

Figure 13.6 Image of child
By Ziv Shiloach

therapeutic conversations that take place alongside it. Regarding therapeutic conversations, this model has nothing new to offer: Therapeutic conversations are a time for clients to investigate the video art work and discover themselves.

Editing as a Therapeutic Tool

This model suggests the use of editing as a therapeutic tool. Editing brings clients' personal stories, pain, conflicts, and wounds into an organized arrangement that did not exist previously. The audio and visual images allow clients to symbolize and organize inner chaos in some form. Editing requires that clients themselves choose what comes first, what comes second, and so on, until the end. Clients decide what will go beside what, what will be in front and what will be on the sides, and what will receive a great deal of screen time and what will receive less.

Editing is a process that takes time. It does not happen in a moment. It requires imagination, contemplation, attentiveness, thought, planning, and decision making, including the ability to decide what will be left out of the final work. Editing involves making choices and concessions, and being able to delay gratification in order to see that something new has been created after all the concessions have been made. Editing permits repeated approaches at various levels of processing that promote inner observation and internalization. It is a crystallizing experience.

In an extraordinary way, editing allows for the playspace that Winnicott (2010) spoke of. The time line in the editing software in which the materials are placed and edited is a wonderful playspace for an adult (Winnicott, 2010). In addition, editing allows clients to see, experience, and hear themselves or their stories in various ways. Every change in editing results in a change in the way the person observes himself/herself because the change requires a different kind of observation. Therefore, editing allows therapists to ask clients questions in many ways and from various angles. Each change in editing invites observations and questions for the clients.

When the work is ready and clients no longer wish to change and edit it, they take responsibility for the story described in the work. If the work dealt with the parts (the images and soundtrack) up to that point, now a work of video art exists that clients stand behind and to which they are committed. It is as if clients are saying, through the work: "This is who I am. This is my situation." They are no longer dealing with the small details but with a work, and a situation, as a whole.

Focusing as a Therapeutic Tool

Gendlin (1996) claimed that when individuals experience their own felt sense, they do not need to do anything other than remain with the feelings and symbolize them. Gendlin asserted that the very experience of the felt sense leads to forward movement, that is, to a change in clients' situations:

"Every experience and event contains implicit further movement. To find it one must sense its unclear edge. Every experience can be carried forward" (1996, p. 15). The meeting with the felt sense is a healing meeting because the felt sense contains understanding or knowledge about the next step. Gendlin wrote that despite the complexity of the felt sense, it contains a demand to move forward in a particular direction. In other words, individuals who pay attention to the felt sense know what the right next step is.

The process is therapeutic because all explicit symbolization moves individuals forward. Gendlin stated that in the original physical feelings, there is always more than can be conceptualized or portrayed in symbolization. However, presenting the feelings in symbolization moves individuals out of their current situations and into new ones:

> A felt sense contains a maze of meaning, a whole texture of facets, a Persian rug of patterning—more than could be said or thought. Despite its intricacy, the whole felt sense also has a focus, a single specific demand, direction, or point. It can "add up to" or "come to" a single further step. Then we know and can say "what it really is," and saying this seems to carry the whole intricacy . . . one single thing, one statement, or one next step can arise from whole of it all, if we allowed it to form.
> (Gendlin, 1996, p. 58)

The goal of felt sensing video art therapy is to have clients experience the feeling that the images that they have created in the editing software are exactly what they felt and wanted to express. This is the relief that comes once the feelings have been given symbolization (Gendlin, 1996). Once the feelings have been given exact symbolization, they have less of a grip on the clients, and the feelings can change, dissipate, and communicate with the clients in new ways. Exact symbolization is a moment of change: The body can let go of something old in favor of something new.

The role of therapists in the process is to listen to clients and to echo what the clients say back to them. Echoing is therapeutic because it supports and helps clients to examine their inner feelings on their own and decide whether the feelings are appropriate for the audiovisual images that they have brought for editing. Echoing expresses the therapists' listening, their presence beside the clients, and their acceptance of anything that clients bring, experience, or say during therapy without judgment or criticism. Echoing helps clients attend to their inner worlds, which allows clients to engage in relationships between themselves and their sensory experiences.

One might assert that the goal of all therapy is to increase clients' levels of freedom, to enable them to become more self-aware so that they will take more responsibility for their lives, project less onto others, and be more internally flexible—less rigid and stuck in one position and free to see various points of view that exist in every situation. Levy (2012) wrote that the goal of therapy is to release feelings with their old representations in favor of new representations:

> The goal of therapy is releasing fixations and obvious, fixed links between feelings and their representations in order to create new representations which, like new colors and new words, can enrich the spirit and liberate it from previous patterns of thought and experience. Old feelings that are given new names create a person who is new to himself. (p. 254)

Focusing offers a more profound option. If the goal of therapy is to give new representations to old feelings (Levy, 2012), focusing holds that old feelings will dissipate and new feelings that, in most cases, are healthier, will replace them. Usually, the new feelings contain higher levels of freedom for the individuals. For example, if they gave particular symbolizations to depression for years and can now find different or perhaps even more complex symbolizations for it, change has taken place. However, focusing allows the feelings themselves, not only their representations, to change. Focusing opens doorways to deeper change. Here, change takes place in the depression itself.

As noted previously, video art is important in cases where words cannot symbolize or represent feelings. An inner cry, for example, can receive more precise symbolization with the sound of a cry than via the words "inner cry." Individuals can find the symbolization of a cry in the many libraries that have sounds available for free download over the Internet. People also might create cries themselves by, for example, recording cries at low volume and altering them digitally with the tools available in video- or sound-editing software. Using these tools, individuals might make the cry sound frightening, disturbing, distorted, distant, close, and so on, according to their feelings. The moment when individuals create or find the symbolizations that describe the feelings, something basic in those feelings changes. Feelings that have been given symbolizations are no longer the same feelings, and the individuals change as a result (Gendlin, 2001).

FOR WHOM IS THIS MODEL APPROPRIATE?

This model is appropriate for the following clients and situations:

- For those who are interested in video art therapy and find this mode of expression interesting and right for them.
- In situations in which it is difficult to describe feelings in words, such as primal fears (fear of being dropped; fear of dripping, leaking, or falling to pieces); existential fears (fear of death, emptiness, a feeling that nothing has any meaning); mind-body feelings that are difficult to put into words (pain, suffering); emotions that have no verbal outlet (i.e., overwhelming feelings toward parents or children; in many cases, these feelings go far beyond words).

- In situations where terms such as *depression, anxiety*, and *fatigue* feel overused to the point of being personally meaningless. These words are too general and inadequate to describe specific experiences, which are different for each person, even if the same words are used. Audiovisual symbolization can describe feelings more deeply and precisely.

Figure 13.7 Upside down fish head
By Moshe Ben Yaish

Figure 13.8 Fish head with background of knives
By Moshe Ben Yaish

- In situations of feeling stuck in life or stuck in talk-based therapy.
- In dealing with trauma.

Working With Traumatic Situations

Levine (1997) developed a method of working with people who had experienced trauma and discovered that his model was appropriate for any situation of flooding, stress, or tension. The work is with the felt sense, as Levine wrote (1997) that the felt sense is the tool that enables human beings to experience themselves as organisms.

The focusing process takes place in the order in which the client brings in the topics he/she wishes to address. The client looks within the experience, and describes it in words (or in a different symbolization, such as visual or auditory symbolization, as suggested in this chapter). The therapist then echoes the symbolization back to the client, who experiences the words in order to find and describe the next sensation, and the session continues further. Although working with situations of trauma involves working with the felt sense, therapists who use the somatic experiencing method are more active in session management than those who use the focusing method.

Therapists who use the somatic experiencing method are more active in this way out of fear that the client will sink into the sensations connected with the traumatic event. In this case, the therapist's role is to remind the client of his/or her inner strengths and make sure that the traumatic energy leaves the client's system. The main purpose of this process is the release of the traumatic energy from the body. In comparison, the focusing approach gives clients time to be with their feelings, allowing the next step that is right for them to come from within those feelings. In focusing, the therapist does not ensure the release of energy from the body.

According to Levine (1997), trauma is a fact of life, but it does not have to be life imprisonment: "Trauma is hell on earth. . . . Trauma resolved is a gift from the gods—a heroic journey that belongs to each of us" (p. 28). Levine stated that trauma is an expanding fact of modern life, even if people are not aware of that fact. Trauma is not experienced only by soldiers or the victims of abuse or attack. It also includes responses to road accidents, severe illness, the sudden loss of a loved one, a difficult birth, a high level of tension during pregnancy, various kinds of surgery, and exposure to violence.

Levine (1997) claimed that the trauma lies not in the event itself, but in the body. Even though a painful event has passed, its residue remains in the body, expressing itself in physical and emotional symptoms. This is because, when traumatic events take place, people are on high alert, and their bodies have high levels of energy. Once the events are over, people suffer from trauma and do not know how to release the large amount of energy inside themselves. The trauma becomes the frozen residue of unreleased, undissipated energy. Levine mentioned three possible responses in such cases: fight, flight, or freeze.

In situations where life is in danger, the first instinct is to escape. If a person escapes successfully, it is likely that traumatic residue will not be created. If fleeing is not possible, the human instinct is to fight. If fighting is not possible, then high levels of energy within the body are released. However, for some reason, if the individual cannot run away or fight, then the energy in the body freezes (Levine, 1997). When the physical or emotional welfare of individuals is in danger, two vortexes of life are aroused: healing and trauma. The healing vortex comprises the healthy parts within human beings that wish to recover. The trauma vortex is created by the surplus energy of the trauma trapped in the body, which causes the reptilian brain to believe that the threat is still present and that the release of stress hormones is still necessary.

Ross (2008) wrote that in freezing, individuals are in a constant state of defensiveness, even though they are no longer facing external dangers. The nervous system continues to give an internal response signaling that the dangers are still present. The individuals have internalized the threats, and their attention is trapped in the traumatic event(s). When a person is in danger, there is an exceedingly high level of energy in the body. The purpose of this energy is to enable the person to defend himself by fight or flight. If the person freezes because fight or flight is not possible, then once the danger has passed, the body needs to discharge the high level of energy frozen within it. Animals tremble after danger has passed, but human beings have lost this ability. The energy remains stuck within the body, and the person lives in a continuous state of alert, as if still in danger. Those who discharge the energy recover, but those who do not suffer from various symptoms. The traumatic situation affects their bodies and changes their brain chemistry (by manufacturing adrenaline, cortisol, and other hormones, and by closing down the activity of the neocortex, which throws the nervous system off balance). Ross (2008) asserted that in such situations the endocrine system, which is responsible for creating natural painkillers, or endorphins, becomes exhausted, as do the adrenal glands. The body loses its natural rhythm and swings between hyper alertness and apathy—that is, from stormy emotional outbursts to dulled sensations and then to a comatose state.

The therapists' role is to make sure that clients are not in the trauma vortex and do not experience their difficulties in ways that are overwhelming. The goal of somatic experiencing is to have the clients encounter positive feelings together with the negative ones so that the body can unload the energy of the traumas, difficulties, or stress and create a new mix. Some of the difficulties are still there, but now, they are combined with good feelings and the clients' own capabilities. Levine (1997) suggested starting therapeutic sessions by finding a pleasant felt sense and then moving on to the client's difficulties while making sure to return to the positive felt sense. Using this method enables clients to find ways to release the problems that they have been holding in their bodies for years (Ross, 2008).

Felt sensing video art therapy in cases where clients are dealing with trauma

When video art therapy is combined with somatic experiencing, clients are asked to find good-feeling audiovisual images, that is, images that calm the nervous system and create good feelings. The therapists can go with the clients to film the positive images, or they can ask clients to prepare them and bring them to their therapy sessions. Clients can search the Internet for images that make them feel better during the sessions, with the therapists beside them, and check their feelings about the images together with their therapists. When clients are able to anchor good physical feelings inside themselves, and once they have found positive images, clients and therapists can then move on to the images of the painful feelings. As clients work with the editing software, therapists can work on loading positive and pleasant healing images into it, images that make the clients feel good, as well as images associated with the wounds.

The therapy happens in the editing room. It includes working with the bodily sensations about the images that clients have brought and uploaded into the editing software. The role of therapists is to ensure that the clients experience the positive images in their bodies via the felt sense, and afterward, briefly experience the images that gave rise to the trauma responses. The therapeutic process in this case emphasizes the editing: What do the clients feel when their videos start with positive images? Where are the proper points to insert the images associated with the wounds? How long will each image be visible in the editing software? Would the clients like to create editing effects for each image? What about creating a picture in which two images are superimposed (an effect that allows both images to be visible at once)? Does one of the images in this sort of picture cancel out or overpower the other? Can images that have been cancelled out come back? Because the work consists not only of observing the artwork but also of listening to the felt sense, creation takes place during the therapeutic work of listening to the felt sense. Therapeutic work and change happen at the same time as the creative work takes place.

According to Levine (1997), the work that takes place in therapy is the release of the energy created by the traumas that have built up in the body; the release enables the nervous system to return to a state of balance. The goal is to provide the nervous system, the body, and the brain with feelings of good health and security (Ross, 2008). Because visual and auditory images affect the human body, the connection between bodywork and image is a logical one. Clients need to create a positive felt sense within themselves as well as benefit from images that make them feel calm and secure and enable them to find new strength in life. The images also can make it easier for clients to deal with their traumas because the painful images are closed within frames and are under the control of the clients who created them or brought them to therapy. The clients decide where the images will be on the time line, the length of time that they will be shown, and when they will be replaced with other images. The editing work allows clients to control that which had been beyond their control before.

Music video clips. Sacks (2009) wrote that music has a great deal of power that works on almost every human being, whether musically inclined or not. He believes that the tendency to listen to music is such a deep part of human nature that it can be considered inborn. In addition to the model described in this chapter, which proposes various stages of working with sound, Pearlmutter and I also suggest another model for working with adolescents, as well as adults who are young at heart, that involves creating images for song clips selected by clients. Because it might be difficult to invite adolescents to conversational therapy, using something that interests them is a wonderful way to communicate effectively. Adolescents enjoy listening to music, and they allow the music to touch them. This is another working model that has no connection to focusing, somatic experiencing, or finding the felt sense.

The clips can be created for songs with lyrics that the clients can connect with or relate to. Whether the lyrics are profound, simple, or even banal, they interest the clients and perhaps even reflect their feelings, providing an alternative mode of expression to the words that they cannot find on their own. In addition, song or musical excerpts bring with them particular feelings and emotional spaces that are relevant to clients. The song choices themselves contain auditory symbolization.

In this model, clients are asked to create video clips, that is, visual images that will be put to music. By working with the clips, adolescents feel more comfortable discussing issues in their lives, current feelings, past experiences, and desires and fears for the future. Wise therapists can give clients dramatic therapeutic experiences during the process of creative work.

CONCLUSION

Clients who describe their inner worlds in symbols of sound and image allow themselves to experience issues in different ways, something that usually occurs naturally once symbolization has been done. The power of images is different from that of words. Walter Benjamin wrote in his 1931 work, *A Short History of Photography*, that images take us one step closer toward a new understanding. Images stop the flood of old associations and make room for a new understanding. Benjamin saw photography as something that reveals a secret, something that shows us things we had not known before. He claimed that photography contains an aura of magic and mystery because it keeps us away from the familiar and allows us to leap one step ahead, toward something new. Flusser (2014) also wrote about the image as a magical world in the sense that, unlike the spoken word and the perception of a linear world, with images there is no need to understand cause and effect. In an image, everything is connected to everything.

I think that we are still in the earliest stages of understanding the moving image (as opposed to the still images that exist in still photography) and its significance in modern life. I think that video brings the photographed image back to written language by telling a story. There is no frozen moment in abstract video art either; a video, too, is something whole, an entire story, a statement. To me, video, together with a soundtrack, brings together the two worlds of image and language, which philosophers such as Benjamin and Flusser saw as different worlds. Video connects the language of image with the language of speech by showing a relationship between cause and effect, or at least what came before and what came after. Although we are still beginning to understand whether video changes people—and, if so, how—and the new options that video may open, close, or reduce, I will write briefly of my own experience with videotherapy: I never stop being surprised and impressed by the enormous power of creativity and by the fascinating images that clients bring to therapy from week to week. This work leads to a sharp, clear meeting with the life forces of clients, and the growth of clients as artists and creators—both of the artwork and of their own lives.

REFERENCES

Barthes, R. (1981). *Camera lucida: Reflections on photography* (Hebrew ed.). Jerusalem, IL: Keter Publishing House.

Benjamin, W. (1931/2004). *A short history of photography* (Hebrew ed.). Tel Aviv, IL: Bavel Publishing.

Bowie, M. (2005). *Lacan*. Or Yehuda, IL: Kinneret Zmora-Bitan Dvir.

Flusser, V. (2014). *Toward a philosophy of photography*. Tel Aviv, IL: Resling Publishing House.

Gendlin, E.T. (1962). *Experiencing and the creation of meaning: A philosophical and psychological approach to the subjective*. Evanston, IL: Northwestern University Press.

Gendlin, E.T. (1996). *Focusing-oriented psychotherapy: A manual of the experiential method*. New York, NY: Guilford Press.

Gendlin, E.T. (1997). *A process model*. Nyack, NY: The Focusing Institute.

Gendlin, E.T. (2001). *Focusing*. Safed, IL: Mirkam Publications.

Levine, A.P. (1997). *Waking the tiger: Healing trauma*. Berkeley, CA: North Atlantic Books.

Levy, R. (2012). Bion and Nietzsche: Self-creation in therapy (Hebrew). *Sihot/ Dialogue: Israel Journal of Psychotherapy, 27*(3), 248–257.

Perl, S. (2004). *Felt sense: Writing with the body*. Portsmouth, NH: Boynton/ Cook-Heinemann.

Rice, H. (2008). *Language process notes: Using words to get beyond words*. Philadelphia, PA: Quaker Books.

Ronen, R. (2010). *Art and its discontents: Lectures on psychotherapy and art* (Hebrew ed.). Tel Aviv, IL: Am Oved.

Ross, G. (2008). *Beyond the trauma vortex into the healing vortex*. Los Angeles, CA: International Trauma-Healing Institute. (Hebrew ed. Tivon: The Nord Institute)

Sacks, O. (2009). *Musicophilia: Tales of music and the brain* (Hebrew ed.). Or Yehuda, IL Kinneret Zmora-Bitan Dvir.

Winnicott, D.W. (2010). *Playing and reality* (Hebrew ed.). Tel Aviv, IL: Am Oved.

14 Expanding the Scope of Traditional Art Therapy With Green Screen Technology

Joe Kavitski

INTRODUCTION

While living as an artist and filmmaker in New York City, I came to work on a documentary about a Holocaust survivor returning to the concentration camps that he had been placed in as a young boy. Traveling to Auschwitz and Birkenau, I went inside the gas chambers, touched the ovens, and sat with a survivor and his family, witnessing firsthand how telling his story allowed him to reclaim his power. After 2 years of conducting interviews, completing research, editing, and connecting individually with young Poles and American descendants of genocide victims, I felt that this work had only begun to scrape the surface of the complex and multifarious workings of trauma. Yet, I was able to witness how art and digital media served as a universal language that could promote healing and growth. While finishing the film, I had the opportunity to assist residents in painting a 15-foot mural at a nursing home in Brooklyn. Working with the residents, many of whom had undergone amputations or were suffering from Parkinson's, Alzheimer's, or kidney disease, only solidified my increasing aspirations to work in medical settings and with psychiatric populations. It was as if something clicked, and I soon found myself pursuing this calling, enrolling in graduate school at NYU to obtain a master's degree in art therapy.

In hopes that I could integrate media into the art therapy process, I began interning under the guidance of Jon Ehinger, a board-certified and licensed art therapist with an interest in media arts. This case study highlights some of the work that we did together, and using a depth psychology perspective, I focus on the implementation of green screen technology in an art therapy context. This media arts group, as it came to be called, demonstrated how a woman with bipolar disorder on an adult in-patient psychiatry unit was able to interact with a green screen, thereby exploring psychological themes relating to internal symbolic material.

BIPOLAR DISORDER

Bipolar disorder has been categorized as a mood disorder with symptomatology that includes episodes of mania and depression (Marohn, 2003).

During an episode of mania, the individual experiences a specific period of elevated, expansive, or irritable mood as well as increased energy or activity (American Psychiatric Association [APA], 2013). The episode also might include inflated self-esteem or grandiosity and excessive participation in activities that have potentially dangerous consequences. Periods of depression are typically characterized by feelings of sadness or hopelessness and a loss of interest in otherwise pleasurable activities. Additional symptoms can include feelings of guilt or worthlessness, psychomotor agitation, indecisiveness, changes in sleep and eating patterns, and persistent thoughts of death/suicide.

THE GREEN SCREEN PROCESS

Green screen technology is a special effects technique used in film and video production. Also known as chroma keying, or compositing, the process entails layering two images on top of each other and removing a specific color, the key color, from the top layer (Wohl, 2002). Green is commonly used because it is on the opposite end of the color spectrum from human skin tones, thus allowing it to be easily recognized and separated from the colors of human skin by computer software. When green areas in the top layer are keyed, the green is removed, rendering those areas transparent and allowing the bottom layer to show through. This process is familiar in daily weather reports: While a meteorologist stands in front of a green backdrop, the green is digitally removed, and images of weather maps and other graphics are displayed where the green once was.

For the purposes of this case study, the use of green screen technology was different from its conventional employment in television and motion pictures where graphics are added during postproduction, meaning that even though the actors interact with the green screen, they do not see the imagery that will be substituted in its place. As Academy Award–winning actor Benicio Del Toro, who is renowned for his green screen work in films such as *Sin City* and *The Wolfman*, stated, "Green screen is really like doing some stage work. You have to make believe that there is a window, make believe that something is there that is really not there and convince the audience. It's part of acting" (as cited in Murray, 2010, p. 1). However, even though actors might typically pretend in this sense—that is, they perform while unable to witness what image is going to be substituted for the green until the postproduction phase—in this case study, the addition of a computer screen facilitated the use of live streaming techniques that enabled patients to see themselves interacting with digitally substituted backgrounds in real time. Both green screen approaches have therapeutic value, but understanding the distinction is important because this case study incorporated live streaming technology.

According to Jung (1948/1970), myths comprise archetypes, or inherent psychological configurations, in the unconscious. Comparing the parallels in myths that span different cultures led him to believe that certain archetypes, along with their resulting myths, are universal. He also believed in the value of personal myths (i.e., archetypal models similar to those often found in fairy tales and mythological stories that have the potential to influence and direct one's individual existence), so elevating unconscious, or subsurface, myths to conscious thought is a primary objective of analysis (as cited in Roesler, 2006). In art therapy, the aim is similar, namely, to facilitate the creation of a symbolic object that in some way contains, expresses, and communicates inner material through the art-making process (Kramer, 1993).

Green screen technology is yet another artistic medium that can be used on the journey of self-expression. Perhaps its most interesting characteristic is its potential to do more than generate symbolic objects; it also can produce mirror experiences that can then be enacted and processed to explore conscious and unconscious psychological themes. As participants engage in live streaming digital processes while watching themselves on a monitor, the monitor functions as a mirror, literally reflecting back the participants' actions in real time. The addition of green screen compositing during live streaming allows the participants to select digital backgrounds that also are displayed on the monitor. This process of interacting with one's own mirror image within a digital environment of one's own choosing generates a transitional space in which to access personal symbols, roles, and archetypes.

CHLOE

Chloe (a pseudonym), was a woman in her early 30s who had expressed an interest in participating in an experimental media arts group in addition to art therapy. Subsequent to being diagnosed with bipolar disorder, she was admitted to a psychiatric unit by her partner after expressing increased depression and suicidal ideations with a plan of overdosing. According to the *Diagnostic and Statistical Manual of Mental Disorders* (5th ed., APA, 2013), "The lifetime risk of suicide in individuals with bipolar disorder is estimated to be at least 15 times that of the general population" (p. 131), and prior to the development and accessibility of lithium, suicide was committed by one in five people diagnosed with manic depression (Jamison, 1995).

Research has indicated that up to 48% of individuals with bipolar disorder either partially or completely do not adhere to prescribed antipsychotic medications and that this noncompliance might result in longer and more frequent hospital stays (Gianfrancesco, Sajatovic, Rajagopalan, & Wang, 2008), as well as hinder the individuals' ability to stay healthy. Negative stereotypes and internalized stigmas about mental illness often influence maladaptive behaviors, including the willingness to seek and adhere to prescribed medication and other forms of treatment (Livingston & Boyd, 2010).

One benefit of using a green screen is that it does not present like other previously stigmatized therapies. The bright green color draws attention, often from patients and staff who are curious about the process. The overwhelming majority of patients with whom I have worked had never interacted with a green screen before, so engaging with it often begins as a novelty that lends itself to a unique, fun, and creative experience. Thus, while in the midst of a session, clients might show less resistance to therapeutic moments when they arise, and under the guidance of facilitating therapists, processing these therapeutic moments in a safe space can help to alleviate depression and ultimately reduce suicidality.

Statistically at an increased risk to follow through with her suicidal ideations, Chloe cited life stressors such as work-related anxiety and her mother's recent diagnosis of cancer as the main causes of her depression. In addition, Chloe's history of substance abuse and difficulty maintaining sobriety complicated her situation. When compared to the general population, individuals with bipolar disorder are three times more likely to have substance abuse and alcoholism problems, and studies have indicated that over 60% of individuals with bipolar disorder abuse alcohol or other substances (Reger, Farm, & Rae, 1990). In such instances, individuals might be abusing alcohol to cope with mania or depression (Marohn, 2003), but substance abuse comorbidity with bipolar disorder increases the risk of suicide (Hawton, Sutton, Haw, Sinclair, & Harriss, 2005). It was while exploring these issues that Chloe disclosed that she was struggling with her gender identity and expressed an interest in wanting to undergo female-to-male gender reassignment surgery. She believed that gender identity issues were at the root of her depression.

I was glad that Chloe had begun to express her feelings and vocalize specific areas that she wished to work on. While actively participating in verbal and creative arts therapy group sessions, Chloe took an interest in art therapy. While in the safe confines of the art studio, she found comfort in the artistic process and the self-expression techniques that the art therapy groups encouraged her to explore. Research has shown that major mood disorders, including manic depression, can heighten the creativity of certain individuals (Jamison, 1995). Because she was invested in her treatment, Chloe was receptive to directive and open studio art therapy methods. Having undergone previous psychiatric admissions, she was interested in discovering new coping skills and healthy habits that would allow her to manage her symptoms more efficiently. This interest made Chloe an ideal candidate for media arts sessions, and when informed of the group, she was willing and eager to engage with the green screen process.

MEDIA ARTS SESSION I

Media arts sessions were held in addition to regularly scheduled groups when time permitted. A description of what the session would entail was provided prior to each group and patients attended on a volunteer basis. All approved patients were aware that they would be filmed prior to the session and had to sign a release form preceding any filming. Patients experiencing psychosis or violating any proper behavioral conduct on the unit were not approved to attend the media arts sessions. For these reasons, group sizes varied. In addition to Chloe, two other patients attended the initial 45-minute media arts session: Kevin (a pseudonym), a man with schizophrenia, and Robbie (a pseudonym), a man who was visually impaired and had schizo-affective disorder, asked to listen to the group members' interactions. My supervisor, Jon, and I served as coleaders.

As the session began, Chloe sat down between a large backdrop of green fabric, which acted as the green screen, and a table, upon which rested a video camera and a computer. After giving a brief introduction to the green screen process, we explained to Chloe, Kevin, and Robbie that there was no "right" or "wrong" way to interact with the green screen and no set goal that needed to be accomplished; instead, we told them that the objective of the exercise was to interact with the green screen in whatever ways they wished. Chloe nodded in understanding. She seemed pleased with the freedom to interact with the green screen, but she opted to give Kevin the first chance to be filmed.

Chloe looked on with a smile as Kevin waved to the image of himself on the monitor. She verbally validated Kevin's movements and appeared more eager to engage with the green screen as time progressed. When it was Chloe's turn, she sat down in front of the camera and laughed. While she was being filmed against the green screen, software for digital editing (Final Cut Pro) and video streaming (Conduit Live) enabled Chloe to see herself on the computer monitor and interact with a digitally substituted background in real time. She grinned while watching herself on the monitor and moved her hands in small motions.

For this session, various still images were used to acclimate Chloe to the process. Excited to engage with new technology in an otherwise structured routine on the unit, Chloe's first interactions with the green screen served as a novelty. Pleased, she watched the mirror image of herself on the computer screen superimposed over a New York City skyline. Chuckling, she then made a joke about whether the video would be put on YouTube. Although Jon and I knew that she made this remark in jest (we had discussed at the opening of the group that the video would not be placed online), the question of how media arts projects are used once filming has been completed has ethical and legal implications: It is illegal to use a patient's image without written consent. The public display and use of media arts projects are valid concerns of many patients. Honest disclosure about confidentiality, release forms, and how the video will be used (e.g., if it will be shown for educational purposes) is imperative. Assuring the group that the video would not be placed online, we told Chloe that we could meet her halfway, superimposing her over a still image of the YouTube homepage.

In addition to building a closer rapport with Chloe, this media arts session marked the formation of a transitional space that was simultaneously fake and real (Winnicott, 1971). Because of the addition of a special effects background, an element of fantasy was incorporated into reality within a safe context, encouraging the component of play to happen. Such a transitional space then led to a greater level of freedom for Chloe, allowing her to open up in new and different ways.

Jon then suggested that for the next session, Chloe should consider interacting with a moving image. She enthusiastically welcomed this idea and suggested a scene from *Days of Our Lives*, a popular soap opera among patients on the unit. Chloe also had a personal connection to the program and recalled fond memories of watching it as a child with her mother. While discussing this concept, Chloe mentioned Stefano DiMera, the villain of the show, and asked whether she would be able to superimpose her arms onto Stefano's body, already defining what her experience might look like while interacting with the green screen and setting the stage of the session with a meaningful context.

Rolling up one cuff of her shirt, Chloe revealed a full sleeve of tattoos on her right arm, the central figure of the tattoo depicting a phoenix enveloped by flames. Chloe, whose history included substance abuse, explained that the tattoo represented her sobriety. She explained, "It says, 'Out of the ashes I rise,' so that out of any situation, I can overcome." She continued to elucidate her strong connection with Stefano's character, explaining that he was notorious for enacting numerous "fake" deaths on the show, thus earning him the moniker of "the Phoenix." The myth of the phoenix has a long and rich history that has evolved across numerous cultures, dating back to 34 A.D. in which the phoenix is depicted in the writings of Tacitus, who believed that the bird existed in Egypt (as cited in Fitzpatrick, 1933). The ancient Egyptians referred to the phoenix as *bennu* and connected it with the appearance of the sun. As the sun disappeared and reappeared again, so did the phoenix, which was symbolized as a returning traveler in hieroglyphics. Phoenix lore has since developed into the modern myth that describes the phoenix as a bird that burns within a fire of its own making, rises from the ashes, and is reborn. As Van Den Broek (1972) stated, "By dying, it obtains new life" (p. 10). Chloe recounted the entirety of her life as the story of the phoenix: She burned in the fire of her drug habit and suicidal ideations, sought treatment, was reborn, and repeated the cycle perpetually. Reiterating this sentiment, she stated that each psychiatric admission was another chance for a new beginning.

Jung called the union of known and unknown elements into one symbolic form a transcendent function that frequently appears as a symbol (as cited in Stevens, 1999). In this case, the symbol for Chloe was the phoenix, which was central to the individualization of who she was and what she wanted to become (Miller, 2004). The individuation process (Jung, 1939/1959a) is a natural and unconscious progression toward self-realization, that is, the finding of purpose and significance in one's life (as cited in Schmidt, 2005). Jung emphasized that symbols are not indicative of disease; rather, they are a way for individuals to preserve their well-being as the unconscious becomes conscious in ways that do not overwhelm the individuals (as cited in Brink, 1976). By associating herself with the phoenix, Chloe distanced herself from associating with her problems directly, projecting her sobriety onto the phoenix myth while finding strength in the magical bird that, in Chloe's eyes, correlated to her own difficult situation.

In ancient Chinese tradition and art, a male phoenix was termed a *feng;* a female phoenix was termed a *huang* (Welch, 2014). Over time, the male and female distinctions of the bird were merged, forming the *fenghuang*, the Chinese term used to describe the phoenix today. Just as this joining of masculine and feminine energies created equilibrium in the Chinese phoenix tradition, similarly, Chloe might have been attempting to use the phoenix as a symbol to balance her animus archetype, the internal masculine qualities of her unconscious mind (Jung, 1959b). The phoenix is a bird of perpetual transformation, being reborn from its own ashes. Although Chloe never expressed this thought verbally, I could not help but wonder whether the phoenix resonated with her on a deeper level than representing her journey of sobriety alone and potentially embodied her own state of transition from female to male and being reborn.

MEDIA ARTS SESSION II

Jon and I retrieved several digital (.mov) files from YouTube of scenes from *Days of Our Lives* that included Stefano. We attempted to select scenes that were only a few minutes in duration and did not appear pixilated. Chloe sat in front of the green screen, and her body, with the exception of her tattooed arms, was cloaked with green fabric. The software showed the *Days of Our Lives* clip in place of the color green so that only Chloe's head and arms became visible on the computer screen. Seeing herself on the computer screen, Chloe became excited and stated, "This is my mom's favorite show. . . . I don't know if you guys know this . . . but she's going through cancer right now, so this project might be something I could show her." Chloe's words marked an important moment in her treatment. In contrast to her recent suicidal ideations, Chloe was now able to formulate and express plans for the future.

As the session progressed, Chloe wished to remove her face from the image and have only her arms interact with the scene by being superimposed on Stefano's arms. It was necessary to cover Chloe's head with green fabric, an action that posed an interesting dilemma. Would Chloe's inability to see herself on the computer screen undermine the therapeutic value of the session, or would this new self-imposed obstacle allow something new and positive to emerge? At first, Chloe appeared hesitant while adjusting to her lack of vision, but it was not long before her intuition took over and she began to physically embody Stefano's character, listening to his dialogue and becoming very animated by using large hand gestures.

In the *Days of Our Lives* clip, Stefano, who was imprisoned in a cell, had a visit from his daughter. Chloe began to behave as if she were actually incarcerated, trying to hold onto the bars. After a minute or so, she began to grope and claw with her hands, as if she were reaching through them to get at someone on the other side. Although Chloe's mirror image on the computer screen gave her a new perspective of herself, her inability to see obliged her to rely on other physical senses in conjunction with implicit feelings and desires.

Watching Chloe interact with the clip, I could not help but notice the symbolic value of the scene, that is, father and daughter (as well as Stefano/digital image and Chloe/live human) divided by an immoveable barrier amid themes of entrapment and freedom. Chloe appeared restless. Shifting the green fabric so that it covered only half of her face, and positioning herself at an angle so that she could see the monitor yet still remain covered by the green fabric, Chloe was able to see her arms without her head appearing on the computer.

> [On computer screen: Stefano is behind jail bars.]
> Stefano's daughter: Father! What happened?
> Stefano: Trafficking . . . illegal arms.

Chloe laughed aloud at the double meaning in Stefano's reply, seeing her tattooed arms superimposed on Stefano's body. This completely coincidental dialogue in the clip led to an open verbal discussion of what it would be like to provide "illegal arms," literally and figuratively, to Stefano. In addition, it called into question the role of the villain, why Chloe associated herself with this role, and how the role was able to coexist simultaneously as the phoenix.

Although Chloe was able to control her arms over the image, she had no control over the prerecorded clip and had to accept Stefano's actions and facial expressions. However, even though her face was not seen digitally on the computer screen, her countenance and body language changed considerably during the session, displaying a range of various emotional states. The sentence would read: In traditional art therapy sessions, observing the artistic processes of a patient creating artwork is just as important as examining the physical artwork that is produced. In other words, the importance does not reside only in a mark made on the paper but also in how the mark was made, the affect and emotions conveyed during the making of the mark, and the words that were expressed.

The same line of thinking applies to media arts groups. By observing Chloe throughout the session, we were able to witness diverse affect states in response to the actions and statements made by Stefano. These observations provided useful information in understanding how far Chloe had progressed since admission and how she was responding to her medication and treatment plan. Our observations also offered potential material for future processing.

POSTSESSION

While recounting her experiences following the green screen sessions and prior to her release from the in-patient unit, Chloe requested a DVD of the final video product. It is important to note that the use of media arts therapy products must be handled with the same, if not even greater, care as any finished work produced by traditional art therapy means, especially if a patient's identity is clearly captured in the video. Therapists practicing media arts must be careful not to breach Health Information Portability and Accountability Act codes or violate laws regarding patient confidentiality. Therapists must ensure that patients always sign the proper release forms before being filmed.

Chloe explained that she often felt herself progressively spiraling out of control before a major depression and that if she could view the DVD, she might be able to prevent the depressive episode. When asked why watching the DVD would help to address the problem, Chloe responded that it would mentally bring her back to the experience of the session and give her an awareness that looking at her other artwork created on the unit would not be able to incite. She commented, "I can watch it again if I feel that I'm slipping, and everything I felt during the session will come flooding back. It brings up so much stuff for me."

While I often remark in art therapy and media arts sessions that the focus should be the process of expression, not the production of a final product, I know that it also is important to recognize the value that the final product might hold. This value likely is different for each patient, but every final product holds the potential to incite continued processing of the artistic expression that created it. Chloe recognized this potential and believed that having access to the final product would aid in her ongoing treatment.

Although I was not able to immediately process with Chloe what "stuff" was brought up for her during the media arts session because another group session was beginning on the unit, Chloe continued to express her belief that participating in the group had been a powerful experience. Chloe was discharged the next day while I was on the unit, and armed with her DVD, she thanked Jon and me for the media arts experience before she left. Only Chloe knows whether the DVD provided her with the relief that she hoped for after discharge, but I believe that the act of creating the live video composite might be seen as a transitional phenomenon, helping Chloe to make sense of her inner experience and the outside reality of the world. The final DVD, as Chloe said, might act as a defense against her anxiety or downward spiral that she can view repeatedly, thus serving as a type of transitional object (Winnicott, 1953).

DISCUSSION

This case study depicted a unique approach to a creative therapeutic experience. While working with the green screen in a safe space and a judgment-free environment, Chloe was able to effectively explore psychological themes relating to internal symbolic material. By selecting a part of her body that held significant symbolic meaning, namely, her tattooed arms, and by digitally superimposing them onto a man's body, she was able to gain insight and, in some ways, move closer to fulfilling the fantasy of transitioning to a male body.

In addition, Chloe was able to develop a deeper understanding of the mythological symbol that she identified with (i.e., the phoenix); project this identifying characteristic onto an archetype (i.e., Stefano, the villain); and process the symbols together, ultimately gaining heightened personal awareness and new perspectives through the experience. While considering how the phoenix transitions from ashen remains to a bird of flight, I hope that Chloe, in like fashion, continues to elevate herself to the skies of her choosing, whether with wings or tattooed arms.

REFERENCES

American Psychiatric Association. (2013). *Diagnostic and statistical manual of mental disorders* (5th ed.). Arlington, VA: Author.

Brink, T.L. (1976). Joseph Smith: The verdict of depth psychology. *Journal of Mormon History, 3*, 73–83.

Fitzpatrick, M.C. (1933). Lactanti de ave phoenice: With introduction, text, translation, and commentary. Philadelphia, PA: University of Pennsylvania.

Gianfrancesco, F.D., Sajatovic, M., Rajagopalan, K., & Wang, R. (2008). Antipsychotic treatment adherence and associated mental health care use among individuals with bipolar disorder. *Clinical Therapeutics, 30*(7), 1358–1374.

Hawton, K., Sutton, L., Haw, C., Sinclair, J., & Harriss, L. (2005). Suicide and attempted suicide in bipolar disorder: A systematic review of risk factors. *Journal of Clinical Psychiatry, 66*(6), 693–704.

Jamison, K.R. (1995). Manic-depressive illness and creativity: Does some fine madness plague great artists? Several studies now show that creativity and mood disorders are linked. *Scientific American, 272*(2), 62–67.

Jung, C.G. (1959a). Consciousness, unconsciousness and individuation (R.F.C. Hull, Trans.). In S.H. Read, M. Fordham, & G. Adler (Eds.), *Collected works: Vol. 9, Pt. 1: The archetypes and the collective unconscious* (2nd ed., pp. 275–289). Princeton, NJ: Princeton University Press. (Original work published 1939)

Jung, C.G. (1959b). The syzygy: Anima and animus (R.F.C. Hull, Trans.). In S.H. Read, M. Fordham, & G. Adler (Eds.) *Collected Works: Vol. 9, Pt. 2: Aion: Research into the phenomenology of the self* (2nd ed., pp. 11–22). Princeton, NJ: Princeton University Press.

Jung, C.G. (1970). On the nature of dreams (R.F.C. Hull, Trans.). In S.H. Read, M. Fordham, & G. Adler (Eds.), *Collected Works: Vol. 8: The structure and dynamics of the psyche* (pp. 281–300). Princeton, NJ: Princeton University Press. (Original work published 1948)

Kramer, E. (1993). *Art as therapy with children.* Chicago, IL: Magnolia Street.

Livingston, J.D., & Boyd, J.E. (2010). Correlates and consequences of internalized stigma for people living with mental illness: A systematic review and meta-analysis. *Social Science & Medicine, 71*(12), 2150–2161.

Marohn, S. (2003). *The natural medicine guide to bipolar disorder.* Charlottesville, VA: Hampton Roads.

Miller, J.C. (2004). *The transcendent function: Jung's model of psychological growth through dialogue with the unconscious.* Albany, NY: SUNY Press.

Murray, R. (2010). Benicio Del Toro discusses "The Wolfman." Retrieved from http://movies.about.com/

Reger, D.A., Farm, M.E., & Rae, D.S. (1990). Comorbidity of mental disorders with alcohol and other drug abuse: Results from the Epidemiologic Catchment Area Study. *Journal of the American Medical Association, 264*(19), 2511–2518.

Roesler, C. (2006). A narratological methodology for identifying archetypal story patterns in autobiographical narratives. *Journal of Analytic Psychology, 51*(4), 574–586.

Schmidt, M. (2005). Individuation: Finding oneself in analysis: Taking risks and making sacrifices. *Journal of Analytical Psychology, 50*(5), 595–616.

Stevens, A. (1999). *Ariadne's clue: A guide to the symbols of humankind.* Princeton, NJ: Princeton University Press.

Van Den Broek, R. (1972). *The myth of the phoenix, according to classical and early Christian traditions.* Leiden, NL: E.J. Brill.

Welch, P. (2014). *Chinese art: A guide to motifs and visual imagery.* North Clarendon, VT: Tuttle Publishing.

Winnicott, D.W. (1953). Transitional objects and transitional phenomena: A study of the first not-me possession. *International Journal of Psycho-Analysis, 34*, 89–97.

Winnicott, D.W. (1971). *Playing and reality.* Middlesex, UK: Penguin.

Wohl, M. (2002). *Editing techniques with Final Cut Pro: Learn to edit video like a professional.* San Francisco, CA: Peachpit Press.

15 Technology, Art Therapy, and Psychodynamic Theory

Computer Animation With an Adolescent in Foster Care

Brian Austin

The personal computer is in the process of becoming the interpersonal computer.

—Timothy Leary, as cited in Laurel, 1990, p. 230

TO COMPUTE OR NOT TO COMPUTE

Some art therapists object to engaging youth by means of computer technology. Gerity, Henley, Kramer, and Williams (as cited in Kramer, 2000) cautioned art therapists to refrain from making use of seductive technology, such as video games and computers, which they believe robs children of genuine creative experiences. They argued that art therapists should not engage clients with the enticing qualities of technology, suggesting that tactile experiences with traditional media are needed to counterbalance the unreal, easy, and stagnating aspects of digital media. These authors believe that computer-generated art making does not engage clients in true creative processes because technology lacks the resistive qualities that give art making an important physical dimension.

Gerity et al. (as cited in Kramer, 2000) claimed that the tension between a material's tangible properties and the artist's aspirations is a key component of the creative process. It could be concluded on this basis that digital art lacks the essential tension requisite to creativity. Artists working in the digital realm, however, are not free from constraints imposed by their medium. Computer artists, like artists in all media, work with materials that offer resistance. For example, 3-D computer animators must work within the constraints of an existing human-computer interface design as they manipulate digital form. Using sophisticated computer software, computer animators struggle to translate their understandings of real-world properties like weight, physical dynamics, movement, timing, light, reflection, and material properties into an artifact that Manovich (2001) referred to as "digital on the level of its material" (p. 180). Writing on the topic of digital craft, McCullough (1996) presented a compelling case for the richness of digital art:

> Think of a digital artifact, shaped by software operations, made up of data assemblies. Although lacking in physical substance, it is a thing with an appearance, spatiality, structure, workable properties, and a history. Although it does not bear the mark of someone's hands, as a clay pot does, neither is it the product of a standardized industrial process, like an aluminum skillet. It is individual, and reveals authorship at the level of its internal organization. It is unique, for although flawless copies can be made, nobody is going to make another just like it unless by copying. It is abstract: a symbolic structure, a workable construction, in a digital medium, showing the effects of manipulation by software tools. (p. 155)

Although nearly all American teens play with electronic media (Lenhart, 2008), mental health practitioners are only beginning to understand the ways in which these ubiquitous technologies are shaping children's lives. Given adolescents' enthusiasm for technology and the degree of resistance to therapy normally encountered in adolescent populations, art therapists should understand the therapeutic potential of these emerging technologies.

THE ADOLESCENT

> There is nothing more difficult than to decide whether one is seeing a healthy boy or girl who is in the throes of adolescence or a person who happens to be ill, psychiatrically speaking, in the puberty age.
>
> —Winnicott, 1989, p. 326

Adults often perceive adolescents as difficult to explain, hard to understand, and dismissive of adult concerns. For adolescents, cognitive development occurs simultaneously with an intense surge in biological maturation. These changes often take place within an environment of intense social and emotional pressure. Adolescents are challenged to delay gratification, channel impulses, master emotions, sublimate issues, develop cognitive capacities, develop motor skills, and visualize the future (Colarusso, 1992). In the ideal scenario, mastery of these challenges culminates in the adequate handling of adult responsibilities, including work and relationships.

According to Piaget (2000), as adolescents develop, emergent cognitive abilities foster rationality in decision making as a counterbalance to emotion. Cognitive-emotional competency, deemed essential for a healthy transition to adulthood, is achieved when the adolescent develops the ability to self-soothe independently, to manage intense emotions without resorting to denial and repression, and to negotiate and maintain new interpersonal relationships at the same time (Rosenblum & Lewis, as cited in Adams & Berzonsky, 2003).

Adolescents have a predisposition for discord because they are able to use their developing cognitive capacities to contemplate their often bewildering lives.

As affective and cognitive experiences become increasingly complicated, encounters with the external environment become ever more confusing for adolescents (Fonagy, Gergely, Jurist, & Target, 2004). They can become overwhelmed by this newfound mental awareness and respond by using defense mechanisms to withdraw from reality.

While defense mechanisms may become maladaptive and interfere with cognition (Vaillant, 1993), they are also adaptive in that they help keep intolerable emotions under control. For example, repression of a painful psychological trauma can protect the adolescent from experiencing the full weight of emotions associated with the trauma. For adolescents in particular, defense mechanisms may become rigid, contributing to the challenge of engaging in insight-oriented talk therapy (Mishne, 1986) and limiting their overall capacity to fully experience life. Therapeutic progress in verbal therapy may be compromised by adolescents' tendency toward "overemphasis of the action component" (Blos, 1962, pp. 117–118) and corresponding difficulty with sitting still to talk (Riley, 1999). Therapists working with this population are challenged to find effective ways to help adolescents manage and symbolically represent psychological states rather than acting them out in destructive ways (Fonagy et al., 2004).

THE ADOLESCENT IN ART THERAPY

Art therapists often use art as a projective medium (Riley, 1999), a way to bypass resistance to talking about feelings. Using art therapy, unconscious, repressed, or denied emotions can be made visible and potentially discussed at a safe remove, which lessens the client's anxiety. The client may gain psychological relief because the image functions to contain affect. One therapeutic value of a projective medium, particularly in relation to highly defensive adolescents, is that it provides a unique opportunity for the expression of feelings, thereby engaging adolescents in a psychodynamic process to which they are normally resistant.

Case and Dalley (2006) expanded on the concept of the art product as a container for affect by including art materials and the art therapy studio as containing influences. They noted that art materials provide options for seeking out private psychological space, while the session room itself serves as a container for the development of the relationship between client and therapist.

Art making does not automatically lead to psychological development or insight (Wilson, as cited in Rubin, 1987). However, each sequential stage of art development correlates with developments in motor skills, perception, language, symbol formation, sensory awareness, and spatial orientation

(Lowenfeld & Brittain, 1970; Malchiodi, 1998). As children reach adolescence, art making often takes a back seat to other forms of expression (Malchiodi, 1998). The reasons for this decline in artistic development are complex. One explanation may be that children in this age group have developed other avenues for self-expression, such as sports, music, fashion, sexual relations, and, of particular relevance to this discussion, video games and other electronic media.

MIRRORING

> The precursor of the mirror is the mother's face.
>
> —Winnicott, as cited in Scharff, 2005, p. 265

Winnicott (1971) theorized that the emergence of a sense of self is the result of the primary caregiver's capacity to accurately reflect feeling states to the child. When a caregiver responds to a child's expressions of affect, the child perceives a close-enough version of his or her emotional state reflected back. This *mirroring* by a sensitive, consistent, emotionally available caregiver organizes the child's experiences, which in turn fosters the child's awareness of internal affective states (Fonagy et al., 2004). Knowing what one feels is a necessary foundation for the emergence of a coherent sense of self. This is what Winnicott (1971) referred to in stressing the importance of "the mother's role of giving back to the baby the baby's own self" (p. 118).

Mirroring also lays the foundation for the capacity to use symbolic expression (Fonagy et al., 2004). As the child sees a representation of his or her affect in the caregiver, the potential exists for that feeling to become part of a shared affective experience, which can be emoted, given symbolic form, or both. The capacity for symbolic representation is therefore an outcome of the relationship with a well-attuned caregiver. The capacity to use language to represent emotional states fosters the self-regulation of emotions. According to Anna Freud (1966), "The association of affects and instinctual processes with word representations is stated to be the first and most important step in the mastery of instinct which has to be taken as the individual develops" (p. 162).

Inadequate mirroring experiences limit a child's capacity to give affect an appropriate verbal, emotional, or symbolic valence (Fonagy et al., 2004). The child is denied the opportunity to share affective experiences with another person, which in turn interferes with the developmental task of organizing emotions. Without such opportunities for sharing affective experiences, development of a coherent self-structure is inhibited, and the capacity for symbol formation is hampered.

Therapeutic interventions to repair faulty mirroring amount to a re-creation of the child-parent relationship in the client-therapist dyad (Fonagy et al., 2004). Accordingly, the therapist must be attuned to the client's state of mind and reflect back the client's affect. Clients may then begin to see themselves in the other as a coherent self with discrete emotions, much like an appropriately mirrored infant. As this process unfolds, the therapist is increasingly able to help the client organize unmanageable anxiety-provoking emotions into manageable entities. Case and Dalley (2006) likened works of art created in art therapy sessions to mirroring. They suggested that, as the client recognizes a part of himself or herself in the image, coupled with the awareness that the art therapist also sees this aspect of the self, a re-experiencing of the earliest caregiver mirroring takes place.

NEW MEDIA AND VIDEO GAME THEORY

> Today, the mirror is replaced by the screen.
>
> —Filiciak, as cited in Perron & Wolf, 2003, p. 100

Computer use patterns have shifted from the 1970s to the 21st century. Turkle (2005) tracked the transition from socially shared programming and hardware manipulations, which characterized much of the early use of computer technology, to today's computer use, wherein users spend their time in virtual environments designed by others. Turkle expressed regret for the loss of this earlier mode of interaction, in which programming on a computer became a projective act. In Turkle's 1970 study of the attitudes and beliefs of early computer users, a 13-year-old commented, "When you program a computer there is a little piece of your mind, and now it's a little piece of the computer's mind. And now you can see it" (p. 146). While today's media users no longer know or care about the underlying mechanisms of technology, Turkle claimed that current electronic media offer rich opportunities for identity experimentation.

Several video game scholars have attributed the appeal of video games to the experience of control. Bernstein (as cited in Wolf, 2001) noted that, in contrast to the unpredictability of the real world, one can use electronic media to revisit the same problem, anxiety, or blockage; apply an identical solution; and experience the same result, ad infinitum. A primary means of enhancing this sense of control in video games has been through the development of the video game avatar. An *avatar* is the video game player's on-screen image—a body-double that combines participation and spectatorship (Rehak, as cited in Wolf, 2001). A sense of agency is established for the player via control over this on-screen self-representation, creating the feeling that the player is inside the game (Taylor, 2003). Video game development has been driven by this desire to immerse the user in technology and in the game's environment (Lahti, as cited in Perron & Wolf, 2003). Player control over the avatar is one of the core features of the video game experience and is essential to creating the illusion of power and control for the player (Wolf, 2001).

Filiciak (as cited in Perron & Wolf, 2003) used applied psychology to evaluate the implications of a game player's relationship to his or her avatar. In particular, Filiciak interpreted the desire to be rendered visible on the screen using Lacan's (2006) theory of the mirror stage. According to Lacan, the image an infant sees in the mirror has a formative effect on ego development as the infant playfully experiences the relationship between reflected image, corporeal body, and reflected environment. The mirror reflection offers the infant a gratifying image of self as an integrated body that is developmentally ahead of its current "motor impotence and nursling dependence" (p. 95). As such, the reflected image gives the infant relief from experiences of fragmentation, offering the illusion of a unified and controllable body (Elliot, 2002). Filiciak locates video game player engagement in the interplay between the player's controllable avatar and his or her tenuous position in the real world.

Video game players, as they project themselves onto the screen and navigate through game space, are involved in two additional processes of the video game experience. The first is the repetitive cycle of birth, death, and rebirth (Perron & Wolf, 2003), which can be repeated countless times in the simple acts of turning off the machine and restarting the game. According to Sigmund Freud (1989), repetition is an attempt to change from the position of passive observer to that of active agent. Repetitive play is therefore an attempt to become "master of the situation" (p. 601).

The work of mastering a particular video game has its own reward system. The second additional process of the video game experience has to do with this reward system, referred to as *earned enhancements* (Lahti, as cited in Perron & Wolf, 2003). As players complete tasks and reach certain predetermined stages within the game, they are presented with new weapons, vehicles, armor, and level advancements. Repetitive play leads to mastery and, through the promise of rewards and level advancement, adds to the set of features programmed into video games that keep players interested in gameplay for long periods of time.

THE ADOLESCENT CLIENT: ROBERT

Robert, a 15-year-old boy, was placed in a foster home because of parental neglect, family violence, and threats of abandonment. Therapy was recommended because of his constricted affect and lack of peer relationships. When I first met Robert, he presented as concrete in his thinking. If not interrupted, he would speak without pause, filling sessions with monotone monologues. Robert would recount, with equal detachment, experiences as diverse as his traumatic history and his day-to-day activities at school.

Robert was clearly excited about one thing: video games. At the start of each session, he reported on his successful level advancement within the video games he was playing outside of the sessions. He was always eager to show me the new levels to which he had advanced on his portable handheld video game. With this in mind, I decided to offer Robert a chance to create his own video game scenario using computer animation. He repeatedly expressed excitement at this prospect.

In our first session, Robert outlined the scenario and created the characters for what would become the first level of a two-level video game world. He created a military figure, a snake, a monster, and a monkey (Figure 15.1) (also found on www.filmandvideobasedtherapy.com). Robert said the monkey character was the game's avatar, and the other figures were monsters. He said that players had to fight their way off an island by beating monsters. The game would end with players lost in space, in an alien world.

In subsequent early sessions, I struggled to adapt the hands-on use of the computer to Robert's unforeseen cognitive limitations. He was unable to stay focused on the process of creating recognizable form in a virtual environment. He became engrossed in creating shapes, one on top of the other, until I redirected him (Figure 15.2). Although he repeated every new technique he learned, he did so without generalizing his knowledge. Robert was unable to make connections between techniques to advance the form of his game design. Often, he simply moved the mouse cursor around the screen without an apparent goal until I intervened. The need for a shift in treatment plan was evident.

During the fifth session, Robert seemed particularly constricted in affect and detached from the surrounding environment. I made an attempt to connect him to the space we were in by showing him an animation I had made during one of his absences: a virtual 3-D model of the room we met in (Video Clip 15.1 can be found at www.filmandvideobasedtherapy.com). "Wow!" he said, leaning forward. On the edge of his seat, he asked, "How did you do that?" I explained, step by step, how I made the virtual room

Figure 15.1 Robert, untitled, colored pencil on paper

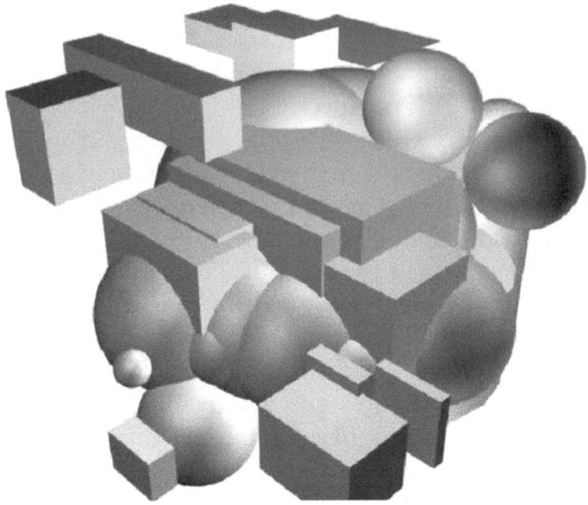

Figure 15.2 Robert, untitled, 3-D computer rendering, screen capture

by putting separate 3-D shapes together. I noticed I had his full attention. He was present in the room with me as he looked around for items I had neglected to include in the model. "You forgot that," he commented, pointing out the phone and other details missing from the virtual room.

Before the next session, I learned that Robert was being transferred to another foster home, and therefore to another agency. The implication of this impending transfer was that Robert and I had only two appointments remaining. This news coincided with Robert's increased immersion in video game playing. His level of interpersonal interaction, minimal to begin with, decreased still further. My therapeutic focus shifted to finding ways to draw Robert out.

Robert came to the sixth session fully immersed in his portable handheld video game, stubbornly refusing to switch it off. As the session progressed, he repeatedly rebuffed me in my attempts to disengage him from the video game. I decided to share with him that I was angry our work together was ending. He then switched off the video game, placed it on the table, and said he was angry, too. I asked Robert what he did with these feelings. He quickly answered that he played his video game so intently that the feelings eventually went away and he did not have to deal with them. I worked with Robert to frame his situation realistically, pointing out the appropriateness of his anger, articulating and modeling it with and for him. We spoke about how he felt that he had little control over anything, except perhaps his emotions, which he turned off by turning on the video game.

After a pause, Robert asked if I had done more work on the animation of the room he saw last week. I showed him the session room model again; since our last meeting, I had added to it an image of Robert's monkey character, which I had previously scanned into the computer (Video Clip 15.2 can be found at www.filmandvideobasedtherapy.com). Smiling broadly, Robert pulled his chair closer to the table, looked at the screen, and asked to continue working on his video game.

Robert drew more props and characters, creating what he referred to as "the second level" of his video game. He said that, once in space, having successfully beaten the set of characters created in our first session, game players would advance to a spaceship (Figure 15.3) in which they would battle more monsters (Figure 15.4). Once they had beaten all the monsters, players would go to the moon, which Robert described as a quiet place with friendly aliens ruled by a protective king.

For our seventh and last session, I met Robert in the waiting room. As expected, he was immersed in playing his handheld video game. Once in session, he sat down and, without raising his eyes, kept playing, resisting my appeals for interaction. After I made several requests, he switched off the game, but kept fidgeting with it in his hands.

I wondered aloud whether he was using video game playing to distract him from uncomfortable feelings. He remained silent, turning the game over in his hands, and opened the case as if to turn it on. His compulsion to play

Figure 15.3 Robert, untitled, pencil on paper

Figure 15.4 Robert, untitled, colored pencil on paper

the game was evident in the nervous manner with which he handled the machine, repeatedly putting it down and picking it back up.

After a few minutes, taking a cue from what I perceived to be his sadness, I told Robert I was sad that this was our last session. "Yes," he commented, making eye contact for the first time in the session. I said I could understand if he was also sad, given some of the recent events in his life. Robert was quiet but attentive. I wondered aloud what he knew about the current state of his foster home transfer. He put the video game on the table, looked directly at me, and asked what I knew about his situation. He also asked me what I knew about foster care. The handheld video game stayed on the table for the remainder of the session as we talked about what was happening to him. Robert appeared sad, which was also how I felt during our conversation.

I told him all I knew about his past and his current situation, from his removal from his biological parents because of neglect, to his upcoming move to another foster home. I reminded him that, as a result of his impending move, this was to be our last session. He listened, leaning forward in his seat with sustained eye contact. Next, I explained that he had used his intelligence and creativity to survive difficult situations, managing his feelings by turning to video game playing.

We discussed that one unintended result of this coping strategy was that it isolated him; turning to video games, albeit adaptively, was not bringing him closer to people. He told me he was lonely. I encouraged him to seek out and talk to people he could trust. He said he liked coming to see me. I told him that he was likely to get another therapist where he was going and that I hoped he would feel comfortable relating to that person, as well. The computer was, as usual, on the table between us. Looking at it, he spoke about how much he wished we could still work together so he could finish his video game.

THE ADOLESCENT: INTERPRETED

The appeal of video games for Robert was essential to his participation in treatment. He initially displayed emotion only in relation to his enthusiasm for playing video games and his excitement about making his own video game scenario. From his gleeful accounts of level advancement to his final wish that we continue to work together so he could finish creating his video game, Robert's interest in and use of video games were central to our relationship.

> To abandon a defense is to expose a conflict.
>
> (Vaillant, 1993, pp. 23–24)

By his own admission, Robert turned to video games, at least in part, because he experienced feelings that were intolerable. Robert was struggling to manage overwhelming affective states. Because he was able to command the avatar in his game, the handheld device may have given Robert a sense of control that he felt to be lacking in other aspects of his life. For adolescents like Robert who have not received favorable responses from the environment, new media represent sites where near total control can be achieved (Bernstein, as cited in Wolf, 2001). No matter how unmanageable the adolescent perceives his or her life to be, mastery is possible in a virtual world.

Despite the fact that Robert's game playing kept many feelings from entering our early sessions, it served him in a role related to an important developmental task: gaining mastery over emotions (Colarusso, 1992; Piaget, 2000; Rosenblum & Lewis, as cited in Adams & Berzonsky, 2003). As Robert's self-reports indicated, he played video games to control his affect, successfully engaging in what Freud (1989) identified as repetitive play aimed at mastering emotions. When his life circumstances became emotionally charged to an uncomfortable degree, he could flip a switch and turn on his electronic coping device.

In session five, the computer screen acted as a mirror. The 3-D model I created did not yet reflect Robert himself, but it did reflect the therapy room. A screen that often held a video game environment now held the therapeutic environment. Robert had experienced pleasurable and controllable play on an electronic screen; it represented a site where he had achieved considerable success managing intense emotions. By equating the therapeutic environment with the video game, the model demonstrated to Robert that the sessions offered the possibility of pleasure and control in a space less fraught with anxiety. In such a space, the relationship between client and therapist could develop (Case & Dalley, 2006).

The mirroring of the environment on this screen also awakened Robert's awareness to his surroundings. His relationship to the environment changed as he challenged me with questions. His question, "How did you do that?" was a turning point in his use of therapy. He was present in the room, paying attention to details, and making demands.

In the following session, Robert made a breakthrough, momentarily suspending a defensive pattern and sharing his affective experience with me. The session began with Robert unwilling to turn off his portable video game. With the transfer to another foster home looming, Robert's cognitive-emotional competency was under renewed pressure to manage intolerable affect. As Robert witnessed me managing my anger, which represented a feeling state "analogous, but not identical" (Fonagy et al., 2004, p. 36) to his own experience, he began to verbalize previously guarded emotions. When he admitted to hiding his anger behind video game playing, his trust in the therapeutic relationship became evident; Robert apparently felt safe enough to share his feelings. His capacity to tolerate and label an intense emotional state (his previously denied anger) provided evidence that his cognitive-emotional competency was improving. Through the therapeutic process, he had established a link between affect (anger) and its representation (words). Thus, the foundation was set for the more creative use of symbol formation that would emerge at the close of the session.

In asking to see more of the therapy room animation, Robert was asking for the mirror again. This time, the screen held a reflection of Robert within the therapeutic environment. The self-reflection to which Robert as video game player was accustomed, wherein the self is represented as an on-screen avatar enveloped within the environment of the video game space, was replaced by a representation of the self as enveloped within the therapeutic environment. Therapeutic space now had a deeper connection to game space, a site where Robert experienced mastery of medium, control over affect, and considerable pleasure. Just as Lacan's (as cited in Elliot, 2002) mirror stage is said to enable a less fragmented, more unified self-perception, Robert's projection into this therapeutic space (an image of himself playing in therapy) had the immediate consequence of engendering self-directed creative control over the session.

As a result of therapeutic mirroring, the metaphor in the second level of Robert's game displayed considerably more development than the material created for the first level. While Robert's first concept for the video game represented a psychologically relevant and historically accurate projection (Riley, 1999) of his experience, it offered little beyond this experience. Robert was born into an environment of neglect and isolation, which is reflected in the fact that the imagined game player begins his in-game journey on an island. Robert survived and managed to make it out of the neglectful environment and into foster care, just as the game player must escape the island in order to make the journey into space. Like the game player who ends up in an alien world, Robert arrived in an unfamiliar city, without friends, unacculturated, and separated from his biological parents. In meaningful ways, Robert's experience in the real world was similar to the detached, ungrounded world of his first video game level.

The second level of the video game scenario, which developed at the close of our work together, provides evidence of a psychological shift within Robert. The previously adrift game player acquires a spaceship for protection, perhaps a sign of Robert's emerging sense of safety within the walls of the session room. The player's final journey to the moon, which Robert described as a safe planet full of friendly aliens, is a significant change in relational potential from the first installment, which left the game protagonist isolated and adrift in space. The protective king, ruler of the player's final destination, may be a symbol of the therapist (me) as someone who could provide a safe place, where feelings could be tolerated, and likely represents a wish for and acceptance of a positive relationship with an adult.

In addition to providing evidence of a more expressive use of representational systems (Fonagy et al., 2004), one interesting interpretation of the transformation from the first level to the second level of Robert's video game scenario utilizes the idea of earned enhancements (Lahti, as cited in Perron & Wolf, 2003). Immediately prior to Robert's creation of the second video game level, he experienced improved cognitive-emotional competency within the session. Just as video games reward players for successful play, Robert may have rewarded himself for this achievement with a new spaceship, a new planet, new friends, and a protective father figure in the form of a king.

In the seventh and final session, therapeutic mirroring established further links between feeling states and representational systems. Robert was expressing sadness in affect and words while asking pointed questions about what his situation would be within the foster-care system; this provided evidence of his improving cognitive-emotional competency to manage intense emotions while maintaining interpersonal relationships. Admitting that he was lonely, Robert evidenced what was, for him, unprecedented insight into the maladaptive repercussions of his rigid coping strategies. His final wish that we could continue to work together so he could finish his video game perhaps expressed his desire for continuity in his relationships. It also may have been a veiled longing for the mirror, a wish to repeat the new experience brought about through the screen he had been using to cope with his condition.

CONCLUSION

Adolescents face myriad developmental challenges. Each of these challenges burdens individuals in different ways. Robert suffered extreme emotional neglect, which he survived by using a rigid defensive strategy. Therapeutic mirroring aided in loosening this defensive pattern. Although Robert's cognitive impairment prevented him from taking advantage of the full potential of animation software, the use of the electronic screen as a mirror assisted him in experiencing the therapeutic process as controllable and pleasurable, much like the video game play to which he was accustomed. This led to his tolerating and sharing previously intolerable affect. Capitalizing on Robert's interest in and use of video games, I introduced him to a creative process whereby he expressed feelings metaphorically and envisioned a more interpersonally related future.

Whatever the underlying causes, any moratorium on artistic development during adolescence represents a lost opportunity. I believe it is a disservice to youth and society at large to fail to offer age-appropriate and compelling opportunities for continued artistic development. Art therapists are in an ideal position to use emerging technologies in a context wherein adolescents can creatively employ electronic media, such as video games and 3-D computer animation, as a means to improve mental health.

Future developments in technology will likely continue to offer increased potential for therapeutic applications. More engaging and physically responsive input options will augment the current human-computer interface (the point-and-click of the mouse). Physical computing, in which a computer responds to body movement and pressure, is to the 21st century what microprocessor speed and memory were to the last decades of the 20th century (McCullough, 2005). The challenge for art therapists is to embrace these emerging forms of technology as vital components of practice, especially technologies in which clients who are resistant to treatment are invested.

REFERENCES

Adams, G., & Berzonsky, M. (Eds.). (2003). *Blackwell handbook of adolescence.* Cambridge, MA: Blackwell.

Blos, P. (1962). *On adolescence.* New York, NY: Free Press.

Case, C., & Dalley, T. (2006). *The handbook of art therapy.* New York, NY: Routledge.

Colarusso, C. (1992). *Child and adult development: A psychoanalytic introduction for clinicians.* New York, NY: Plenum Press.

Elliot, A. (2002). *Psychoanalytic theory: An introduction.* Durham, NC: Duke University Press.

Fonagy, P., Gergely, G., Jurist, E., & Target, M. (2004). *Affect regulation, mentalization, and the development of the self.* New York, NY: Other Press.

Freud, A. (1966). *The ego and the mechanisms of defense.* New York, NY: International Universities Press.

Freud, S. (1989). *The Freud reader* (P. Gay, Ed.). New York, NY: W.W. Norton.

Kramer, E. (2000). *Art as therapy* (L.A. Gerity, Ed.). London, UK: Jessica Kingsley.

Lacan, J. (2006). *Ecrits.* New York, NY: W.W. Norton.

Laurel, B. (Ed.). (1990). *The art of human-computer interface design.* Reading, MA: Addison-Wesley.

Lenhart, A. (2008). *Teens, video games, and civics.* Retrieved October 8, 2008 from http://www.pewinternet.org/2008/09/16/teens-video-games-and-civics/

Lowenfeld, V., & Brittain, W.L. (1970). *Creative and mental growth.* London, UK: Macmillan.

Malchiodi, C. (1998). *Understanding children's drawings.* London, UK: Guilford Press.

Manovich, L. (2001). *The language of new media.* Cambridge, MA: MIT Press.

McCullough, M. (1996). *Abstracting craft, the practiced digital hand.* Cambridge, MA: MIT Press.

McCullough, M. (2005). *Digital ground.* Cambridge, MA: MIT Press.

Mishne, J. (1986). *Clinical work with adolescents.* New York, NY: Free Press.

Perron, B., & Wolf, M.J.P. (Eds.). (2003). *The video game theory reader.* New York, NY: Routledge.

Piaget, J. (2000). *The psychology of the child.* Paris, FR: Basic Books.

Riley, S. (1999). *Contemporary art therapy with adolescents.* London, UK: Jessica Kingsley.

Rubin, J. (Ed.). (1987). *Approaches to art therapy: Theory and technique.* New York, NY: Brunner/Mazel.

Scharff, D. (Ed.). (2005). *Object relations, theory and practice: An introduction.* Lanham, MD: Rowman & Littlefield.

Taylor, L. (2003). When seams fall apart: Video game space and the player. *The International Journal of Computer Game Research, 3*(2). Retrieved November 1, 2007, from http://www.gamestudies.org/0302/taylor/

Turkle, S. (2005). *The second self.* Cambridge, MA: MIT Press.

Vaillant, G. (1993). *The wisdom of the ego.* Harvard, MA: Harvard University Press.

Winnicott, D.W. (1971). *Playing and reality*. New York, NY: Brunner-Routledge.
Winnicott, D.W. (1989). *Psychoanalytic explorations*. Harvard, MA: Harvard University Press.
Wolf, M. (Ed.) (2001). *The medium of the video game*. Austin, TX: University of Austin Press.

Contributors

Kim Anderson, PhD, LCSW, is an associate professor in the School of Social Work at the University of Missouri–Columbia, USA, where she teaches clinical practice and evaluation courses at the graduate level. As highlighted in her book *Enhancing Resilience in Survivors of Family Violence* (2010), Dr. Anderson's scholarship bridges gaps between theory and practice by offering mental health practitioners conceptual frameworks that capture the interplay of trauma and resilience in survivors of family violence.

Brian Austin, MPS, holds a master of professional studies degree in art therapy. He is the founder and program director of the Animation Project, a program that utilizes animation and video to help at-risk youth focus on their futures by developing skills to improve their lives as well as their careers. Based in New York, NY, Austin is also a professional 3-D animator and art therapist.

Natalie R. Carlton, MA, is an avid collage artist and researcher who creates with fabric, paper, glue, tape, scissors, and digital media including photography, video, and sound. She is an art therapy adjunct professor at Southwestern College in Santa Fe, NM; Saint Mary of the Woods in Terre Haute, IN; and Lesley University in Cambridge, MA. Natalie is also a private practitioner in Taos, NM, where she works and learns alongside children, youth, families, and dedicated colleagues.

Joshua L. Cohen, PhD, received a PhD in clinical psychology with an emphasis in depth psychology from Pacifica Graduate Institute, a master's degree in general psychology from Walden University, and a bachelor's degree in film and anthropology from Colorado College where he hosted a seminar on Cinematherapy in 1997. In his clinical training, he addressed many conditions in the *DSM*. He presented his dissertation findings on film-based therapy at the APA Convention in 2013 and as a guest speaker in a medical setting. He works in Beverly Hills, California.

Jon Ehinger, ATR-BC, LCAT, is a licensed and board certified art therapist, multimedia artist, and educator who works in Brooklyn, New York. He developed a new media mental health art therapy program integrating hands-on computer activities, video green screening, digital photography, and Photoshop technologies for treating acute psychiatric patients. Using his creative arts therapy specialization in electronic arts/video, he combines traditional therapy modalities with new media for child, teen, and adult psychiatric populations.

Elizabeth Hamilton, PhD, earned her BA from Vanderbilt University (honors in psychology), her MS from Tulane University, and her PhD in clinical psychology from UCLA. She was the recipient of an APA dissertation grant, and more recently, is co-investigator on a school-based intervention grant awarded by Division 53 of APA. In addition to involvement with clinical training and teaching in the Graduate Department of Clinical Psychology at George Fox University, she maintains an active clinical practice with children, teens and adults, with special interests in eating and mood disorders. Her current research interests include protective and risk factors in developmental psychopathology.

J. Lauren Johnson, PhD, is a filmmaker and a psychologist; she is also the founder of the Therapeutic Filmmaking Institute. After obtaining a bachelor of fine arts in film and video production (York University), she received a master of science (University of Calgary) in applied psychology and doctor of philosophy (University of Alberta) in counselling psychology. She works in private practice, specializing in working with women and members of First Nations in Calgary, Alberta.

Joe Kavitski, MA, is an award-winning filmmaker and artist with a master's degree in art therapy from New York University. His work with individuals suffering from acute mental illness incorporates a variety of creative techniques, including the integration of digital media technologies in an art therapy context. He is also an advanced level Reiki practitioner.

Yarden Kerem, MA, has a master of fine arts degree and is based in Jerusalem, Israel. Yarden is the director of the Videotherapy Department at the Ma'aleh School of Television, Film and the Arts as well as the director and certifying coordinator of the Videotherapy Center in Jerusalem. In addition to this work, she is a trainer and teacher in the therapeutic technique of focusing at the Focusing Institute in New York.

Wanda Lakota, MA, is an Inclusive Excellence Fellow at the University of Denver where her current research interests focus on filmmaking and the intersections of race, identity, and health. In completion of her dissertation, she is writing, producing, and directing a documentary about the first FDA-approved race-based drug. Prior to studying filmmaking, Wanda Lakota was a full-time instructor, director, and academic advisor for the Department of Communication, University of Colorado–Denver.

Carolyn McGurl, MA, graduated from Messiah College where she studied psychology and minored in counseling and children and youth services. She moved from New York to Oregon to pursue doctoral studies in clinical psychology at George Fox University. She completed her dissertation with the assistance of a grief and loss center for children and adolescents where she utilized a unique technological intervention. Carolyn will complete her doctoral internship at Philhaven in Mt. Gretna, Pennsylvania, in the child and adolescent track.

Mark McMinn, PhD, is a professor of clinical psychology at George Fox University. He is a licensed psychologist in Oregon, and a fellow and former president of the Society for the Psychology of Religion and Spirituality (APA's Division 36). He is board certified in clinical psychology through the American Board of Professional Psychology. His research interests include the integration of psychology and Christianity, positive psychology, clergy-psychology collaboration, and technology in psychological practice.

Basia Mosinski, LCAT, ATR-BC, MA, MFA, is an art therapist in Southern California and a licensed creative arts therapist in New York. She was a clinician and assistant director of mental health at Gay Men's Health Crisis in New York and a former chair of the Technology Committee of the American Art Therapy Association. Prior to becoming an art therapist, Basia was a faculty member in the Film/Video/New Media Department at the School of the Art Institute of Chicago. She is currently in private practice in California and New York.

Penelope P. Orr, PhD, ATR-BC, is a board-certified, registered art therapist and an art therapy board credentialed supervisor. Dr. Orr served on the Art Therapy Credentials Board, which credentials art therapists in the United States, and she is the past president of this board. She has taught at Edinboro University in Pennsylvania and Florida State University for the past 10 years, during which time she has published one book, written chapters for two edited books, and authored 15 peer-reviewed articles on digital media theory and use in art therapy.

Marty Otañez, PhD, is an assistant professor in the Anthropology Department at the University of Colorado–Denver. He examines digital storytelling as a research method to promote health equities among communities of color. Also, he studies diverse ways to bring digital media, social justice, and community wellness perspectives to social science and public health applications. Martin is a co-editor of the forthcoming book *Engaging Participatory Visual and Digital Research.*

Benjamin Patton, MA, is the founder and president of Patton Veterans Project (PVP), Inc., a not-for-profit organization devoted to serving veterans and military families who are coping with the consequences of posttraumatic stress. Ben oversees the operations for PVP and leads each I Was There therapeutic film workshop, reaching out to veteran participants before, during, and after participation. The youngest grandson of WWII's General George S. Patton Jr., Ben is co-author of the 2012 book *Growing Up Patton: Reflections on Heroes, History and Family Wisdom.* Formerly a producer and development executive, he also operates Patton Productions, an independent production company. Ben is a graduate of Georgetown University and holds a master's degree in developmental psychology from the Teachers College of Columbia University.

Winston Seegobin, PsyD, received his PsyD in clinical psychology from Central Michigan University. He is currently the director of diversity and a professor of clinical psychology in the Graduate Department of Clinical Psychology at George Fox University. His primary research areas include international psychology, multicultural psychotherapy, psychology and religion, and hope and resilience in positive psychology.

Rivka Tuval-Mashiach, PhD, is a clinical psychologist and a senior lecturer in the Department of Psychology at Bar Ilan University in Israel. She is also the head of the community services unit at the Israel Center for Victims of Terror and War. Her research and clinical work include using narrative approaches to diagnose and treat people exposed to trauma and those with PTSD. She studies collective trauma, gender and trauma, and identity-construction processes following traumatic events, and has published extensively on these topics.

Beatriz Wallace, MA, is a visiting professor in the School of Journalism and Multimedia Arts at Duquesne University in Pittsburgh, PA, USA, where she teaches multimedia storytelling and critical media studies at the undergraduate and graduate levels. Her visual ethnographies have appeared in the Tisch art gallery, *25 Under 25 Up-and-Coming American Photographers*, and the annual Visual Communication Conference. Her research explores digital media curricula and strategic communication for higher education, business, and health.

Index

Note: page numbers in *italics* indicate illustrations or photographs.

Kolibri 360 GmbH
Ferdinand-Jühlke-Straße 7
99095 Erfurt, Deutschland
produktsicherheit@kolibri360.de